The Wines of Italy

THE WINES
OF ITALY

CYRIL RAY

*With colour photographs by Ekhart van Houten
and maps by Audrey Frew*

OCTOPUS BOOKS

This edition published by arrangement with
McGraw-Hill Book Company Inc.
330 West 42nd Street, New York City 36
by Octopus Books Limited
59 Grosvenor Street
London W1

© George Rainbird Ltd 1966

ISBN 0 7064 0176 X

Produced by Mandarin Publishers Limited,
77a Marble Road, North Point, Hong Kong
and printed in Hong Kong

This book on the wines
of the country of his fathers
is dedicated to
CHARLES FORTE
in gratitude for the good meals
and fine wines I have enjoyed in the
CAFÉ ROYAL GRILL ROOM
the outward aspect and the culinary traditions
of which he has so lovingly preserved

Contents

Colour Plates

Maps

INTRODUCTION

ITALY is the greatest wine-producing country in the world. Not in the quality of her wines: few Italian wine-growers, save the most provincial and inexperienced, would claim for their products that they can vie with the greatest growths of France or Germany. (Though there are undoubtedly Italian wines, a few white and more red, that show far greater character and distinction than the coarse Midi reds, the sugared and blended – and sometimes even more dubiously concocted – wines labelled "Niersteiner" and "Liebfraumilch", that owe their place in the British market, and the prices they command, to the reputations earned by noble clarets and elegant hocks.) But, having been accustomed, year after year, to dispute the first place with France for volume of production, in the years when Algeria's output was included with that of metropolitan France, Italy can now claim to grow more wine than any other country in the world,* and this although she is little more than half the size of France and, because of her mountains, with a smaller area, proportionately, suitable for agriculture; to export more wine to other countries; and to have a higher proportion of her population – almost twenty-five per cent – concerned with wine-growing and the wine trade.

Yet the wines of Italy are neither so well known nor so highly regarded in Britain as they deserve to be, and there are many reasons for this.

It is more than a century ago that Cyrus Redding observed that –

> the wines of Italy are all made for home consumption. The interests of commerce, which lead to competition, have not yet interfered to improve them;

* France did, in fact, take the lead again in 1964, for the first time since 1957, with 60·5 million hectolitres against sixty. A slight margin, and in the decade 1950–9 (according to the new, revised edition of Mr L. W. Marrison's Penguin Handbook, *Wines and Spirits*), Italy produced nearly twenty per cent more than France. Since then, it has become more like thirty to thirty-five per cent more. Between them, the two countries provide the world with half its wine.

[adding that] the petty sovereignties of Italy are a blight upon her manufactures no less than upon her civilisation. Many of these are shut up to themselves, as regards their productions, and cannot interchange with the neighbouring states without a great disadvantage, owing to pernicious duties. . . .

It was twenty years after those words were written before the "pernicious duties" finally disappeared; the effects lingered much longer; and the regionalism persists to this day, so that it is difficult for the English or the American visitor to Rome, say, or to Florence to acquaint himself seriously with any Italian wines other than those of Rome or of Tuscany, to compare one with another and to take home with him an informed interest that would stimulate his wine-merchant into enquiry and possibly into purchase.

A climate all too favourable for the production of common grapes with a high yield, combined with a lack of demand from neighbouring regions, let alone from the more discriminating markets abroad, naturally resulted in the peasants taking the easy way – of producing as much wine with as little effort as possible. Meanwhile, France and Germany were consolidating the position of their wines as the world's classics – the wines by which all others were, and are, judged. So that it is difficult now for such fine wines as Italy does produce to establish themselves abroad – for what British wine-lover, brought up in a long claret-and-burgundy, port-and-sherry, tradition, is prepared to pay as much for an old Barolo, say, or Brunello, as a *château*-bottled claret or estate-bottled hock? The best Italian wines cost as much to produce; money must be tied up in them as they acquire the bottle-age necessary to the better Italian red wines; and Italian standards of living and of rates of pay are comparable, now at any rate, with those of the French countryside, and far higher than those of Chile, for instance, which is why Chilean reds of good *ordinaire* quality can come half-way round the world and still undercut similar wines from Europe. Nor does the Italian wine-grower enjoy the Government backing that has enabled Yugoslavia to establish herself so firmly since the war as one of the most important single suppliers of white wines to this country.

Newly introduced wine laws, though, have encouraged the production of finer wines, and ensured at the same time a greater measure of consistency than before in those of the middling sort, which make up the bulk of the wines that Italy sells abroad. Export figures have risen accordingly, with Germany and Switzerland by far the biggest customers – particularly for the red wines they lack themselves – and France taking more Asti

Spumante than any other country. The United States, where a huge Italian population still thirsts for the wine of its fathers, ranks fourth, after France, Germany and Switzerland, among the importers of Italian wine. In the years immediately after this book first appeared (1966) Britain so increased her imports as to move above Austria and Belgium into fifth place, but this is so recent a development that Italian wines are still little known and understood here compared with those of France and Germany. This is doubly disadvantageous to the Italians, for this country is the home of wine-scholarship, and still sets standards of taste and judgement for wine-drinkers everywhere: Italy loses not only what we would pay for her finer wines, but also what we would say and write about them.

Italians are individualists, and find it hard to combine. There has been no concerted campaign by Government, growers and shippers to familiarise Britain with the wines of Italy, and to combat the ignorance and prejudices that undoubtedly still obtain. Otherwise the light-bodied red wines of the Italian lakes might well have established themselves as firmly on the British market as the *vinhos verdes* of Portugal. Italian restaurateurs, ship-owners and airlines could also certainly do more to popularise their own country's wines among their foreign visitors – with eventual advantage to the tourist trade in general, in the way that travel in France increases interest in French wines among foreigners, and interest in French wines in turn sends foreigners to France. Italy has an enormous advantage here: it is quick and easy for British tourists to visit Italy, which they do in vast numbers; the language and the country are both reasonably familiar – much more so than Serbo-Croat and Yugoslavia; there is an immense goodwill. It is a pity for both countries that we know as little as we do about her wines, and that Italy does not try harder to teach us more.

In most parts of Italy the old methods of viticulture still obtain, just as Redding described them:

> Corn is sown between them [the vines], and other grain, or vegetables are grown. The vines are planted upon soils oftentimes the least congenial to their growth, as in the plain of Pisa. They are suffered to run up to any height, and in many places are never pruned at all.* In the Roman States the vines producing

* In the south, in Sicily and Sardinia, in spite of recent improvements in methods of viticulture, many are grown on the *"albarello"* ("little tree") principle, close to the ground, which means that they derive reflected heat from the soil, in a part of the country where the wines are, in any case, coarsened by excessive sunshine.

every quality of wine grow together, without assortment of any kind. They are conducted from tree to tree, generally of the elm species, along the boundaries of enclosures, and even by the high roads, where they run up in wild luxuriance, and waste their vitality, not in the fruit but in leaves and branches. Even where the vine is raised on trelliswork or on poles, it is rarely pruned or trained.

The various Italian systems of land tenure and inheritance have not, in the past, made it easy for Italy to produce fine wines in the same way as those of the Médoc or the Rhine are produced. The great estates were too big, the peasant holdings too small, for any of them to be conducted as a Rothschild conducts Lafite, or a Prüm looks after the Wehlener-Sonnenuhr vineyards. But the noble families of Tuscany, for whom the Baron Bettino Ricasoli had set a pattern of dedicated large-scale wine-growing as long ago as the eighteen-sixties, produce serious wines on the scale in which serious wines are produced by the great firms of Champagne and, in the same way, by buying as well as growing their grapes, and by making wine in big wineries. They do not vary year by year, as the 1952 Lafite differs from the 1961, nor do they vary from vineyard to vineyard, as a Lafite will differ from a Latour, but we do not think any the less of Moët and Chandon or of Pol Roger for producing a non-vintage wine that remains pretty well constant year by year and wherever and whenever you buy it. Just as the great champagne houses produce, as well as the non-vintage wines, their fine vintage champagnes, so now do the big Chianti houses produce their *"riserva"* wines, or wines with an estate name, such as Brolio, or Nipozzano.

A more recent development has been the growth of the co-operatives, particularly in the Oltrepo Pavese at one end of the country and in Sardinia at the other, making it possible to introduce modern methods of vinification that the small growers could never have been able to afford, and to reach a level of consistency all too little known, hitherto, in Italian wines. The same period – roughly since the nineteen-thirties, but much more intensively since the war – has seen the growth of the *consorzi*, associations of growers and wine-makers dedicated to maintaining the standards and, in consequence, the reputation of the wines of their district. The growers of the "Chianti classico" district set the pattern,* according to which each grower in the voluntary association has his output checked each year, both for quantity and quality: if the quality is right; if it has been made of the right grapes in the right district by the right method, then he gets *numbered*

* See page 102.

neck-labels to the number of bottles his yield will fill, and no more. There are now more than fifty such *consorzi* and, in the nature of things, some are better or more rigorous than others; many are new and still feeling their way; many exist in districts where the wine is nothing much to write home about, anyway, even when it is what it says it is, and guaranteed to be so. But the scheme works – I have seen inspectors of the Chianti classico and the Asti Spumante associations at work, and they were very impressive: I have no doubt at all that a bottle of either of these wines bearing the numbered neck-label of its association would be the real thing. The pity is that some shippers in this country import wines that would never qualify for neck-labels at home in Italy, so that we, the consumers, knowing no better, condemn Chianti, say, or Valpolicella, in general, judging it by what is foisted on us under that name here.

I do not think that either France or Germany is stricter in its wine laws than this system at its best, and the new Italian wine law* that has been coming into force in phases since the beginning of 1965 is based on the experience and advice of the *consorzi*, and with their co-operation.

Stricter legal standards do not mean that we now have to pay more in Italy for the highest categories of Italian wine – estate-bottled and, in effect, State-guaranteed. The best Italian wines have been estate-bottled and guaranteed by their growers' associations for the past generation. But it does mean that the British shipper – if he thinks it commercially worth while – is now able not only to buy the best Italian wines but also to assure his customers of their quality. And, of course, there will still, and always, be a market for the cheaper wines, "stretched", or "cut", with the coarser wines of the south, exactly as the cheapest French wines are – often, indeed, with the same Apulian or Sicilian or Sardinian wines, for much of the output of these heavy blending wines goes direct to France (and it ill becomes Frenchmen to disparage the wines of Italy, without which their own wine trade would be hard put to it to provide them with their *vins de consommation*, or their foreign customers with some of their "French" wines).

Even before the new wine law came fully into effect, wine for export was checked for wholesomeness and alcoholic strength (quality is another matter: *chaptalisation* [sugaring] – permitted in France and Germany in certain circumstances and for certain wines – is forbidden in Italy in all circumstances, though not blending, which can, of course, be forbidden by

* See Appendix 1.

15

a *consorzio*). Checking is by sample, and the responsibility of the Istituto Nazionale per il Commercio Estero, usually through local *consorzi* or regional centres of the Ministry of Agriculture. Clearly, the officials can only check that the wine being exported is the wine that the foreign shipper has asked and is paying for – not what he is going to call it when he gets it home. Nor should Italian wines be judged abroad by the so-called "commercial wine" bought by other countries, notably Germany (for making into German "vermouth" and German brandy), which is not reckoned by the Italians to be fit for table wine – it is checked only for alcoholic content, and is permitted to be fortified – but may well be sold as such, or judged as such, when it gets to its destination.

Nor, for that matter, as I have said, should Italian wines of medium quality and medium price be judged by the standards set by the finest single-vineyard wines of France. With few exceptions, they are the equivalent of French district or village wines – of wine entitled only to be called Beaujolais, say, or at best, of some such wine as is named, simply, "St Julien". And, because they are grown under more and stronger sunshine, they resemble the wines of the south or of the Rhône more than those of Burgundy or Bordeaux or the Loire. But the resemblances are not close: Italian wines are *different* – some of them, such as Lambrusco, very different – from anything grown in France, and they should be treated as such, judged by their own standards, not condemned for not being what they do not pretend to be. Nevertheless, they have character, and with the growing demand for wines in Britain, especially for wines of modest price, and with the growing number of British visitors to Italy, it is at least interesting, and possibly useful, for a people that knows so much about the wines of France and Germany – more than most Frenchmen and Germans do – to know something about Italian wines in general, and how they differ in particular. Such, then, are the reasons for offering to the English reader a book on Italian wines that I hope may prove more comprehensive than any that has so far appeared in English, less indiscriminately eulogistic than those written by Italians. My own interest in the wines of Italy dates back nearly thirty years, to the time when, as the *Manchester Guardian's* correspondent with the Eighth Army, newly landed in Italy, I quenched my thirst with the rough wine of the South, and then with the more sophisticated wines (in both senses, sometimes, alas) of Naples, or celebrated our entry into Rome with the sweet sparkle of Asti Spumante. For the last few months of the war, and some months afterwards, a year in all, I lived in Rome, enlarging my experience at such restaurants as Ranieri and Valadier and the Hostaria dell'Orso; imbibing knowledge of Italian wines, as I imbibed other forms of worldly wisdom, from old Carlo Sforza (in the political wilderness at the time, as the result of his quarrel with Churchill); and spending weekends with the Senni family at Grottaferrata, in the country of the *castelli Romani* wines, where in those days the wine of that hospitable household was still trodden, as I suppose few Italian table wines are trodden these days, though there must be a few places in the South, as I know there are in Sicily, where the old practice lingers on, as it does in the Upper Douro.

Since those days I have visited Italy almost every year – in some years three or four times – and have made notes of the wines I have drunk in every part of the peninsula, from the Alps to Sicily, and from Sardinia to the Yugoslav frontier, completing my researches in the course of five visits spread over the fifteen months before this book was finished, renewing my acquaintance with those wines I had not tasted for years; visiting those regions that I did not already know, so that I can now claim to have visited, and to have tasted wine in, every region of Italy;* tasting such wines as were still unfamiliar; and spending the last six weeks in Siena, filling the gaps in my experience, and completing this book, at its wine museum, the Enoteca Italica Permanente.

I have listed here every Italian wine the name of which I know to be in any way officially or even generally recognised, taking as my check-lists the recent Italian works mentioned in the bibliography, notably the *Nuova Enologia* and those by Luigi Veronelli and Bruno Bruni. I have tasted virtually every wine named in this book, some in their native regions, some at the Enoteca; some long ago, but most quite recently. For the sake of completeness, I have included those few that – because they are peculiar to some remote locality to which I have not penetrated – I have not had the chance of tasting, and a few that I suppose I must have tasted in my time, but have forgotten. I have based my entries for them on what Bruni or

---

* In Italy a "region" is one of the historic divisions of the country: Piedmont, Lombardy, Tuscany, the Veneto, are "regions". "Province" – the word that I think one would have been more likely to use in this sense in English – is applied to the districts administered by the main towns in each region. Thus, Siena and Florence are not only cities but provinces within the region, Tuscany. Potenza and Matera are the two provinces in the region of the Basilicata.

Veronelli or the *Enologia* have to say about them, though I have taken no single one of these as gospel – for a wine that is unknown to me to have been included in this book it must have been mentioned in at least two of these three recent Italian authorities.

The names of Italian species of vine will mean little to my readers, as indeed they do to me, save when a species gives its name to a noted wine, as in the case of Moscato, say, or Aleatico. But wherever I have been able to discover the name of the grape from which a wine of another name is made I have included it here, so that students may know what family connections there are between various wines, and trace a resemblance, or puzzle their heads over dissimilarities. So, too, though I am no great believer in vintage charts, and although vintage dates are of far less significance in Italy, where the weather is more constant and more consistent, than in France and Germany, I have included such notes on vintage years as are available (they are derived from Cùnsolo – see the bibliography – who abridged them, omitting the merely passably good years, from a list compiled by Dott. Antonio Niederbacher, editor of the magazine, *Enotria*, and apply to fifty of the more important wines) so that those interested may compare the good and the better years of the various Italian wine-growing areas with those of France and Germany. I do not pretend that these dates are a guide to buying from a wine-merchant, or to choosing in a restaurant, for many of the Italian wines of the greatest years are no longer easily available, but it is of interest to note, for example, that 1958 was so much better for Barolo than for burgundy, 1947 so consistently good throughout Western Europe.

Finally, in most cases I have given the alcoholic strength of a wine: such figures are not regarded in England as being of major importance, but in Italy they are always given, and the price of common wine is based on them. As the figures exist, they are useful in showing relative strengths, and in assessing them the English reader will be helped by bearing in mind that claret is usually rather more than 10°, Sauternes rather more than 13°, Châteauneuf du Pape rather more than 12·5° (these are the minimum strengths for the wines to qualify for their *appellations contrôlées*); sherry about 20°; and that 14° is the point above which the British Customs and Excise exact almost twice as much duty as on "light" – i.e. table – wines: an important point in considering Italian wines, for many are above this strength.

I have found a great deal of pleasure and interest, as well as the inevitably tedious donkey-work, in compiling and composing this reference book: I hope it will help those who consult it to find similar pleasure and interest in the wines of Italy. If so, and they feel grateful to me, they must feel grateful, too, as I do, to the following who, among others, have helped to make the book possible:

Dott. Enzo Malgeri, Commercial Minister at the Italian Embassy in London; Dott. A. Giaroli, of the London office of the Istituto Nazionale per il Commercio Estero, and Dottori Silvio Barocas, Domenico di Paolo, Mario Rizzotti and Cesare Fristelli, of the Rome office; Mr Douglas Whybrow, sometime of British United Air Ferries, so courteously efficient in getting me and my car to Geneva; Dott. Arrigo Musiani, Secretary-General of the Enoteca Italica Permanente, Siena; Mr Gerald Asher, of the London firm of Asher Storey and Company, whose scholarly notes on the Italian wines he is introducing to London have been so useful; and Mr R. M. Scott, of the London firm of Aug. Hellmers and Sons, Ltd., who first introduced me to the charming wines of the Alto Adige. I am indebted to the Baron Bettino Ricasoli of our own time, who carries on so devotedly the tradition established by his distinguished ancestor, Cavour's successor, and who has been my kindly host both at Brolio and in Florence; to my fellow newspaperman, the Marchese de'Frescobaldi – "Dino" – and to his brother Piero, who entertained me so handsomely at Nipozzano with a wine of the house of the year of my birth, before he died untimely, in a car crash; and to the Marchese di Antinori and his brother Piero. Among my guides and hosts in various parts of Italy have been Dott. Nino Anesi, of the Assessorato Regionale Industria e Commercio della Regione Trentino-Alto Adige, Trento; Dott. Guglielmo Anzilotti, Director of the Consorzio per la Difesa del Vino Tipico del Chianti; Signor Dante Carelli of the Camera di Commercio, Potenza, and his sister, Signorina Ada Carelli, of the Ente Turismo there; Signor Carlo Balzi, of the Chianti house of Ruffino; Dott. Arturo Bersano, of Nizza Monferrato; Signor Gaetano and Signor Guglielmo Bertani of the Verona firm of that name; Dott. Andrea Masala, of the Department of the Regional Government of Sardinia in Cagliari; Dott. Luigi Ruffino, Secretary-General of the Camera di Commercio, Pavia; Dott. Vittorio Pasqualini, of the Camera di Commercio, Bolzano, Dott. Richard von Mackowitz, of the Ufficio Estero of the Camera di Commercio, Bolzano, and Dott. Ludwig Kofler, Director of the Consorzio delle Cantine Sociale of Bolzano; Dott. Claudio Poncibo, of the Consorzio per la Difesa d'Asti Spumante; and Signor Antonio Mollo, of Reggio Calabria. Signorina Rita

Ghezzi, of Siena, helped my lame Italian over many a stile; Miss Sian Evans translated the text of the Italian wine law that appears as an appendix to this book; and Esmé, Countess of Carlisle, who knows and loves Italy at least as well and as much as I do, and the Italian language a great deal better, has helped to tidy up some of my worst mistakes. But those that remain, along with errors of commission, errors of omission and errors of judgment, are all my own.

CYRIL RAY

Chapter 1

THE WINES OF THE PAST

✵

THERE was wine in Italy before there was Rome. It is still a matter of scholarly debate whether the Bronze Age inhabitants of northern Italy made wine from the wild grape-vine which is known (from the grape pips found where their lake-dwellings used to be) to have flourished in their time, but it is as certain as can be that the Etruscans were making and drinking wine in the regions we know now as Tuscany and Lazio in the ninth and tenth centuries B.C. (The traditional date for the founding of Rome is 753 B.C.) It is generally agreed, except by Mr H. Warner Allen, that the Etruscans, "in the days of their glory", as the late Dr Charles Seltman put it, "must have made fine drink after the manner of the Greeks and the inhabitants of Anatolia whence this remarkable people had come to settle in Italy" (in about 800 B.C.). And Mr William Younger also held that "they would certainly have known about viticulture in the ninth century and . . . would certainly not have been content to lead a life without wine". They even paid their devotions to a wine god of their own, Fufluns.

Mr H. Warner Allen, in his *A History of Wine* states that "the Etruscans seem never to have mastered the art of viticulture", but he seems to be alone in his belief. It would be fairer to say that the Etruscans, though not by any means completely ignorant of viticulture, were amateurs at it – drinkers of immature wine from unpruned vines – compared with the Greeks who founded a colony at Cumae, on a promontory near what is now Naples, in about 750 B.C., bringing with them "a tried system of viticulture as well as cuttings of their vines and, equally valuable, the art of pottery, which made it possible for wine, favoured by a good year, well-made from fine grapes and stored in an air-tight earthenware receptacle, to ripen into something very different from the best wine then known in Italy". Not long after, it is interesting to note, other Greeks, from Ionia, founded Marseilles, and the art and science of viticulture began to spread along the valleys of the Rhône and, perhaps, the Rhine.

The Greeks of Cumae conquered the Etruscans, and the Sabines conquered the Greeks. By that time, about 420 B.C., the region around Cumae – Campania – was already famous for its wines, and Father Sabinus, the legendary founder of the Sabines, who had appropriated to themselves the culture of the conquered, eventually makes his appearance in Virgil as the Vine-Grower, with his pruning-knife.

All the same, the Romans of the time seem to have imported their fine wines direct from Greece, rather than to have drunk the wines grown in Campania from Greek vines in the Greek way, and to have gone on doing so well into the period when, with the conquest of Greece and the fall of Carthage, Rome became the mistress of the Mediterranean world.

Pliny, in his *Natural History*, writing in about A.D. 70, gives a curiously precise date – 154 B.C. – as the year in which Italy became the greatest wine-growing country in the world, producing about two-thirds of the eighty known varieties of fine wine. Even then, Greek wines were competing with native growths on the Roman market, and still enjoyed such prestige that that great gourmet, Lucullus, a couple of generations earlier than Pliny, distributing Greek wine to the Roman people on his return in triumph from his campaigns in the East, flattered himself on his own open-handedness, for he recalled that in his father's time it was only one cup of Greek wine apiece: guests at public banquets then had to continue with Italian wines. But by this time Falernian from Campania seems to have been prized as highly as the wines of Chios and Lesbos, and in his third consulship Caesar, in addition to Chian and Lesbian, offered not only the now famous Falernian of Campania but Mamertine from Sicily as well.

In his immense, and immensely learned history of wine and of wine-drinking, the late William Younger listed eighteen wines as being regarded by the Romans of the golden age – the latter years of the Republic and the earliest of the Empire – as being the finest in the world. Three were Greek, and all three came from the farthest of the Greek islands – Cos, Chios and Lesbos. At one time, the Greeks used to treat their wines with sea-water, as the Greeks of our own time treat theirs with resin, but the resinated wine that Rome knew, and that Martial inveighed against, came not from Greece but from northern Italy. Greece took to it later. Younger's belief, following Pliny, is that it was only as this sea-watering declined that the Chian, Lesbian and Coan wines became fashionable in Rome, but it is clear that even before they became fashionable, they had been popular when very heavily salted, and enough Romans were fond of them for Cato, in his *De Agri Cultura*, to give more than one recipe for counterfeiting Coan wine, all of them involving the addition of brine or sea-water.

There are four Spanish wines, too, in Younger's list, but it is the eleven Italian wines that concern us here. One was Sicilian – the Mamertine already mentioned, from around Messina, which Julius Caesar made fashionable, and the remaining ten came from the mainland. Most famous of all was – and is, thanks to the frequency with which the classical writers referred to it – Falernian,* which came from the hills forming the boundary between Latium and Campania, near where Mondragone now stands. Like so many modern Italian wines with a single name, there were a dry and a sweet, a red and a white, but Mr Warner Allen is sure that the great classic was the dry red Falernian, "probably not unlike such a Rhône wine as Châteauneuf du Pape", but with a much more powerful bouquet (though Henderson thought that it must be like a sherry or madeira), and he quotes Martial, who "wanted not merely to drink the kisses left in the loved one's cup but to kiss lips moist with old Falernian". Again, like so many Italian red wines of our own time, Falernian seems to have had a remarkable capacity for ageing, probably in glass or earthenware jars, sealed with a sort of plaster of Paris; Petronius, in Nero's time, makes the *nouveau-riche* Trimalchio serve his guests with the most expensive wine obtainable in Rome – Falernian, a hundred years old.†

Similarly, Surrentine, from the Sorrentine peninsula, was said to need at least twenty-five years to lose its youthful asperity; it takes its place among Younger's pre-eminent eighteen wines largely, it seems, because of its reputation in classical times as a tonic, much prescribed by the physicians, though two Roman emperors in succession, Tiberius and Caligula, found it too thin for their tastes – Caligula, indeed, scorned it as *nobilis vappa*.‡

Calenian, a lighter wine than Falernian, but from the same parts (near the

* See pp. 122, 129, 131.

† For the most expensive wine in the Rome of our own times, not all that younger than Trimalchio's Falernian, see p. 99, Brunello di Montalcino.

‡ Badly kept wine turns to vinegar, and the Latin word for vinegar that in its turn had become insipid was *vappa*. The emperor considered Surrentinum to be flavourless vinegar with ideas above its station. By extension, the word *vappa* came to be used for a stupid good-for-nothing: it persists as *voppo* in Neapolitan slang, and entered the American vocabulary by way of immigrants from the South, becoming "wop" in the process – all this according to the late Dr Charles Seltman, *op. cit.*

present-day Calvi), is mentioned time and again in Horace – though Horace admits that he offers it to Maecenas only because he cannot afford Falernian; and so is the dry, full-flavoured Caecuban, which before the time of Augustus was tremendously fashionable, though it must have been a coarse, heavy and headachey wine (Henderson believed it to be a rough sweet wine), from vines trained up the poplars that grew in the marshes between Terracina and Formiae. As Mr Warner Allen observes, vines grown in a marsh can never produce really fine wines, and Cyrus Redding goes farther, in excluding "soil infected by stagnant waters" as the only ground in which the vine will not grow. In any case, Caecuban ceased to be produced when Nero drove the Baiae–Ostia canal through its native swamps.

Setine must have been finer: it came from notably beautiful vineyards overlooking the Pontine marshes, and was thought by some of his courtiers to be Augustus's favourite wine, which meant, of course, that it became theirs. Others, though, claimed the distinction for the north-Italian Rhaetic, which must have pleased Virgil, for it came from the hills above Verona, near his birthplace, Mantua, and he loved it dearly. With the Sicilian Mamertine, Rhaetic is the only Italian wine of the eighteen not from either Campania or Latium, and is the exception to the general opinion of the time that no wine worth drinking came from north of Rome. Opinion in modern times is all the other way, and Rhaetic came, in any case, from just about the same region as the Soave of our own time, and may perhaps have been a similar wine – we know it to have been light and delicate, a pleasant change for Augustus from the heavy wines of Latium and Campania, the admirers of which found it mawkish.

Of the remaining wines, Alban was the precursor of the present-day *castelli Romani* wines, coming from the Alban Hills: there were a sweet and a dry, both perhaps white. Massic came from the same area as Falernian and Calenian, which it resembled, and Fundanian was very similar to the heavy Caecuban; Statanian came from the fringe of the Falernian country and was lighter than most.

🦋

"In ancient times," wrote Cyrus Redding a century ago, "the Romans trained their high vines as they now do in Tuscany, along palisades, or from tree to tree." In Tuscany, this pattern is only now beginning to change*
* See p. 97.

and far more vines than not in central and south-central Italy are still trained in this way, so that the twentieth-century holiday-maker, on his way to Florence and Siena, to Verona or Bologna, can see how Horace's Calenian, or Virgil's Rhaetic, was grown, by the system known to the Romans as the *arbustum*.

A variation of this method was the *compluvium*, a rectangular trellis raised above the ground, forming a sort of arbour – still a "high vine" system, and with the same advantage as the *arbustum*, in that either under the trees or over the trellises the vines could be trained in such a way as to be shielded by foliage from too great a measure of sunshine.

Then as now, on the other hand, the vines of Southern Italy were trained low, by the system now known as *albarello*, perhaps brought in by the Greeks – an easier and cheaper method, for it obviates the expense of trees or of trellises, and much of the trouble of training, but produces coarse wines because of the reflection of heat from the soil, and in Roman times was said to encourage the depredations of foxes, rats and mice.

Cellaring must have been well understood by the Romans, even though they seem to have kept their wines above ground, in what the French would call *chais* rather than *caves*, but various writers, Henderson points out:

> . . . generally advise a northern aspect, and one not much exposed to the light, in order that it may not be liable to sudden vicissitudes of temperature; and they very properly inculcate the necessity of placing it at a distance from the furnaces, baths, cisterns, or springs of water, stables, dunghills, and every sort of moisture and effluvia likely to affect the wine.

The better wines were matured in a *fumarium*, and references in Latin authors to "smoky" wines have suggested to some historians that the wine itself was smoked, and led to curious speculations as to what it could have tasted like. But it seems reasonable to suppose that the reference was not to a sort of kippered claret but simply to the process to which the wine had been subjected. Rather, it must be thought probable that Roman wines were subjected to heat, as Madeira is to this day, for the purpose both of mellowing and stabilising it.

From Cato, who flourished around 200 B.C., to Columella, between two and three hundred years after – as it might be from Isaac Newton to our own time – a great number of Latin authors produced treatises on agricultural methods, and from them William Younger made tentative identification of some of the grapes of classical times with some of present-day

Italy, notably the Aminean with the Greco Bianco and the Trebulan with the Trebbiano, both producing white wine.

Columella preferred the Aminean to the more prolific Nomentan for precisely the same reason that in Burgundy, for instance, the Pinot is a "noble" grape and the more prolific Gamay is not. By this time (in the early years of the Empire, under Claudius or Nero), wine-growing on the sizeable estates of Latium and Campania was well-informed and highly sophisticated, which is not to say that the greater part of Italian wine-production did not come from smallholdings on which peasant farmers made rough wines from common grapes by the simplest methods, and drank them young. But a wine-grower such as Columella himself took great trouble over his cuttings and graftings, picking each variety of grape individually, and laying it down that "we judge to be best every kind of wine which can grow old without any treatment, nor should anything at all be mixed with it, which might dull its natural flavour. For that wine is immeasurably the best, which needs only its own nature to give pleasure."*

Macaulay wrote that –

> *This year the must shall foam*
> *Round the white feet of laughing girls*
> *Whose sires have marched to Rome.*

But that was in the time of Tarquin, which is pre-history, and there is plenty of evidence that the finer wines of classical times were pressed, not trodden, before fermentation in great earthenware jars, and that the Romans knew a great deal about fining and racking, as well as having devised a sort of *chaptalisation*, making use of honey or of boiled must, for thin wines lacking in natural grape-sugar. Boiled must was also used to produce fortified dessert wines, as is done with *vin cotto*;† some wines were preserved, or flavoured, or both, by the addition of herbs, spices or, as in Greece, resin; and there are unappetising recipes in Cato, Virgil, Pliny and others for cheap wines, many of them made from a second pressing, as rations for farm-workers. Pliny, indeed, writing in the first decades A.D., complained that even the nobility were fobbed off with coloured and adulterated wines.

No doubt there were genuine wines, carefully produced by wine-growers as dedicated to quality as Columella, but as William Younger has deduced

* Mr H. Warner Allen's translation.   † See pp. 95 and 165.

from the cookery books of the time, those Romans who were not given to country dishes and the simple life, as Horace was (or, at any rate, as Horace sang), lusted after pungency and richness, their dishes spiced and peppered, and enjoyed wines to match. Spiced and aromatic wines, or the Roman version of *retsina*, would no doubt go well with such dishes as dormice fattened on chestnuts and cooked in a sauce made of the entrails of salted Spanish mackerel and pepper. And we know that there were wines made specially to be drunk as aperitifs or as dessert wines, by flavouring with honey, with violets, with roses or with pepper, as well as an absinthe (*absinthites*) made of wine and wormwood.

Most of the true, unadulterated wines, such as Falernian, were probably, as we have seen, big, full-flavoured heavy red wines – the light, dry Rhaetic, possibly white, was one of the few exceptions: perhaps the Romans drank it with the oysters they loved so much – and the Roman love for rich dishes would explain their popularity, though there are many references to their being drunk diluted with water, or with snow. There were drinking-parties, and there were heavy drinkers, but the Romans generally, in the great days of the city, were an abstemious people, and to drink wine undiluted was to go it, rather. Catullus sang the promise of a drinking bout with a hard-drinking companion in his *Minister vetuli puer Falerni*:

> *Bearer of old Falernian wine,*
> *Good boy, a stronger glass be mine.*
> *Mistress of toasts (as drunk as she*
> *Not ev'n the drunken grape can be)*
> *Postumia will have it so.*
> *You, water, wine's destruction, go:*
> *Away with you to folk austere:*
> *The god of wine himself is here.*

– which suggests that Falernian was usually offered diluted, and that this was a special occasion.

All the same, the great wines, even if destined for dilution, were handled with some connoisseurship, for they were usually decanted, strained either through linen or through metal wine-strainers that may perhaps have resembled those made by the great Georgian silversmiths.

They would need decanting, too, for the best and most highly prized of these big, heavy wines spent many years in cask (or, more likely, in earthenware jars, though wooden casks were not unknown), and in smaller glass or earthenware bottles, before being served. There are endless references in the classical authors, from Cato onwards, to the age of wines of the better sort – such lines as Horace's promise to Maecenas that a jar of mellowed wine had long been waiting for him, and Columella's assertion that almost all wine improved with age. Not that there were vintage years as such: as in Italy now, it is how many years a wine has aged in cask and bottle that matters, not in what year it was made.* True, most of the wine of Italy was for immediate consumption by the farmer who grew it, and for his family – wine of the country that was drunk within the year. But even Horace's modest Sabine wine, which no doubt bore about the same relation to Falernian as a common Beaujolais would to a Romanée-Conti, or a Blayais to a first-growth of the Médoc, and was by no means, it would seem, a "big" wine, was ready to drink, wrote Horace, after from seven to fifteen years; the marsh-grown Caecuban took many years to mature; and we have already recorded the quarter of a century that was needed to smooth away the harshness of Surrentine. We cannot know now, for certain, what any of these wines tasted like, but it is clear, at any rate, that the best wines of classical Rome were grown, made, cellared and decanted as carefully as any first-growth claret that reaches the table of a twentieth-century connoisseur, and that although much of this skill and care and devotion were forgotten, along with much else, for centuries after the fall of Rome to the barbarians, much remained. It is not so much that the arts of living were all lost in the Dark and the Middle Ages as that a great deal went unrecorded: there is a link between the vineyards that Virgil knew, in northern Italy, and the Vernage, or Vernaccia,† that came to England from those parts in the fourteenth and fifteenth centuries; and Trubidiane, recorded as having been imported into London in 1373, is a corruption of Trebbiano, which has been at any rate tentatively identified with the Trebulan that was grown in Campania in Julius Caesar's time.

* Though the Romans usually knew a wine's year, and some were especially highly thought of. "The ancients noted the years of celebrated growths, as that of the Opimian year, or the year of Rome, 632, when Opimius was consul. It was in high esteem a century afterwards. The Romans marked their amphorae, or wine vessels (containing seven gallons and a pint modern measure), with the consul's name, which indicated the year of the vintage. Many amphorae now exist with the legible mark of the vintage" (Redding). The Opimian year was 121 B.C., and it was the Opimian wine that Trimalchio offered his guests (see p. 23). But it was age rather than vintage that usually impressed.
† Not to be confused with the Sardinian Vernaccia.

We know little of Italian viticultural techniques in the Middle Ages, but Italy always remained a wine-growing country: M. André Simon, in his *History of the Wine Trade in England*, records the capture by French pirates in 1472 of a Venetian carrack bound for England with more than four hundred casks of sweet wine on board. It may well be that this particular cargo was of wines from Greece or the Levant, for Venice enjoyed the carrying trade between those parts and the west and north of Europe, but that there were sweet Italian wines being carried to this country at the same time is shown by the monopoly granted to the port of Southampton by Henry IV for the importation of "Malmseys, Muscadels, and all the sweet Levant, Greek or Italian wines, imported either by foreigners or by natives". And in modern times, by the seventeenth century, "Florence wine", white and red, meaning in fact the wine of Tuscany, is being constantly mentioned in English literature, from Lady Sandwich's present of two bottles to Pepys to take home for his wife to Salmon's complaint that although red and white Florence wines are both very good stomach wines, "the red is something binding". The same period sees mention of Lacrima Christi and of "Leattica" – Aleatico – both to be found in the following pages among the familiar Italian wines of our own time.

The Florence wines were apparently exported in uncorked flasks, sealed with olive oil and packed in chests: they were very popular in England. A silver wine-label, or bottle-ticket, inscribed "Flore" is listed in Dr N. M. Penzer's book, where an offer in a *London Gazette* of 1707 is noted of "A Parcel of extraordinary good Red Florence at 6s. a Gallon", and there is reference in a letter of Horace Walpole's to the British ambassador at the court of the Grand Duke of Tuscany, asking him to send Fox "two chests of the best Florence wine every year". A century earlier, according to Henderson, "in the time of our own James I, to have drunk Verdea is mentioned among the boasts of a travelled gentleman".*

It seems clear, though, that Italian wines were no longer so sturdy, or so capable of ageing, as in the days of the great Falernians. Mr Warner Allen quotes Dean Swift's complaint, in 1711, of going to a tavern, after "a scurvy dinner", to drink Florence "at four-and-sixpence a flask; damned wine". The same irascible cleric was given one of the chests that the Grand Duke of Tuscany had sent to Bolingbroke, which he "liked mightily" at first, but which began to spoil within a fortnight, causing Swift to write to Stella: "Do you know that I fear that my whole chest of Florence is turned

* See p. 142 for the Verdea of our own time.

sour, at least the first two were, and hardly drinkable? How plaguy unfortunate am I! And the Secretary's own is the best I ever tasted!"

There can be little doubt that Italian wines were made less carefully than in classical times and that, as William Younger wrote, there was no scientific viticulture between the fall of the Roman Empire and the agricultural innovations of the eighteenth century. Even then, technical improvements came more slowly on the Continent, and especially in Italy, than in the England of the enclosures, of Coke of Holkham and "Turnip" Townshend. Indeed, by Cyrus Redding's time, in the eighteen-fifties, Italian wine had gone completely out of favour in England, simply because, as Redding observed, "Italian wines have stood still and remained without improvement, while those of France and Spain . . . have kept pace to a certain extent with agricultural improvement and the increasing foreign demand."

After examining the difficulties that the wine-grower of a still disunited Italy found in the way of producing good wines for export ("trampled by the Austrian military tyranny, or by the feet of Church despots, destitute of adequate capital, and weighed down by a vexatious system of imposts, what has he to hope for by carrying towards perfection an art which can bring him no benefit?") Redding went on:

> There are places, however, where very good wine is made, and something like care bestowed upon its fabrication; but those exceptions are the result of the care of the proprietor for his own individual consumption. The curses of a foreign yoke and of domestic exaction blight the most active exertions, and render that land, which is the gem of the earth in natural gifts, a waste, or a neglected and despoiled heritage to its inhabitants. The Italians would soon make good wine, if good wine would repay the making – if they might reap that reward due to industry and improvement, which common policy would not withhold in other countries. The peasantry generally are not an idle race.

Though Redding somewhat qualifies that final tribute in going on to give another of the reasons why Italy lagged so long behind France in producing wines worthy of her soil and her long tradition:

> A fine climate, to which the wine seems wedded, produces a large quantity of rich fruit with little trouble, and why should the peasant not enjoy, without extra care and labour, that which, on his bestowing care and labour, will yield him no additional benefit?

Even while Redding was revising his book, though, there were reforms on foot in the Chianti country.* He admitted himself that –

* Redding's classic work first appeared in 1833. The third edition, added to and revised, consulted for this present book, appeared in 1860.

. . . in Tuscany, indeed, things have been at times somewhat better. [and went on] In particular districts in Italy it is by no means a rare thing to meet with good wine. The general neglect of a careful and just system of culture, and the want of that excitement that interest creates, have not prevented the capabilities of the Italian vineyards from being known. In certain instances much care is bestowed upon the vine. In spots among the Apennines the vines are carefully dressed, terrace-fashion, and were they well pruned, and the fruit taken in due maturity, and regularly assorted, which it rarely or never is, a vast deal of excellent wine might be made, without altering anything essential besides, in the present system of vine husbandry. There is good-bodied wine to be produced in Naples for twopence-halfpenny English a bottle, and at Rome and Florence for four-pence.

The Austrian military tyranny, the temporal despotism of the Church, the imposts between petty principalities have all long disappeared, and now, with the new wine law, with the growers' associations, viticultural stations experimenting with French vines and German hybrids, and new co-operative wineries, another era is dawning for Italian wines, possibly as golden as in the days when Horace, over his glass of modest Sabine, knew that he was at the centre of the wine-growing world.

Chapter 2

PIEDMONT AND THE VAL D'AOSTA

As a wine-producing region, Piedmont – with which I include, for convenience's sake, the autonomous French-speaking Val d'Aosta* – usually comes third for volume of output among the provinces of Italy: after Apulia, and often after the Veneto. But no province – not even Lombardy, with such red Valtelline wines as Sassella; not even the Veneto, with its charming lakeside wines and its Soave; not even Tuscany, with its old Chiantis – produces more distinguished or more varied *vini pregiati*, fine wines.

My Italian friends would not thank me if I suggested that this might be due partly to French influence, though there are western and northern fringes of the old kingdom of Savoy – Antico Piemonte – that are still French-speaking, and Italians from farther south or farther east have been known to speak tartly of Turin as "the most Italian city of France". Certainly, Francis I was showing enough interest in Piedmontese wines in the sixteenth century to have them imported into France.

But more especially it is soil, long tradition and climate.

The vine has been established in Piedmont certainly since Roman times, and the more settled history of the kingdom in the past century or so, compared with those other parts of Italy still under Austrian or Papal or Bourbon rule, enabled the royal family – notably King Charles Albert (reigned 1831–49) – to take a practical interest in establishing and improving cellars and vineyards, setting an example followed by Cavour (whose

---

* The Val d'Aosta ranks as a separate region, but its production of wine is far too small for it to be listed separately: 50,000 hectolitres in 1963, compared with Piedmont's more than 5 million, and only one-eighth as great as that of Liguria, the next lowest.

successor as prime minister of united Italy, Ricasoli, followed the same example in his turn, but in Tuscany).

The softly rounded hills that lie east and south of Turin, on either side of the Tanaro river, tributary of the Po – the Monferrati to the north and the Langhe to the south – are where the great Piedmontese wines come from. They are the gentlest of mothers of the noble Nebbiolo grape,* and lie in the same latitude as those slopes of the Rhône valley that grow Tavel and Hermitage and Châteauneuf du Pape, but are protected by the great sweep of the Alps from the winds that harry the French vineyards. It is a sunny, smiling countryside, not scorched and seared as are the vineyards of the south of Italy, the wines of which, like those of the sunbaked south of France, under too fierce a sun, are prolific and undistinguished.

Yet again, the proximity of big, rich and stable markets must have encouraged not only intensive but painstaking production, and the maintenance of high standards: the Monferrat and the Langhe vineyards lie largely within a triangle of which the corners are the great cities of Turin, Milan and Genoa, none of them more than fifty or sixty miles from the centre of the area, and the holiday coast of the Italian Riviera is a shop-window as well as a market.

🐝

Given a more benign climate and more sunshine than the classic wine-growing areas of France and, to an even greater degree, of Germany, Italy tends in the nature of things to produce, in general, bigger and fuller red wines and the grapes from which sweet, aromatic whites can be made without late-gathering. This is not true of all Italian wines, of course: there are dry whites and delicate reds, for climate is not the only factor – there are methods of vinification, too, as well as soil and altitude. But it tends to be true of Italian wines in general; and the wines of Piedmont, even though its climate is more temperate than that of other wine-growing regions of Italy, are good examples.

The red wines are usually big and full-bodied, similar in character to the French Rhône wines, but requiring to be aged in cask for far longer, and improving notably with greater bottle-age still. And although only ten per cent of the total wine production of Piedmont is of white wine, that

* The word is related to *nebbia*, mist, perhaps because it is gathered when the season of mists has begun.

small proportion includes one of the great white wines of the world – Asti Spumante, not only sparkling but sweet, and not only sweet but sweet without (as in sweet champagne) added sugar, and without being made from over-ripe and sun-dried grapes (as in Sauternes and the German *trockenbeerenauslesen*). Asti is sweet simply out of the sweet nature of the muscat grape it is made from.

🔊

France (except for Alsace) names its wines after the regions, sub-regions, communes, villages or vineyards in which they are grown – no mention of Merlot or Cabernet in labelling or demanding a Lafite, for instance, which, besides being a Lafite, no less, is also entitled to be called by such lesser names as Pauillac, Médoc and Bordeaux. Alsatian wines, on the other hand, are Rieslings or Sylvaners, Traminers or Gewürztraminers. But some Italian wines are one thing, some the other, which is confusing, and particularly so in Piedmont, for of the familiar Piedmontese wines Barbera is a grape, whereas Barbaresco is a village, after which a wine is named that is made not from the Barbera but from the Nebbiolo, the noble grape that also produces Barolo – which is confused in its turn with the Brolio of the Chianti country.

One can but speak generally in dealing with the names of Italian wines, for such rules as there are differ from region to region, and are applied, without anything like the sanctions that the French are able to apply in enforcing their laws of *appellation*, by the various *consorzi*, or voluntary associations of growers and merchants, which differ enormously in earnestness and vigour. Speaking generally, then, those Piedmontese wines which bear place names are protected as to the use of those names by associations: when a wine made from the same grape is known only by the name of the grape – Nebbiolo, for instance, instead of Barolo – it is grown outside the delimited and protected region. It may be no worse a wine: it may (though this is unlikely) be better: one cannot be sure.

🔊

Drive into Italy by way of the Great Saint Bernard (quite the easiest way of taking one's car to Italy is to fly it to Geneva by air-ferry, and then through the new tunnel) and the first vines you see are Nebbiolo, trained

34

into pergolas over trellises on terraced hillsides high up in the valley of the Dora, in the autonomous French-speaking region of Val d'Aosta, against a background of snow-topped Alpine peaks and themselves a couple of thousand feet above sea-level. (Some, I am told, flourish at three thousand. Even in the Langhe, vines from which fine wines are made grow at over two thousand feet: fifteen hundred is common in Piedmont.) The Nebbiolo here produces red wines – Donnaz and Carema, after communes in the region – lighter in shade and in style than those made from the same grape, trained more in the French way, in the gentle hills – the Vercelli, the Monferrati and the Langhe – on either side of the upper reaches of the Po and its tributaries: wines such as Gattinara, Barolo, Barbaresco, and those known simply as Nebbiolo, or Nebbiolo Piemontese.

These, with Asti Spumante (made from the Moscato, which used to provide most of the white-wine base for the vermouths of Turin, though more, nowadays, come from Apulia), are the noblest grapes and greatest wines of Piedmont. As will be seen, the Nebbiolo and the Moscato flourish, too, in Lombardy. Other Piedmontese grapes are the Barbera, the Grignolino, the Freisa, the Brachetto, the Cortese, the Dolcetto, the Bonarda and the Erbaluce, each of which has a place in the list of officially recognised Piedmontese wines that follows. Some French Pinot and some German (or Alto-Atesino) Riesling are also grown in the province, but only tentatively and in small amounts, and not producing wines named as yet in any official or semi-official list.

I do not regard vermouth, a manufactured, blended wine, as falling normally within the scope of this book, but it would be absurd to discuss the wines of Piedmont without any mention of it. Vermouth has been made in Turin since the late eighteenth century, the Moscato of the region proving itself an admirable base with which to blend extracts from the aromatic herbs of the neighbouring mountains. (It is significant that the centres of French vermouth manufacture, Marseilles and Chambéry, are also within reach of never-ending supplies of mountain herbs.) Turin is still the centre of the industry, with firms such as Martini, Cinzano, Carpano, Gancia and others earning immense amounts of foreign exchange for Italy.*

* The export trade in vermouths and similar aromatised wines is worth the equivalent in various foreign currencies of some five or six million pounds sterling a year to Italy – most of it in U.S., British, German and French currencies.

Nowadays, wines from the south are more widely used – Piedmont could hardly produce enough for the great vermouth houses of Turin – but the basic principles are the same, and Italian law lays it down that seventy per cent of anything called "vermouth" must be pure natural wine (which does not mean that there are not other aperitifs under other names, which are made of alcohol, sugar and flavourings, without any wine at all).

The various brands of vermouth differ, but the main styles are *bianco* and *rosso*, both sweet; and another white vermouth, made after the French style, which is not called *bianco*, but "dry". The firm of Carpano makes a distinctively bitter variety called Punt è Mes, (allegedly because it used to be served at a café near the Turin Stock Exchange where, on one occasion, an excited broker went on shouting to the waiter the phrase, "point and a half", that he was hammering away at in the business deal he was trying to clinch), and Campari is another bitter aperitif, not strictly speaking a vermouth, though used in the same way, and a particularly good aperitif with soda. Many wines of the region are quinined into an appetising bitterness as aperitifs – Barolo Chinato is the best example.

The great vermouth houses have the resources and the facilities for making Asti Spumante and other sparkling wines.

The Wines of Piedmont and the Val d'Aosta

Ara. Dry *frizzante* red wine from Grignasco.

Asti Spumante. Almost the whole yield of the Moscato grape, which is widely grown in Piedmont, is made into a delicate, sweetish, aromatic sparkling wine, generally considered too sweet for the more sophisticated English tastes, but delicious with fruit or sweets after a meal, for a mid-morning drink or at parties. The finest quality is Asti Spumante, production of which is rigorously supervised and controlled by inspectors of the consortium of growers, which grants a neck-label showing San Secondo, patron saint of the town of Asti, mounted, in blue on a gold ground: Moscato d'Asti (*q.v.*) also carefully controlled, is less fine and sweeter.

One firm – Contratto – still makes a very little Asti by the *méthode champenoise* (involving secondary fermentation in bottle; *remuage* to settle the sediment on the cork; *dégorgement* of the sediment by quick freezing of the neck of the bottle; and subsequent liqueuring by filling the gap with sugar dissolved in champagne). But virtually all production of Asti, and all the production of Moscato Spumante – the centre of which is not in Asti itself but in the small neighbouring town of Canelli – is by the Charmat, or *cuve close*, method of fermentation in closed vats, and bottling under pressure. Not only is this method much cheaper (it is forbidden in France to any wine that is to be called champagne), but the makers claim that it preserves much better the fragrance of the muscat grape, which suffers under the lengthy *méthode champenoise* – the *cuve close* method takes days as against months.

Indeed, many of the big houses – and Asti is largely produced by big houses and co-operatives – do in fact maintain the *méthode champenoise* for the production of *dry* sparkling wines made from the white Pinot grape, and sold under brand names. These wines are increasingly popular in Italy, but are not exported, as they could not be expected to compete with champagne in foreign markets. In Italy, though, they are considerably cheaper than champagne, though about twice the price of sparkling Asti and Moscato. Typical examples are the Fontanafredda firm's Contessa Rosa; the Cinzano Principe di Piemonte; the Gancia Royal Cuvée, the Martini Riserva Montelera; the Contratto Bacco d'Oro, and many others.

Curiously enough, even though these very acceptable wines are made from French grapes in the French way, my experience of them is that they share with the sparkling Asti and Moscato the characteristics of having a much smaller, weaker and shorter-lived bubble than champagne.

Barbaresco. Red wine made, in small quantities, of the Nebbiolo grape in Barbaresco and neighbouring communes in the gently hilly country just to the east of the great white-truffle centre of Alba. A full-bodied, rich, fragrant wine, deep in colour and acquiring slight amber tinges with age, it matures more quickly, losing its harshness earlier, than its close relative, Barolo (*q.v.*), made in the same way, of the same grape, only a few miles away. Protected by an association of growers of Barolo and Barbaresco, the approved wines bear a neck-label showing the tower of the ancient township of Barbaresco in gold on a blue ground. 12·5°–14°. Good years: 1946, 1947, 1950, 1955. Very good: 1945, 1951, 1952, 1957, 1958.

Barbera d'Asti; Barbera di Cuneo; and Barbera with other district names. Quite the commonest vine in Piedmont – twenty times as common as the aristocratic Nebbiolo – is the Barbera, producing red wines that vary widely in quality, many of them made in co-operatives. Harsh when young, Barbera mellows with age to about the quality of a modest Rhône wine, which it resembles in style. Mr Gerald Asher, of the London firm of Asher Storey, which ships them, has observed that while the Barbera wines "do not have the strength and nerve of Nebbiolo", they "lack none of its colour, nor its robust earthy flavour". The finest, grown chiefly round Asti, are accorded an association neck-label showing blue grapes superimposed on the old city's tall, part-Roman, part-medieval tower, in red, and allowed to be styled "d'Asti". Others are permitted to be styled Barbera Riserva or Barbera Extra and are also full-bodied, and improve with bottle-age, though they are usually sold after four years in wood and only six months in bottle. Wine that is styled Barbera, simply, is a common wine, often slightly *frizzante* and sweetish, like a subdued Portuguese *vinho verde*. 12°–15°. Good years (for Barbera d'Asti only): 1945, 1946, 1953, 1954, 1957. Very good: 1947, 1950, 1955. Exceptional: 1958.

Barberati. A name given to wine made in the Langhe of a mixture of Dolcetto and Barbera grapes.

Barengo. Very limited production of a straw-coloured dry wine made in the Novara region from the Greco Bianco grape. 12°–14°.

Barolino. A name given to wine made in the Langhe of a mixture of Dolcetto and Nebbiolo grapes.

Barolo. One of the great red wines of Italy – many experts consider it the greatest – made of the Nebbiolo grape in compact, smoothly hilly areas, strictly delimited by the two associations, around the commune of Barolo, near Alba. Deep red in colour, full and fragrant. (Writers in official publications claim to detect the mingled aroma of tar and violets.) It spends at least three years in cask before bottling, and ages as well and as long in bottle as a good claret* (longer than burgundy), taking on a similar tinge of orange-brown at the rim of the glass. Considered rather superior to its close relative, Barbaresco, because of its greater capacity for ageing in bottle, it is usually very slightly the fuller and heavier. It carries a neck-label showing either a golden lion or a helmeted head, according to the particular district it comes from. 13°–15°. Good years: 1946, 1950,

---

* Indeed – as will be observed, too, of the finest Tuscan wines – these full red Italian wines have an immense capacity for ageing in bottle. Paolo Monelli records having tasted a Barolo 1858 that had lost colour, but of which the bouquet was "still racy and generous". At the end of 1964 the 1952 seemed very backward.

1954, 1955. Very good: 1945, 1951, 1952, 1957. Exceptional: 1947, 1958.

Bianco di Castel Tagliolo. White wine made in Tagliolo Monferrato: the common sort made of Cortese grapes and sold as a café wine, but a finer variety, the Cortese mixed with Riesling and Sauvignon, is bottled, and is a pleasant, dry, straw-yellow table wine, 10°–13°.

Blanc de Morgex. Dry white wine, with a faint suggestion of herbs in scent and flavour, made from local varieties of grape in the highest vineyards of the Val d'Aosta, some as much as 3,000 feet above sea-level. 8°–10°.

Boca d'Asti. Dry, ruby-red table wine made from Vespolina, Spanna, Bonarda and Croatina grapes: drunk locally after a couple of years in bottle, and also exported to Switzerland. 12°–13°.

Bonarda d'Asti. Sparkling, semi-sweet, red wine made near Asti from a grape of the same name. Deep in colour, but light in alcohol (10°–11°) and refreshing, served cool. Rarely found outside its own region.

Brachetto d'Asti. Similar to Bonarda, but made from the Brachetto grape, lighter and much sweeter – a sort of cherry-red Moscato Spumante. Becoming rare. 12·5°–13·5°. Good and very good years: 1945, 1946, 1947, 1949, 1951, 1952, 1953, 1954, 1955, 1956, 1957, 1958.

Bricherasio. See under Nebbiolo.

Camarino. Rare red wine, similar to Ghemme (*q.v.*), but credited with aphrodisiac qualities that it was difficult to put to the test in the cloistered quiet of the tasting-room. 12°–13°. There is a Camarino Rubino, said to be "most gentle" – presumably for patients in not such dire need.

Camiglione. See under Nebbiolo.

Canavesano; Campiglione. Roughish red wines made near Turin of mixtures of Barbera, Freisa and Avarengo grapes; fairly common wines of no great merit. 10°–11°.

Carema. Red Nebbiolo, close kin to Barolo and Barbaresco, but lighter, perhaps because of the altitude at which it is grown – up to about 2,000 feet – in the valley of the Dora, around the village of Carema in the Val d'Aosta, where a grape festival is held every year at vintage time. Here the vines are trained into pergolas, as in the Alto Adige. 12°–13°.

Cari. *Rosé*, semi-sweet wine from a grape of the same name. 9°–10°.

Castel la Volta. A charming, dryish white *frizzante* (sometimes *spumante*) wine, made in some years, not all, from what is really a table grape, with few pips. Comes from the neighbourhood of Santa Vittoria and Monticello.

39

Castel Tagliolo. Similar to Cortese dell'Alto Monferrato (*q.v.*).

Castello di Sommariva. Dry, fragrant, delicate white wine from the Cortese grape. (See Cortese dell'Alto Monferrato.)

Cesnola. A local Nebbiolo, lighter than most, and drunk fairly young.

Chiaretto di Cavaglia. Sweetish, *rosé* wine, of no great distinction, from near Vicelli.

Chiaretto del Viverone. Light red, almost *rosé* wine, slightly *frizzante*, from same area.

Cortese dell'Alto Monferrato. Dry white wine, light and fragrant, made in the Monferrato hills from the Cortese grape: to be drunk young, and excellent with fish. (Some is used as a base for vermouth.) A sparkling version is sometimes to be met with: the semi-sweet is called Gavi (*q.v.*). 10°–12°.

Dolcetto; Dolcetto d'Alba; Dolcetto delle Langhe; Dolcetto di Strevi; Dolcetto d'Ovada. A red wine that is dry or dryish, despite its sweet-sounding name, which is that of the grape it is made from, one of the commonest in Piedmont (next only to Barbera and Freisa). Pleasant country wine, sometimes with a little sugar retained, by temperature control, to render it *amabile* – very slightly sweet, though not rich or luscious – and there is a sparkling version. Dolcetto d'Alba is the finest – a dry wine with a bitter tang; the others are commoner and cheaper. 10·5°–11·5°. Good years (for better qualities): 1945, 1951, 1952, 1957. Very good: 1947, 1950, 1955, 1958.

Donnaz. Another Val d'Aosta version of the Nebbiolo: see under Carema.

Enfer. Clear red, common wine of the Val d'Aosta.

Fara. A Gattinara (*q.v.*) of Fara, near Novara, but not of the highest quality.

Freisa di Chieri; Freisa d'Asti. The garnet-red wine made from the local Freisa grape is one of the commonest of the region: that made in the Chieri district near Turin is more highly regarded than that of Asti, though the latter has the protection of an association's neck-label (black grapes superimposed on a yellow tower of Asti). Dry, and all the smoother for a couple of years in bottle, when it offers a pleasant raspberry bouquet. There is also a sweet, sparkling version. 10°–12°.

Frossasco. See under Nebbiolo.

Gattinara. Made, like Barolo, from the Nebbiolo grape, in a very restricted region near the town of Gattinara (near Vercelli, in the low-lying

Plate I Vineyards near Barolo, A
Piedmont

Plate II Alba, Piedmont: vineyard
Moscato grapes, from which Asti
mante is made

Po valley), and preferred by some experts to Barolo itself, as perhaps the greatest of all Italian red wines. (Indeed, it has acquired so much prestige for a wine produced in such small quantities, that reputable bottles are very hard to come by, as unscrupulous dealers have taken to blending it with inferior wine from the South.)* Tends to be lighter in colour than Barolo, a garnet rather than a ruby red, less strong and rather more elegant in style. In some bottles I have thought to detect a hint of the flavour of fennel – not unpleasing, but odd. Needs at least three years in bottle. 12°–13°. Good years: 1947, 1949, 1954, 1957. Very good: 1945, 1946, 1950, 1958. Exceptional: 1952.

Gavi. Semi-sweet version of the white Cortese (*q.v.*).

Ghemme. Similar to, but not so fine as Gattinara (*q.v.*), being made with Bonarda and other grapes, as well as Nebbiolo. From commune of Ghemme, near Novara, where they also make a sweetish white wine consumed locally, called Greco di Ghemme – the Greco di Sizzano is similar.

Grignasco. Similar to Ghemme (above).

Grignolino d'Asti. Red wine, from Grignolino grape, grown in the Alessandria–Asti area, lightish in colour and style, usually drunk young and cool, like Valpolicella and Bardolino, though Mr Gerald Asher, who describes it as, "fine in style and attractively perfumed", considers it can be, "drunk young with pleasure, and old with delight". (There is also a sweet, sparkling version.) 11°–13°. Those who would wish to try drinking it "old with delight" should note that the good years were: 1945, 1950, 1951, 1952, 1957. Very good: 1947, 1954, 1955, 1958.

Lessona. Similar to Gattinara (*q.v.*) though not quite so fine, and also sometimes called Valdengo or Vigliano, according to its commune of origin.

Masserano. Similar to Gattinara (see above).

Moscato d'Asti. The commoner, cheaper, usually rather sweeter, but still quite respectable version of Asti Spumante (*q.v.*). About ninety per cent of the total production of the Moscato vines in the Asti area goes to making sparkling wine, but a very little still white wine is produced; a little goes to Turin as a basis for vermouth, as in the old days, though the great vermouth firms rely more and more on cheap wines from the South (notably Apulia); and a very little indeed is made from semi-dried grapes into a richly luscious dessert wine, the Passito di Moscato, now very rarely seen.

* But now has a *consorzio* of growers, which presumably will be able to withhold labels from such wines.

According to the delimited region it comes from, Moscato d'Asti bears a neck-label showing the mounted San Secondo of Asti in red on a blue ground, or a helmeted head in blue on gold. 7°–10°.

Moscato di Canelli; Moscato di Strevi. A very small amount of dry but highly perfumed still Moscato is occasionally found in this region. Good years: 1945, 1946, 1947, 1950, 1953, 1954, 1957, 1960. Very good: 1955, 1958.

Mottalciata. Similar to Gattinara (*q.v.*), but not generally thought to be so fine.

Nebbiolo. The finest Nebbiolo wines are Barolo, Barbaresco, Gattinara and the others listed here as being similar to Gattinara. Minor but good examples are Camiglione, Bricherasio and Frossasco. Red wines from the same vines grown in other areas are not so fine and are styled simply Nebbiolo, or Nebbiolo Piemontese. But Nebbiolo is a sound, decent wine, and goes well with meat. There are sweet, semi-sweet (*amabile*) and sparkling versions. 12°–13° dry; 10°–11° sweet. Good years: 1946, 1947, 1949, 1952, 1953, 1954, 1956, 1959. Very good: 1945, 1948, 1950, 1951, 1955, 1957, 1958.

Passito di Caluso. In Italy *passito* wines are made from grapes that have been part-dried in the sun after picking (cf. the French *vins de paille*), so that their sweetness and flavour are concentrated, making rich, fragrant dessert wines. This particular example is made in very small quantities from the Erbaluce grape (and is sometimes known simply as Erbaluce, or sometimes Albaluce), in the high sub-Alpine country south of Ivrea – a golden wine with a pronounced bouquet. A dry Erbaluce is sometimes found. 12°–16°.

Passito di Moncrivello. Dessert wine from Vercelli.

Passito della Val d'Aosta. Dessert wine from Moscato grapes produced near Chatillon and Aosta itself.

Pellaverga and Quagliano. Produced in small quantities from the Pellaverga grape in the mountains north of Cuneo: light, sweet red wines of only small importance. 9°–10°.

Prunent. Rare red wine, from a grape of the same name; dry and rather sharp, grown near Trontano, not far from Novara.

Ramiè. Local name for a rather ordinary, lightish Barbera.

San Marzano. Red, slightly *frizzante* wine made of ninety per cent Barbera and ten per cent Nebbiolo, peculiar to the communes of San Marzano and Nizza Monferrato, near Asti. Bottled in the spring after picking, and kept in bottles for two to three years before rebottling. Fresh, frothy and fragrant, and something of an oddity.

Sizzano. Similar to, but less fine than Gattinara (*q.v.*). Other wines of the same sort, usually made by mixing other grapes with the Nebbiolo, distinguished only by place names, are:

> Briona (or Caramino)
> Fara
> Grignasco
> Maggiora
> Ronco del Frate

Torretta di San Pietro. Rich dessert wine found rarely, and in small quantities, in the Val d'Aosta.

Vino della Serra. Red and white wines from the Serra d'Ivrea – high country north of Ivrea. The white is made from Erbaluce grapes, dry but full (9·5°–11·5°), the red from Barbera, Freisa and others, including a little of the better-bred Nebbiolo, which gives it some finesse. 10°–12°.

❧

Minor wines of Piedmont and the Val d'Aosta, usually found only in the localities where they are grown, include:

Agliè. The sweetish light red wine from near Turin.

Candia Canavese. A sweetish red wine, made from Barbera, Brachetto and Freisa grapes.

Chambave (also Grand Cru de Chambave, or Moscato de Chambave). A Val d'Aostan strong, sweetish white wine, made from Moscato grapes.

Chiomonte. A dryish red table wine.

Malvasia di Nus. Dessert wine, highly esteemed but rare, produced by one grower in Val d'Aosta.

Malvasia Rosa. Rather more common (in both senses) than the above; *frizzante* or *spumante*, and sweet. 10°–12°.

Meana di Susa. Red, sweetish, semi-sparkling wine.

Mesolone. Full-bodied red wine, with strong bouquet, made of seventy-five per cent Nebbiolo, twenty-five per cent Bonarda. 13°–14°.

Montouvert. The only place I know of outside Germany where they sometimes make an *eiswein** – otherwise the wine of this little place near Villeneuve is like that of Chambave (*q.v.*).

Rosso Rubino del Viverone. Full red wine made from a mixture of Barbera, Bonarda, Dolcetto and Freisa grapes.

* Wine made from grapes that are fully ripe but have been frozen on the vine, so that the grape-juice is highly concentrated, giving a wine of very high quality in very small quantities.

Chapter 3

LIGURIA

✿

LIGURIA, the narrow coastal strip that runs between mountain and sea, from the French frontier to La Spezia, with Genoa at its middle, is the smallest of the regions of Italy. Its production of wine is small even in proportion to its size, for so much of the region is given up to olives and carnations;* so much of its manpower to fishing and to the tourist industry; though Genoa itself is, perhaps, the major centre of the Italian wine trade, both for home and for export, much of the wine of the south of Italy reaching it by sea.

Although the passing tourist may notice many vineyards as he drives – or waits in the traffic jams – along the coastal road, most of these are small plots only, cultivated to provide a family with its own simple table wine, and not for sale. What commercial wine-growing there is in Liguria is concentrated mainly between and around Genoa and Savona, and near La Spezia. Few Ligurian wines are to be found far from where they are grown.

The Wines of Liguria

Arcola Bianco; Arcola Rosso. Quite undistinguished table wines, red and white, produced between La Spezia and Lerici, and unlikely to be met with much farther afield.

Ameglia. Similar to Arcola, above.

Barbarossa. Rather pretty pink wine, made from a vine of the same

* Some wines, indeed, once well-known, no longer exist, or not on any commercial scale, because the ground where once they grew has been given over to the more immediately profitable flower-growing: Piematone, once grown very near to Ventimiglia, springs to mind.

name that is so called because of the long branches of red grapes that it bears, considered to be like long red beards. This vine grows on the slopes above the stretch of holiday coast between Noli and Pietra Ligure, on either side of Finale Ligure. There is a sweet variety called Barbarossa Dolce: the drier Barbarossa is described by an Italian writer on wine as being "full of *brio*" – which seems just the thing for a carefree holiday region. 12°–14°.

Busetto. Very much a local white wine, dry and drunk young in the fish restaurants around Finale Ligure.

Campochiesa Bianco. A full-flavoured and heavily scented, but dryish white wine, made chiefly from the Pigato grape, which has the unusual characteristic, for a white wine (and a not very strong white wine, at that), of not only lasting but even improving for very long periods in bottle – some writers say for twenty to twenty-five years, though I have no experience myself of a Campochiesa of so great an age. But it is, at any rate, the local custom, in the region between Ceriale and Albenga (just to the west of the Barbarossa district, see above), and in the hills behind, to lay down a demijohn on the birth of a son, with a view to drinking it at his wedding. 10°–11°.

Campochiesa Rosso. Not so fine a wine, and neither so well known nor so plentiful as the white, nevertheless the red Campochiesa is also extremely fragrant, and ages well in bottle. Made from a mixture of many types of grape including the white Pigato. 11°–12°.

Casteldoria. See under Dolceacqua.

Chiaretto del Faro. Just outside the Cinqueterre district (see below), on the Spezia side, they produce an interesting pink wine by adding to the *cépage* used in the white Cinqueterre wines a certain amount of red must from Sangiovese and Canaiolo grapes. Dry and delicate.

Cinqueterre. Quite the most famous of all the wines of Liguria comes from the five villages, or "lands" – *cinque terre* – of Corniglia, Biassa, Monterosso, Vernazza and Tiomaggiore, which lie between rocky cliffs (tunnelled by the railway) and the sea, between Cape Mesco and Cape Cavo, west of La Spezia. The villages are still difficult to get at for the visitor: the vineyards seem impossible – some can be reached only by boat, others from the cliffs above by ropes and ladders. But what is grown there is very fine wine indeed – or rather two fine wines: a Cinqueterre Bianco (14°), full-flavoured yet dry, almost salty, which I have drunk with pleasure as an aperitif, served cold, though the relative dryness depends on the year: most of it is drunk very young indeed, the year after the vintage. It is made from the Vernaccia grape which, when dried or semi-dried (*passito*) makes the much rarer sweet wine of the district. This is done by leaving the grapes spread out in the sun on the flat roofs of the village houses, pressing them when they are almost raisin-like, and leaving the must to ferment on the skins for seven to fifteen days, producing a rich, luscious wine, deep gold in colour and extremely rare (only about one-tenth as much of it is made as of the dry Cinqueterre), and therefore, alas, much counterfeited commercially elsewhere. It is difficult to find the genuine sweet Cinque-terre anywhere but in the district itself, and especially at Monterosso (even the Enoteca at Siena does not have one), where it is known as Sciacchetra (16°) – the same word being applied to the local drunks, for it is powerful stuff, fit for heroes, even if some Italian gourmets do say that it is the only wine to drink with ice-cream. (There is also a wine here called Schiacche-trau – the extra letter at the end apparently indicating lower strength, though I cannot be sure, for the authorities differ.)

Coronata. Dry white wine, produced only in very modest quantities and consumed locally, made from the Vermentino, Bosco, Bianchetto and Rollo grapes, along a small stretch of coast just to the west of Genoa, from one of the villages of which it takes its name. It has a faintly lemony taste, which makes it an especially pleasant and suitable accompaniment to the local fish. 11°–12°.

Cortese di Liguria. Strongish and rather coarse white wine, found at various points along the coast, made from the grape of the same name, and suitable to drink with fish. 13·5°–14°.

Dolceacqua (or Casteldoria, or Rossese di Val di Nervia). After Cinqueterre, undoubtedly the best-known Ligurian wine, perhaps because of the mild jokes that can be made about a wine that is called "sweet water". It comes from the handsome hill country that lies behind Venti-miglia and Bordighera, almost on the French frontier, and is a deep ruby red, made from seventy per cent Rossese grapes and thirty per cent of three or four others. Dolceacqua is found in most of the restaurants of this holi-day area, as well as in Monte Carlo, and goes well with the rich local dishes, especially if it has had four or five years in bottle, for it is a full, heavy, flavoury wine, with a rather sweetish under-taste (though it is by no means in itself a sweet wine) and a strongly aromatic bouquet. 12°–14°.

There is a tradition that Napoleon drank it in these parts in 1794, at one of the Doria palaces, and liked it so much that he used to have it sent to

Paris. Hence, the claim on some labels that it was "Preferito di Napoleone", though this is to say little for any wine: Napoleon was no judge, and used to water his Chambertin.

Note that other, neighbouring, districts make a wine from the same *cépage* that ought to be – and sometimes is – called Rossese, simply, but that Dolceacqua is considered the best, with the obvious result that a lot of it gets called Dolceacqua, anyway. A pale pink, very dry wine from the same grapes, taken earlier from the skins, is made at Ventimiglia and called Vino di Latte – certainly not because it is as mild as milk, for its alcoholic strength is 14°.

Dolcetto Ligure. Similar to the Dolcetto of Piedmont (*q.v.*), though the wine made here from the same grape usually shows a rather deeper colour, and is not quite so dry.

Limassina or Lomassina. The same wine as Busetto (*q.v.*).

Marinasco. Dry and semi-sweet white wines are made from the Trebbiano grape in the commune of this name near La Spezia, very similar in style to the white wines of Arcola (*q.v.*).

Massarda. Precisely similar to Busetto (*q.v.*).

Mattaosso. Precisely similar to Busetto (*q.v.*).

Morasca Cinqueterre. A dry white wine, not precisely from the Cinqueterre itself (*q.v.*), but from the area immediately adjacent, and neither so fine nor so rare as those that bear that name alone. 12°–13°.

Moscatello. A light, sweetish, semi-sparkling white wine, made from Moscatello grapes at the western end of the Ligurian coast, notably near the picturesque village of Taggia, in the Argentina valley behind San Remo. A mere 8° of alcohol, which makes it eminently suitable, served as cold as possible, for family picnics. Sometimes called Moscato di Ventimiglia.

Pigato. A sound, full-flavoured dry white wine, and also a sweeter semi-sparkling one, are made from the grape of this name near Alassio. The former is one of the most reliable of the white wines of the coast for drinking with fish meals (11°–14°), and the other is light and fresh, and only 8°.

Polcevera. White wines from near Genoa, some dry, some semi-dry, made from Vermentino, Bosco, Bianchetta and Rollo grapes, and often served in Genoese fish restaurants. 11°–12°.

Portofino. Modest dry white wine, of which few would probably have heard had not so many heard of the self-conscious, picturesque and over-frequented little place it comes from. 11°.

Riviera, Bianco della. Much the same may be said of this wine as of the Portofino: it is found at Santa Margherita.

Rossese. See under Dolceacqua.

Rubino di Canavisse. A bright red wine from near Savona, dry with a sharply bitter finish.

Sarticola. In the valley of the Magra river, from which one can see the white Carrara marble quarries, they grow a sweet, semi-sparkling white wine and also a full-bodied red, both with this name, and both highly prized in and around La Spezia, though unlikely to be found elsewhere.

Sciacchetra. See under Cinqueterre, but note that there is also a less important and quite different wine of the same name, pink and dry, from near Imperia.

Verici. A dry and a sweet wine, both deep gold in colour: both made from Bosco, Bianchetta and Rollo grapes – the same *cépage* as the wine of Portofino (*q.v.*) producing much better wines – around the village of this name near Sestri Levante. The dry goes well with fish, the sweet as a dessert wine. 11°–12°.

Vermentino; Vermentino di Pietra Ligure. White wines from the grape of this name are made in the hills just behind the middle stretch of the Riviera coast, roughly between Savona and Imperia. All are dry, some are slightly sparkling. Among the best and most delicate are those that have been made from grapes more shaded by the foliage than others, and so less lusciously ripe: there is a faint suggestion of the Riesling in their fragrance. 10°–13°.

Vernaccia di Corniglia. Another name for the sweet Sciacchetra of the Cinqueterre (*q.v.*), often made from the Vernaccia grape, which is said to derive its name from Vernazza, one of the five villages of the Cinqueterre. (To make up the five, Vernazza and Corniglia are counted separately, though I think that officially the one is a part of the other.) No connection with, or any resemblance to, the Vernaccia of Sardinia: it may well be that the vines are quite different.

Vezzano. Similar to Arcola (*q.v.*).

Chapter 4

LOMBARDY

❧

IN 1963 wine production in Lombardy declined sharply – from three and a half million hectolitres in 1958 to only half that amount, a much bigger proportionate fall than that suffered by Italy as a whole, even from a fairly good year, quantitatively, to what was quite a bad one, here as everywhere else in Europe, and greater, too, than that in the neighbouring provinces of Piedmont and the Veneto during the same period – an indication that the decline in Lombard wine production was not entirely due to the weather.

The decline, indeed, was chiefly in the production of the thin, foxy wines of the wide, flat Po valley, where rice matters more than the vine, and where the *contadini* can now afford the better wines grown in the hillier parts of the province: the Valtelline, the Oltrepo Pavese and those western and southern shores of Lake Garda that lie within the boundaries of Lombardy.

In the Valtelline, between the Alps to the north and the mountains behind Bergamo to the south, the hills are terraced with vineyards, some as high as 2,500 feet above sea-level, though the best wines come from the lower terraces, facing south, along the right bank of the Adda. Here, and throughout the region generally, the noble Nebbiolo is the chief vine, as it is in Piedmont, though it is often known locally as the Chiavennasca, and some of the Lombard wines, unlike the fine wines of Piedmont, and in the same way as the commoner ones, mix the Nebbiolo with others – with the Rossola for the lower-quality wines from the mountain vineyards, and with the Brugnola and, in some places, the Pignola, even for such distinguished wines as the Inferno.

At their best, then, such wines of the Valtelline as (in particular) the Sassella, the Grumello and the Inferno – all red wines, of course – are comparable with the great Piedmontese Nebbiolo wines, Barolo and Gattinara themselves. But for various reasons they are harder to come by, not so easily recognisable, and less consistent. For one thing, the custom prevails in the Valtelline of separating the bunches of grapes after the vintage into three qualities – the two better qualities making two grades of, as it were, *auslese* wines, that find their way more frequently into Switzerland, a notable market for the finer red wines of Northern Italy, than into the *trattorie* of Lombardy. Then again, the better wines are frequently sold under brand names, which tend to confuse the foreign visitor who is looking for the name of a grape or a region; and there is not the same measure of control over the quality of the Valtelline wines as is exercised by the Nebbiolo growers of Piedmont over Barolo and Barbaresco, nor by another of the three main wine-growing districts of Lombardy, the Oltrepo Pavese.

Nevertheless, a Sassella or a Grumello from a good grower, with five or six years of bottle-age, such as ought to be found at any of the good wine-merchants or better restaurants of Milan or, nearer to their birth-place, in Sondrio or Bergamo,* is one of the fine red wines of Italy, and well worth the amateur's leisurely consideration.

Lighter red wines, and wines more rosy than red, are grown along the south-western shores of Lake Garda, between Brescia and Desenzano – wines very similar in character to those from the south-eastern shores, which lie in the Veneto – as well as one notable white wine, the Lugana.

But it is in the Oltrepo Pavese – the part of the administrative province of Pavia, that is to say, that lies over the Po (to the south) from the city of Pavia itself, in the hill country rising to the foothills of the Ligurian Apennines, that the greatest progress in the viticulture of Lombardy seems to have been made in recent years, and that the strictest control over quality seems to be exercised. Big co-operative wineries have established high standards for cheap table wines, while at the same time a small number of dedicated individual proprietors, as in Tuscany, are producing wines of high and – in Italy at least as important – consistent quality. In addition, there is a vigorous association, the Consorzio Volontario per la Difesa dei Vini Tipici e Pregiati dell'Oltrepo Pavese, sponsored by the Pavia Chamber of Commerce, that jealously watches standards of production, and grants numbered neck-labels (showing the end of a wine-butt, tapped and flowing) to the approved wines of the district. The Oltrepo wines in the following list are all entitled to the label.†

* Where the Ristorante Moro, starred in the Michelin for Italy, lists Grumello as one of the wines of the house.
† More recently an association has been formed to protect the wines of Brescia.

The Wines of Lombardy

Angera. A fruity red wine with tawny highlights after it has aged in bottle, made from a mixture of Barbera, Bonarda and Nebbiolo grapes in the extreme north-west of Lombardy, rather outside any of the three main wine-growing areas, near Lake Varese, which lies between Maggiore and Como. Luigi Veronelli speaks highly of a variety known locally as Roccia Rossa.

Barbacarlo. Very like the Piedmontese Barbera (*q.v.*) though to some tastes not so firm, and sometimes to be found semi-sweet and semi-sparkling. This deep-red wine is made in the Oltrepo Pavese, and named after a commune there, from a mixture of Barbera, Ughetta, Croattina and Maradella grapes. 11°–13°. Good years: 1945, 1949, 1951, 1953, 1956, 1957. Very good: 1947, 1952, 1955. Exceptional: 1958.

Barbera. See under Piedmont. A fair amount of this red wine is made in the Oltrepo Pavese, one of the finer ones being Pezzalunga, clear in colour and fresh in scent and flavour. There is also a good Riserva Oltrepo Antico Piemonte which, in spite of its name, is made at Stradella, in Lombardy, between Piacenza and Pavia. 12·5°–13·5°. Good years: 1945, 1946, 1950, 1951, 1953, 1957. Very good: 1952, 1955. Exceptional: 1947, 1958.

Bellagio. The red wine of Bellagio, on Lake Como, is made from grapes the names of which are hearteningly familiar to all lovers of French wines – Malbec, Merlot, Cabernet and Pinot. Not that this wine reaches Bordeaux heights, but it has a certain finesse, and makes an agreeable and, at its best, even rather elegant light luncheon wine, very suitable for summer picnics in this beautiful lake district. Griantino and Tremezzino are pleasant red wines from this part as is also a Chiaretto di Bellagio, a *rosé*, semi-sparkling wine made from the same *cépage*, which tends to be stronger alcoholically than the red; also a sparkling white Bellagio Spumante.

Bonarda. Made from the same Bonarda (or Croattina) grape as the Bonarda of Piedmont, but a still wine where the Piedmontese Bonarda is usually sparkling. A light red wine from the Oltrepo, to be drunk young, and not taken too seriously.

Botticino. A sweetish, brilliantly red wine from near Lake Garda, made from a mixture of grapes that includes the Barbera of Piedmont and the Sangiovese of Tuscany. Drunk young and, locally, cool. Sometimes found under the more general heading of Colline Rocciose.

Buttafuoco. A softish, fruity, mild red wine from near Pavia, made largely from Barbera, along with Bonarda (Croattina) and others. Dry but frothy and semi-sparkling (hence its name – it is said to crackle like *fuoco* – fire). 12°.

Cabella. A local variant, from between Pavia and Piacenza, of the Bonarda (*q.v.*) of the region, given rather greater distinction by an admixture of Barbera and Croattina – a smooth, velvety red wine, with a pronounced bouquet.

Canneto Amaro and Canneto Dolce. The "bitter" (or dry) and the sweet, frothy red Canneto wines are made (in the Oltrepo) from exactly the same mixture of Croattina (mostly), Barbera and other grapes, the difference between them being due to vinification. These *frizzante*, frothy red wines are strange to English eyes, and palates, but served cool, as they should be, they are both pretty and refreshing under a hot Italian sun. There is also a Canneto Gran Spumante.

Casteggio. A general name for a wide range of the white wines of the Oltrepo, most of them made from Cortese, Trebbiano and Malvasia grapes, though there are variants. Lightish yellow in colour, dry and refreshing. See also under Clastidio.

Castelli di Calepio. Undistinguished light red and white wines, drunk young, the whites often sweet and the reds *frizzante*, but offering a rather confusing inconsistency.

Cellatica. Precisely similar to the other Lake Garda red wine, Botticino (*q.v.*).

Chiaretto di Cellatica. Pink version of the above, very popular in Milan and Brescia.

Chiaretto del Garda. The distinction is not always clear in these parts between *chiaretto*, *rosato* and even *rosso*. The red wines of this Riviera Bresciana coast of Lake Garda are light in colour: the *rosés* deeper in shade than comparable French wines. All are drunk cool, like their very near relatives, the Bardolino and the Valpolicella of the opposite, Veronese, shore. Delightful light luncheon wines, all the more refreshing for the slightly bitter after-taste offered by some, made from Groppello, Schiava, Berzamino and Corva grapes, and drunk young.* Some are found under the name of Moniga del Garda, and there is a wide range of precisely or

* According to Mr Gerald Asher, the London shipper, a great deal of Chiaretto del Garda is now being made exclusively of Merlot.

almost similar wines offered under such names as Retico, Manerba, San Felice and others, or more simply and generally as Vini della Riviera del Garda. The red wines of the Valtenesi region, just inland from the lakeside riviera and higher (and not to be confused with the Valtelline) are very similar. See also under (Vini delle) Colline Mantovane e del Garda.

Chiaretto del Lago d'Iseo. Very like the Chiaretto of Lake Garda.

Clastidio Bianco; Clastidio Rosato; Clastidio Rosso; and Clastidium Gran Riserva. Clastidium was the Latin name for the small town of Casteggio, centre of the wine-growing area of the Oltrepo Pavese. In three of these wines the old Roman name has been partly re-Italianised into Clastidio: it retains the old form for the Gran Riserva, a fine, sweet, golden dessert wine made from Pinot Nero and Pinot Grigio grapes, and made *"in bianco"* – the must taken off the skins before it can take on their colour. 12·5°.

The white Clastidio is made from a mixture of the Italian and the Rhine Riesling (Riesling Renano), and although it never achieves the delicacy of a fine German or Alsatian wine, it is crisp and fresh. The red and the *rosato* are made from the Barbera, Croattina and Uva Rara grapes, the *rosato* being taken off the skins earlier. 11°–12°.

Colli dei Frati. Red wines from near Bergamo, made of Corva, Sangiovese and Barbera grapes, fairly light and dry, and usually drunk young. Similar wines are called Giuramento, Pontida and Val San Martino.

Colline Mantovane and Colline del Garda (Vini delle). A wide range of red, white and *rosé* wines from the region that lies between the southern shores of Lake Garda and the city of Mantua, linking those vineyards that lie between the lake and Brescia (whence come the wines already referred to under Chiaretto del Garda), and the Bardolino–Valpolicella area, to be listed later in the section devoted to the wines of the Veneto. All three regions produce similar wines: clear, light or lightish red wines, to be drunk cool, like the whites and the pinks. Some of the best wines of this particular district are also referred to generally as *"vini del Serraglio"*,* and other minor commune names to be noted include those of Monzambano, Cavriana, Volta and the battlefield of Solferino. In his *Dizionario del Gourmet*, Felice Cùnsolo claims to detect in the reds of this region a slight taste of almonds, and in the whites (which, incidentally, tend to throw a deposit, unsightly but harmless) a scent of lemons.

Colline Rocciose. See under Botticino.

* There is no exotic significance: Serraglio is the name of a township in the district.

Croattina. Some of the red Oltrepo wines made from this grape are sold under that name alone, but those with any distinction have a more precise district, commune or brand name.

Domasino. Local white wine, rather light, made near Como from a mixture of Trebbiano, Cortese and other grapes.

Doppo Secco. See Montevecchia.

Forzato di Valtellina. Strong, sweet red dessert wine from the mountain country near Sondrio, almost at the Swiss frontier. Tirano is a centre of its production – an ancient town that suffered heavily in the massacre of the Valtelline Protestants of 1620 that inspired Milton's, "Avenge, O Lord, thy slaughter'd Saints . . .".

Fracia. Red and white wines of the Valtelline. The *bianco* (12·5°–13°) is fuller-bodied than other white wines of the district; the *rosso* (12°–13°) is a fine wine, closely related, though inferior, to Sassella. (See Valtelline Red Wines.)

Franciacorta. A light red wine from the slopes to the south of Lake Ideo, made from Barbera, Berzamino, Sangiovese, along with certain white grapes, and similar to the other lakeside wines of Lombardy and the Veneto, though with perhaps a more marked bouquet than some. 10°–11°.

Frecciarossa. This is one of the relatively few examples in Italy of a widely recognised and widely accepted *appellation* pertaining to a single grower – and one with a much smaller property than the great Chianti families of Tuscany. The vineyards of the village of Frecciarossa, near Casteggio, in the Oltrepo Pavese, belong to the Odero family, having been bought and developed by the father of the present owner, Dott. Giorgio Odero, who has devoted himself for the past forty years to producing the finest possible wines, all estate-bottled, as carefully as by any *château*-proprietor of Bordeaux. (Indeed, Dott. Odero rather fancies the word "*château*", which is what he uses himself on his labels.)

There are four Frecciarossa wines: all have the name Frecciarossa as the most prominent word on the label, but each has its own brand name in addition. The dry white wine (brand name, "La Vigne Blanche") is made from equal quantities of Pinot Nero and Riesling Renano (the German Riesling), though the Pinot is the more noticeable to nose and palate. It is a clear, dry wine (12°–12·5°) with a slightly bitter finish.* Luigi Veronelli,

* "The dry white wine is of particular interest," wrote the late Allan Sichel in *The Penguin Book of Wines*, "being crisp, fragrant and refreshing."

in his great book, *Vini d'Italia*, recommends the white Frecciarossa especially as an accompaniment to oysters – not that these are encountered frequently in the Oltrepo Pavese. But then Dott. Odero's wines are exported a great deal, and can, I understand, be obtained in England, through Messrs. Giordano of Soho (the Frecciarossa vineyards can, in fact, boast two viceregal appointments: to Lord Linlithgow and Lord Willingdon, Viceroys of India, of all odd places to have found Italian wines).

The white semi-sec, "Sillery" (Dott. Odero named it after a friend's racehorse long before he realised that Sillery used to be the English name for a particular still champagne), is only lightly, not lusciously, sweet – rather like one of the more flowery Graves, or a good Entre deux Mers. It is made chiefly of Pinot Nero, with smaller amounts of Riesling Renano and Moscato, the proportions depending on the vintage. 12°–12·5°.

The *rosé*, "Saint George", is crisp, with a fine bouquet, made of Barbera, Croattina and Uva Rara grapes, *"vinificato in bianco"* – taken quickly off the skins. 12°–12·5°. The red "Grand Cru" (the grower insists by his choice of brand names in French on challenging comparisons with fine French wines) is one of the best red wines of Italy, made of the same grapes as the *rosé*, four years in cask before bottling, and well repaying another four or five in bottle. 12°–13°. The high quality of this red Frecciarossa wine is a tribute especially to careful viticulture, vinification and bottling, for the grapes – Barbera and the others – are not considered so noble as the Nebbiolo that makes the fine wines both of Piedmont and of Lombardy (such as the Sassella) or as the Sangiovese of Tuscany. Yet I would place the wine itself in the same class.

Giuramento. See under Colli dei Frati.

Gran Spumante di Canneto and Gran Spumante la Versa. Sparkling wines, dry, semi-dry and sweet (*secco, semi-secco* and *abboccato*), made by the *méthode champenoise* from Pinot Nero and Pinot Grigio grapes, just as the Piedmontese makers of Asti Spumante also make their rather more expensive dry, champagne-type wines.

Grumello. See Valtelline red wines. Good years: 1945. Very good: 1954, 1957, 1959. Exceptional: 1947, 1952.

Gussago. Similar to Botticino (*q.v.*).

Inferno. See Valtelline red wines. Years as for Grumello.

Lacrima Vitis. Strong, luscious, golden dessert wine made from the semi-dried grapes of a particular species of Moscato – the Moscato Fior d'Arancio, or orange-blossom Moscato – grown in the Santa Maria Versa district of the Oltrepo Pavese. Also found under the name of the grape, simply, and also as Gran Moscato.

Lugana. Undoubtedly the best white wine of the Garda district, and one of the best in the whole of Lombardy, Lugana is made from the Trebbiano (sometimes in these parts called the Torbiano) grape, and is aged in cask for as much as four years before bottling – very rare indeed with any white wine. It acquires, with this ageing in wood, a pale golden colour, and some connoisseurs find in it a taste of saffron, which I confess has so far eluded me. However that may be, it is a good wine to drink with fish, and makes a natural accompaniment to the fresh-water fish from the neighbouring lakes. 11°–13°.

Mombrione. See Montespinato.

Monteceresino. Modest wines – a white, a *rosé* and a red – from the commune of the same name in the Oltrepo Pavese. The white is usually made from the Sauvignon and Italian Riesling grapes; the *rosé* and the red from Croattina and Uva Rara. The white and the *rosé*, 12°–13°; the red (which seems to be rather better of its kind than the others), 13°–13·5°.

Montelio. This is the name of a property near Codevilla, in the Oltrepo, specialising in wines of above-average quality – red and white – usually sold under that name, but the reds also to be found under the name of Rosso di Costarsa, a prizewinner at the International Wine Fair at Ljubljana in 1964. The same grower makes a particularly good Merlot, from the French grape, and a Müller–Thurgau from the German hybrid, which is labelled "Müller", simply. (It is a pleasant, well-balanced wine, but not so crisp nor so scented as German wines from the same grape.) These two last wines are not entitled to the Oltrepo Pavese neck-label, as the vines are not yet accepted as being natural to the district, but the Riesling, the Cortese and the grower's other two reds are labelled. (Another grower's Rosso di Codevilla is recorded in Veronelli, along with a Roccasusella and a Rosso Montu, but they are not in the official lists.)

Monte Napoleone. Lightish, sweetish red wine, made from Barbera, Croattina and Uva Rara grapes in a village in the Oltrepo Pavese that used to be called Montebuono until the Corsican passed that way. 13°–13·5°.

Montespinato. The name given in the Cignognola Hills, in the Oltrepo Pavese, to the red wine made from the usual Barbera, Croattina and Uva Rara mixture. There is an *amabile* – semi-sweet – version. 13°–13·5°. The Mombrione of Casteggio is similar but perhaps rather finer. 12·5°.

Montevecchio. Dry red and white wines (sometimes called Rubicchio and Doppo Secco, respectively) grown in limited quantities in the lush Brianza district, south of Como. The white is especially well thought of, but neither is easily found outside the immediate district, where it is drunk by the rich Milanesi with villas there.

Moscato. The Moscato grape – many varieties of it, indeed – is grown all over Italy, and Lombardy produces sweet, scented Moscato dessert wines of varying quality under various local and brand names, among which the Moscato di Scanzo of the Valtelline, which is made from the Merera grape, and the Moscato of the Oltrepo Pavese, from the Moscato grape, are especially worth noting. The Moscato di Casteggio, also from the Oltrepo, has a singularly strong bouquet. See also under Lacrima Vitis, and note, too, that a particularly rich Moscato Passito, from Moscato grapes rendered even sweeter and more luscious by being semi-dried, is also to be found in the region.

A considerable quantity of a Moscato Spumante, similar and not inferior to that of Asti – some people find it lighter and better balanced – though not so well known, is produced at Casteggio, in the Oltrepo Pavese and, in the same district, co-operatives (*cantine sociale*), and private growers make a drier Gran Spumante from the Pinot grape by the *méthode champenoise*. The Santa Maria della Versa *brut* is one of the very best of all the dry Italian sparkling wines and, after the Ferrari Gran Spumante of the Trentino–Alto Adige (*q.v.*) one of the most expensive. Good years (for the Spumante): 1946, 1949, 1951, 1956, 1957. Very good: 1947, 1952, 1958. Exceptional: 1955.

Nebbiolo. A sweet red Nebbiolo is recorded by both Luigi Veronelli and Felice Cùnsolo in their recent books as coming from Retorbido, but it does not occur in the official lists of the regional association of growers, nor have I met it. See also under Valtelline red wines.

Perla Villa. See Valtelline red wines.

Pezzalunga. See Barbera.

Pinot dell'Oltrepo. Good red wine is made from the French Pinot Noir in many parts of the Oltrepo, particularly around Pernice and Santa Maria della Versa, but most are named after an estate or are given a brand name by a co-operative. In general, for the Pinot Nero of the district, good years: 1945, 1949, 1950, 1951, 1957. Very good: 1952, 1955. Exceptional: 1947, 1958.

Pontida. See under Colli dei Frati.

Prosecco dell'Oltrepo. In various parts, a light (10°) semi-sweet and semi-sparkling, refreshing wine, is made from a mixture of Riesling and Pinot grapes.

Pusterla Bianca. A rather bland, though dry, white wine grown near Brescia from the rare Invernenga grape, and not found much elsewhere. A pleasant accompaniment to light dishes. 10·5°–12·5°.

Riesling. The Italian and the German Riesling (Riesling Renano) are both grown fairly widely in the Oltrepo Pavese, sometimes for blending with other grapes, as in the excellent Frecciarossa (*q.v.*), sometimes used together – never separately in this region, to my knowledge – to produce a wine styled simply Riesling, or with some special brand or place name, such as the Riesling Fiore, the Sanrocco Riesling and the Imperial Riesling of various growers and co-operatives in the area. Never so delicate nor so fragrant as the German or Alsatian Rieslings, but pleasant and refreshing wines: there is a Riesling *frizzante* made at Stradella. Good years: 1945, 1949, 1950, 1951, 1957. Very good: 1952, 1955. Exceptional: 1947, 1958.

Rubicchio. See Montevecchio.

San Colombano. "Worth bottling in good years," is Felice Cùnsolo's comment in his *Dizionario del Gourmet* on this light, often *frizzante*, red wine – along with a white wine of the same name, even less distinguished – the only wine grown in the province of Milan itself.

Sangue di Giuda. Rather sweet, frothy red wine, made from Barbera, Croattina and Uva Rara grapes in the Oltrepo Pavese.

Sassella. See under Valtelline red wines. Sassella is the name of a variety of grape, but the wine is made largely of Nebbiolo, with only a small admixture of Sassella. Good years: 1945. Very good: 1954, 1957, 1959. Exceptional: 1947, 1952.

Tre Valli. A deep-red table wine made between Bergamo and the Lago d'Iseo, of a mixture of Barbera, Berzamino, Merlot and other grapes, including an interesting new Italian hybrid, the "Incroci Terzi 1 and 2", which is a cross between Barbera and the French Cabernet. Not a fine wine, but agreeable, with a pleasant bouquet. 10°–11·5°.

Tocai del Garda. A small amount of the Tocai grape is grown near San Martino and Pozzolengo, to the south of Lake Garda. This is a much sweeter wine than that made from the same grape – and deservedly better known – in Venezia Giulia (*q.v.*). 12°–14°.

Val San Martino. See under Colli dei Frati.

Valtelline Red Wines. The River Adda flows east to west into Lake Como, just inside the northern frontier of Italy, entering the lake at Còlico. Its steep northern bank, stretching either side of Sondrio, is terraced with vineyards, the vines trained over frames, benefiting from the southern aspect, the sunshine intensified – as it is in the Rheingau – by reflection from the surface of the water. Here are grown the great red wines of Lombardy: Sassella, Grumello and Inferno being the most highly esteemed, and usually in that order, with Perla Villa (sometimes called Villa, simply), Fracia and Valgella as rather less distinguished members of the family, and Valtellina Rosso as the general name for the common wines of the district.

As in Piedmont, the Nebbiolo is a noble grape here (where it is also known as the Chiavennasca, but none of these wines is made exclusively of the Nebbiolo, as are the finest wines of Piedmont: eighty-five per cent is the usual proportion in Sassella, Grumello and Inferno, with the remaining fifteen per cent made up by Brugnola, Sassella, Pignola and Rossola Dura in varying degrees. The inferior wines of the region have less Nebbiolo.

There is little to choose between Sassella, Grumello and Inferno. None, to my mind, is quite so fine, or quite so full in flavour, as Barolo or Gattinara at its best (perhaps because they are grown higher above sea-level, and farther north; perhaps because of the mixture of Nebbiolo with less distinguished grapes). But they are very good wines indeed, admirable accompaniments to roasts, grills and game, and they sometimes seem to have a more brilliant colour and a prettier nose than the Piedmontese wines, to make up for their shortcomings elsewhere. The Sassella is said to be rougher when young than the others, but with greater bottle-age (up to about six years) to show more breeding. The Grumello is said to be at its best after about four years in bottle (as is the lighter Fracia), and some people prefer it to the Sassella, as being rather softer. The Inferno usually has a greater proportion of the Brugnola grape than the others, and with it a nuttier after-taste.

None of these admirable wines is at all well-known in England, nor indeed are they easily to be found in Italy outside their own region and in Liguria, but a considerable amount is exported to Switzerland, always a good market for the best Italian red wines, and a very close neighbour in this particular case.

Vecchio Piemonte. A Lombard wine, in spite of its name (and not to be confused with Vecchia Romagna, a brandy). This is a dry, but fruity, red wine from near Stradella. 12·5°.

In addition to the wines listed here by name, there are many simple wines offered merely under regional names, such as "Bianco Secco dell'Oltrepo" and the like, which may still bear the association's neck-label. There are also many wines, particularly in the Oltrepo, too many to list here, produced in smallish quantities, but each with its own name, whether that of a village, an owner, or the brand name of a co-operative. They can be identified in shops and restaurants, for they will always bear, in addition, the name of the type and the region, and usually of the grape, on the label.

Chapter 5

TRENTINO–ALTO ADIGE

❦

NLIKE the French-speaking region of the Val d'Aosta, which is administratively separate from Piedmont, and autonomous, the German-speaking Alto Adige – its inhabitants much more different in character and feeling from their Italian-speaking neighbours than are the Val d'Aostans – is combined with the Trentino to form a joint autonomous region that thus has an Italian-speaking majority.

Italy's sound strategic reasons for this, and the equally inevitable tensions and resentments (and international complications with Austria) are not our concern here, but they cannot be ignored by anyone visiting the superbly beautiful Alpine region that stretches from Merano south to Bolzano, for more than ninety per cent of the wine-growers here are German-speaking;* the wines have German names, and are exported mainly to Germany, Switzerland and Austria (in that order of volume, Germany taking more than half of the total export), remaining virtually unknown to the rest of Italy. I have even been told by some, though others have denied it, that it is the unwillingness of the German-speaking growers of the Alto Adige (which in any case they prefer to call the South Tyrol) to collaborate with the Italian-speakers of the Trentino that prevents the formation of a growers' association for the whole province, to protect the names and maintain the standards of all the local wines, as the Trentino itself has recently done for its own.

Nevertheless, there is some measure of co-operation, for the Istituto Agrario Provinciale, at San Michele all'Adige, in the Italian-speaking part of the region, near Trento, a Government organisation, controls the quality of all wines for export, and is a much respected adviser to both parts of the province. Nor would it be impossible for the Alto Adige to set up a *consorzio* of its own, like the Trentino's, as the Oltrepo Pavese district

* And even of the remaining few, some speak not Italian but Ladin.

does within the province of Lombardy – there is certainly sufficient solidarity of feeling and community of interest among the growers.

The Trentino produces rather more wine than the Alto Adige – in the proportion, usually, of about a million hectolitres a year to three-quarters of a million – but the Alto-Atesino wines are finer, more varied, and more valuable, and account for about ninety-seven per cent of the total wine exports of the whole province.

Throughout the province, the vineyards are exceptionally trim and well cared-for, in marked contrast to some of the regions farther south. The vines, whatever their variety, and both in the Trentino and in the Alto Adige, are trained to turn into pergolas at an angle of about 45 degrees or so to their long trunks. One of the most beautiful sights, even in Italy, is in the Alto Adige, where the climate is mild enough to grow oranges, though there is always snow to be seen on the mountains, to see the long lines of golden-leaved pergolas, in the autumn, just after the vintage, catching the sunlight, with the glittering snow-clad peaks of Alps and Dolomites in the distance.

As the two wine-growing regions of the district are so distinct, their wines shall be listed here separately.

The Wines of the Alto Adige

There are so many small growers and co-operatives in this tiny district that there are more than two hundred entries in the list of Alto-Atesino wines at the autonomous joint province's Ministry of Commerce (the *Assessorato Regionale Industria e Commercio* of Trentino–Alto Adige). Most of them, as in the Oltrepo Pavese, are family names, vineyard names, commune names and the brand names of co-operatives. All that we can do here is to list those more general and descriptive names that derive from varieties of grape or from sizeable districts within the area, and those most likely to be met with, whether in Italy or abroad.

More than three-quarters of the production here is of red wine, more than half of which is exported, largely to Germany and Switzerland (and a smaller amount to Austria), both of which countries have a great thirst for red wines, especially those of Italy, and both of which are conveniently placed for commerce with the region and speak the same language. Mostly, the whites stay at home, though a certain amount finds its way to England, where at least one firm makes something of a speciality of the Terlaner Rieslings.

Wine was grown in these parts in Roman times, and the Lex Domitiana of A.D. 90, by which the Emperor Domitian hoped to cure the results of over-production of wine in Italy by forbidding its production in the military provinces of the Rhine and the Danube (where the Romans had in fact introduced the vine) gave a great impetus to wine production in the Adige valley, whence it could be more easily transported to the thirsty legionaries than could those of Spain (whence so many of the legions came) or of the rest of Italy.

Barzemino. A garbled word for Marzemino (*q.v.*).

Blauburgunder. The German name for the black grape of Burgundy, the Pinot Noir (also labelled here as Pinot Nero or Borgogna Nero) which is grown widely throughout the whole of the province, Trentino as well as Alto Adige, but at its best in the vineyards around Caldaro, Bolzano and Terlano, where it produces a smooth, full red wine, more "French" in style than the other red wines of the region, and fairly consistent as to quality.

Cabernet. Grown in the Alto Adige as well as in the Trentino, and vies with the Blauburgunder as producing the finest red wine of the region. Ages well in bottle: a 1955 tasted at the end of 1964 was about the level of a really good minor *château* of the Médoc, and not so far advanced as some, which by then were showing past their best.

Caldaro; Rosso di Caldaro; Lago di Caldaro; Caldaro Appiano. It is under these names that these red wines are shown in all Italian works of reference, and to have four of them is in itself confusing enough: Lago di Caldaro usually indicates a rather higher quality than the simple Caldaro. What makes it all more confusing, though, is that more often than not the wines of the district are labelled Kalterer or Kalterersee, the German name for the lake, south of Bolzano, where they are grown, and in this case an *auslese* label is worth looking for. They are lightish wines, made from the Schiavone, Schiava and other grapes, popular locally and in Switzerland, and said to show some character after a year or so in cask, and a couple in bottle, but I have found the bouquet unpleasing, and the quality very variable. This being so, I attach only slight importance to what are said to be the good years: 1948, 1958. Very good: 1954, 1959. Exceptional: 1949,

Plate IV Wine vault in the Trentino (p
graph by courtesy of the Trentino-Alto A
Tourist Association)

1952. 11°–12°. There is a newly created *consorzio* of growers to maintain the quality of Caldaro wines, and to issue labels.

Caldaro di Collina. From higher slopes above the lake than the wines mentioned above, and both stronger in flavour (though not in alcohol) and sharper. 10°–11°.

Castel Rametz. The name given around Merano to the Blauburgunder (*q.v.*).

Colline Bolzano or Leitwein. General term for the red wines, of varying quality, made from the Schiavone (or Frankenthal) and other grapes grown on the hillsides around Bolzano. Probably the best of these fairly common, but pleasant, wines are the Santa Giustina and the Eppaner Justiner, which in spite of the similarity of name and district, seem to be made of different *cépages.* 11·5°. The Santa Maddalena of the district merits an entry of its own.

Colline di Merano; Meranese di Collina; or Küchelberger. Like the Bolzano wines, but from farther north, and also from Schiavone and Schiava grapes. 11°–12°.

Gewürztraminer or Traminer Aromatico. The people of the region claim that the Traminer of Germany and Alsace derives its name from the South Tyrolean village of Tramin, or Termeno, just south of Caldaro. Certainly, the vine is well-established here, though the Gewürztraminer of the region never seems to me to achieve the full fragrance of its Alsatian namesake, which I have heard Alto-Atesino growers criticise as being opulent to the point of vulgarity. In these parts, it is a full, flavoury and moderately fragrant white wine, none the worse for a little bottle-age. 12·5°–13°.

Girlaner Hugel. The wine is red, mild and dryish, and comes from Cornaiano, near Appiano. 12°.

Guncina or Guntschna. Soft red wine, made from Schiava grapes near Bolzano. Has a heavy bouquet, and improves with bottle-age. 11·5°.

Jungfrau. From various parts of the Alto Adige, made from the Schiava grape – a very light, fresh, dry white wine of 11°, drunk in cafés, between meals.

Kreutzbichler. The Bolzano name for the Blauburgunder (*q.v.*).

Küchelberger. See under Colline di Merano.

Kurtatscher Leiten. A red wine from Schiava and other grapes, very similar to those of Lake Caldaro (*q.v.*).

V Making *fiaschi* covers in the Tuscan Countryside

Lagrein or Lagarina. The Lagrein vine grows right up to the town boundaries of Bolzano and Gries. A very small amount is made fully red, and this is well worth looking for, but the *rosé* (Lagrein or Lagarina Rosato, or Lagreinkretzer) which is a very deep pink, is so popular, both at home and in Switzerland, for its freshness, charm and occasional slight prickle, that less and less of the red is being made. To English tastes it seems quite different from other *rosés*, and some have detected in it a slight and not unpleasing flavour of vanilla. 12°. Good years: 1948, 1958. Very good: 1954, 1959. Exceptional: 1949, 1952.

Leitacher. See under Santa Maddalena.

Moscato Atesino. A sweet, highly scented dessert wine (14°–15°) is made from Moscato grapes around Bolzano, Merano and elsewhere; and an unusual Moscato Rosa, made from a grape which was imported into the region thirty years or so ago from the Adriatic coast near Trieste, cherry red and smelling of roses, is grown in very small quantities at various parts of both the Alto Adige and the Trentino. A special taste, no doubt, but then I once knew a man, lower middle-class by origin, far from being a fop, and determinedly heterosexual, who ate rose-petal jam for breakfast.

Moscato Giallo. Similar to the above, but paler in colour, and weaker in alcohol (13·5°).

Müller–Thurgau. This valuable German hybrid (Riesling × Sylvaner) is being gradually introduced into various parts of Northern Italy (see under Lombardy: *Montelio*) and is to be found in the Alto Adige as well as in the Trentino and the Oltrepo. Never, in my experience, so fragrant here as in Germany, but it makes a wine of obvious quality, and is always worth looking for.

Riesling. Although the whole region – both Alto Adige and Trentino – was under Austrian rule until 1918, and although the Alto Adige is still German both in language and in feeling, it must not be supposed, as I had long myself supposed, that the Riesling Renano – the Rhine Riesling – must have been here since time immemorial: it came to these parts from Germany no longer ago than the 1850s. (It would be interesting to know when the Riesling reached that other part of the old Habsburg Empire which is now Yugoslavia's province of Slovenia.)

It now produces in this region a charming, well-balanced wine, not perhaps so pretty as the young wines of Alsace and the Moselle, but without the underlying coarseness of so many Yugoslav Rieslings, and much to the taste of their admirers – most of them local or, at any rate, in Italy, for it is the red wines of the region that are exported, but British shippers import some very pleasant Terlaner Riesling, from around the picturesque Alpine-valley village between Bolzano and Merano.

The Riesling Renano is grown in the Trentino, as well as in the Alto Adige, and there is also some Riesling Italico in the region, sometimes blended with the Renano, sometimes with other white grapes. Good years: 1948, 1958, 1960. Very good: 1954, 1959. Exceptional: 1949, 1952.

Rülander, Pinot Grigio or Borgogna Grigio. A white wine from this Pinot grape is made in most parts of the Alto Adige, but chiefly in the north. Often *frizzante*. 11°–13°.

Santa Maddalena or S. Magdalena. In every wine-growing region of the Northern Hemisphere there are wines that are grown on the northern bank of a river flowing east and west, or on the northern bank of a lake, deriving benefit not only from the southern exposure, but also from the reflection of sunshine from the water.* In the Alto Adige, the Santa Maddalena, grown on the hills to the east of Bolzano, facing south across the Isarco river, is the finest of the red wines of the region, made largely from the various Schiava and Schiavone grapes, as are the commoner local wines, but with about ten per cent Lagrein, which gives it great finesse, as the sunshine gives greater body and character. Deeper in colour and fuller in flavour than the Caldaro wines, and showing its superiority in both body and bouquet, with a sort of bitter-almond back taste, after three or four years in bottle. 12°–14°. Leitacher is very similar, but with even less Lagrein, and grown on shadier slopes – it is both drier and less strong, and many people prefer it.

Sylvaner. Another import from Germany, which flourishes – as do the Rülander and the Traminer – in vineyards as much as 2,500 feet high in the Alpine valley that stretches up to Bressanone and the Austrian frontier. Makes a light, rather sharp, not particularly distinguished white wine, similar to the more modest Alsatians. 12°–13°. Good years: 1948, 1958. Very good: 1954, 1959. Exceptional: 1949, 1952.

Terlaner. There are both red and white Terlaner wines, from the Alpine township already mentioned. The red is made from a mixture of Vernaccia, Merlot and Lagrein grapes, and should be drunk young. 10°–12°. There is also a Terlaner Merlot, with much more finesse, but not so widely known, nor perhaps so consistent, as the Merlot of the Trentino, farther south. Some of the whites are Rieslings (*q.v.*); some a mixture of Pinot Bianco and

* In Italy itself, cf. the Valtelline red wines of Lombardy.

Riesling Italico, with quite a touch of style. 11°–13°. Good years as with Riesling.

Termeno. Dry, lightish red wine, to be drunk young, made from Schiava grapes in the hills around the village of Tramin (Termeno) – whence the Traminer of the Rhine is said to have come, and to have derived its name – about half-way between Bolzano and Trento, almost at the southern extremity of the German-speaking area. 10°–11°.

Traminer. Most of the Traminer of the district seems to have become Gewürztraminer, or Traminer Aromatico, by the time the label is put on the bottle, but there is some of the more modest wine about, though the village from which the grape is said to derive its name (see above) goes in more for Schiava grapes, and red wine. Good years for Traminer as for Sylvaner (see above).

Veltiner. A favourite wine of the region, but not known outside it, from the grape of the same name; dry, fresh and rather light, both in flavour and in alcohol (10°–12°). Much used as an accompaniment to the excellent local trout.

Weissburgunder, or Pinot Bianco, or Borgogna Bianco. Widely grown throughout the region, both for use as a white *ordinaire*, and also as a base (with other grapes, including the Pinot Nero) for a local sparkling wine – one of the better such, by Italian standards, the best-known and most widely available of which locally, is that with the brand name, Gran Spumante Ferrari,* though there are others, also quite good, made by various co-operatives and private firms in the area, some by the *méthode champenoise*, some by the Charmat, or *cuve close* method.

Note: Many wines of the Alto Adige with names other than those listed above are, in fact, the same or similar wines with brand, district or family names on their labels, as well as the type or the grape names. My tasting notes, for instance, include such wines as Schwanburg, Kolbenhof, Kettmeir and others, which it would be more confusing to list than it is to omit. The use of two languages, with German preferred, is an added complication.

---

* The most admired, and most expensive, of all Italian sparkling wines, the Ferrari di Trento Riserva, costs above three times as much, retail, as the best Asti Spumante, and about half as much again as the other dry *méthode champenoise* Italian wines.

The Wines of the Trentino

There are fewer varieties of wine in the Italian-speaking Trentino than in the Alto Adige and, contrary to what one might expect, the Italian-speaking Trentinesi are readier to co-operate with each other, less individualistic than their German-speaking neighbours. At any rate, there is an association of the Trentino growers, one of the growers of the Isera district, and another of the co-operatives in the district, which issue between them labels for at least three of the outstanding wines of the region: similar recognition of others was being planned as this book was being written.*

Avio. A *rosé* wine grown in the extreme south of the region, not far from Borghetto, just over the hills from Lake Garda, to the *chiaretti* of which it bears some resemblance. Rather bland for a pink wine; made from Teroldego, Merlot and Marzemino grapes, each of which, unblended, produces a rather more stylish wine than this. 12°–13°.

Borgogna Bianco. The same as the Weissburgunder (*q.v.*) of the Alto Adige.

Cabernet. Some is produced north of Trento: see under list of Alto Adige wines; a notable variety is the Castel S. Michele.

Casteller. *Rosé* wine grown in the immediate surroundings of Trento, and sometimes called Vino di Trento. Made from Schiava grapes, which give it its body, and Merlot and Lagrein, which give it delicacy. Marked bouquet, dry and – for a pink wine – rather full. 11°–12°. Some qualities are labelled Casteller Gran Rubino, and the Novaline Casteller and Torre Franca are similar wines.

Castelli Mezzocorona. Soft, mild and rather fruity red wine (mostly Schiava with a large variety of others, separately and in blends – a Pinot Nero from here won a gold medal at Ljubljana in 1964) made in the valley of the Adige, north of Trento, at the limit of the Italian-speaking region, across the river from San Michele all'Adige, where the Istituto Agrario is. 12°–12·5°. Protected by the Trentino *consorzio*, approved bottles carry a neck-label showing one of the *castelli* of the district, in its vineyard.

Garda Trentino. Red, white and *rosé* wines are grown at the northern end of Lake Garda, the whites from Nosiola, Trebbiano and Pinot Bianco

* An association of growers in the Alto Adige has just been set up to control the Caldaro wines.

grapes, the reds and the pinks (taken earlier from the skins) from Schiava, Merlot and Lambrusco. The whites range from dry to semi-sweet, and some are *frizzante*: Perla del Garda is perhaps the best. The reds and pinks are all dry, and the red and pink Val del Sarca are better than most. All about 10°–12°.

Marzemino. Red wine from the grape of that name, grown pretty well all over the southern part of the Trentino, but chiefly around Isera, south of Trento. It has the distinction of having been mentioned by the librettist of *Don Giovanni* as "l'eccelente Marzemino". It is a biggish wine, that has suffered some loss of reputation since Mozart's time, because of over-production, but a *consorzio* of Isera growers is now making serious efforts to rehabilitate it, and awards appropriate labels to approved wines. There is also a *rosé*. 11·5°–12°. Good years: 1946, 1949, 1954. Very good: 1957. Exceptional: 1947, 1952, 1959.

Merlot. The French Merlot grape produces a stronger, fuller red wine in the Trentino than in the Friuli, the Veneto and elsewhere in Italy; certainly ranks with Santa Maddalena (*q.v.* under Alto Adige) as one of the outstanding red wines of the region; and is in great demand from Germany and Switzerland. 12°–13°. Good years: 1946, 1949, 1952, 1954. Very good: 1957. Exceptional: 1947, 1959. One grower is said to produce a dessert Merlot.

Moscato and Moscato Rosa. See under the wines of Alto Adige. Both are produced in the Trento, where the San Vigilio is well thought of.

Negrara. Dry, full red wine made from the Negrara grape near S. Michele dell'Adige.

Nosiola. Dry golden wine from the grape of the same name grown in the Val di Cembra, just north of Trento. Perhaps the most common white wine of the region after Vernaccia (*q.v.*). 10·5°.

Novaline Bianco. Rather full-flavoured white wine, made from a mixture of Pinot Bianco and Italian Riesling grapes, and a sounder table wine than its fancy bottle would suggest. 11·5°–12°.

Novaline Casteller. See under Casteller.

Passito di Arco. Rich, sweet dessert wine, made from dried grapes near Arco, the pretty little resort at the head of Lake Garda.

Perla del Garda. See under Garda Trentino.

Riesling. Grown in various parts of the Trentino: see under wines of the Alto Adige.

San Zeno. See under Vallagarina Rosso.

Sorni Bianco. Rather delicate white wine, made from Nosiola and the hybrid Müller–Thurgau (Riesling × Sylvaner) grapes in the San Michele all'Adige district, mainly for local consumption.

Sorni Rosso. Lightish red wine, with a pleasing bouquet, made chiefly from Schiava grapes, in the same region as the Sorni Bianco (*q.v.*), much of it exported to Switzerland. 11°–12°. Good years: 1946, 1949, 1954. Very good: 1957. Exceptional: 1947, 1952, 1959.

Teroldego (or Teroldico) Rotaliano. Protected by the *Consorzio per la Difesa del Vino Classico Trentino*, and accorded its neck-label, this big red wine, made from the grape of the same name in the beautiful vineyards on either side of the Noce river, north-east of Trento, is the backbone of the region's wine production. It is full-flavoured – even coarse – with a rather bitter, nutty back-taste, and various qualities are produced: to be drunk young, to be aged in bottle, and also for blending with other red wines, to give them body, as are the wines of the South of France. Some consider it the finest red wine of the area, when at its best, but the English amateur, his taste formed by French wines, will hardly rank it as high as the Merlot, the Cabernet or the Santa Maddalena, though it has an enjoyable robustness of character when aged in bottle. (In the winter of 1964, a good 1959 Teroldego seemed by no means ready to drink.) 11°–12°. Good years: 1946, 1949, 1952, 1954. Very good: 1957. Exceptional: 1947, 1959. The local *consorzio* issues a numbered neck-label showing a gold crown and crossed keys on a red ground.

Torre Franca. See under Casteller.

Val del Sarca. See under Garda Trentino.

Vallagarina Bianco. White wine of the Isera region, made chiefly from Vernaccia grapes.

Vallagarina Rosso. Robust red wine (one Italian writer's description of it is *di buona stoffa*), made from a mixture of Schiavona, Marzemino and Merlot grapes, which combine to give it a deep colour with a slightly bitter – some of the locals describe it as being salty – taste, varying in quality, but worthy of attention: the San Zeno Rosso is well spoken of. 11·5°–12°.

Valdadige. The common red wine of the district, rather light and nutty, made from a mixture of Teroldego, Lambrusco, Schiava and Merlot grapes. 11°. A better grade, rather stronger (11·5°–12°), is exported, its quality controlled by the *Istituto Agrario*.

Vernaccia Bianca, Vernaccia Trentina, or Vernaccia di Aldeno. A very light white wine, grown from the grape of the same name, fermented without its stalks, which makes it delicate for so common a wine. Often slightly *frizzante*. Made near Trento. 10°–10·5°.

Vino Santo. Often labelled, and always referred to, as Vin Santo – sometimes even as one word – a sweet dessert wine made in most parts of Italy. But those who like this kind of wine hold that the Vino Santo of the Trentino is outstanding, made from Nosiola, Trebbiano and Pinot grapes, dried on straw after the vintage and not pressed until as late as the following Easter. (Hence the term Vino Santo – made in Holy Week. Though I do not know what happens if Easter is unusually late or unusually early.) Aged in cask for four to six years, the Vino Santo from this region is a heavily scented, amber-coloured dessert wine, with more individuality than most and – considering its lusciousness – some delicacy.

※

Note: A certain amount of Negrara and Lambrusco grapes is grown in the Trentino, producing wines of moderate quality, and there is a sweet, sparkling Recioto del Trentino, so called from the word *recie*, a corruption of *Orecchie* – "ears" – only the "ears" or outermost grapes of each bunch being gathered, these having had the most sunshine, and yielding most sweetness.

Chapter 6

THE VENETO

❧

IN output alone, the Veneto would rank high among the wine-growing regions of Italy – in some years second only to Apulia. But it ranks high in quality, too, for the light red wines of Lake Garda, such as Valpolicella and Bardolino, and of the Valpantena, even if not so distinguished as the fine red wines of Piedmont, or as the best Chiantis, are wines of grace and charm; while Soave, from the hills between Vicenza and Verona, is unquestionably one of the finest white wines of Italy.

Geographically, this is a varied region, stretching from the shores of Lake Garda to the lagoons of the Adriatic; from the foothills of the Lessini Mountains and of the Dolomites to the plains of the Po. It has always been a rich region, too – from Roman times, when Livy was born in Padua; through the golden age when Venice held the gorgeous East in fee; later, when Palladio built villas by the Brenta for those who had inherited the fortunes thus made; and now, when German and American and British and Swedish tourists pour money into the coffers of the hotels and the restaurants of Venice and of the lakeside resorts.

Tourism exacts its penalties: at the smartest hotel in Verona they offer you a "Romeo and Juliet" cocktail (though no steak-house in Venice that I know of advertises a pound of flesh as the speciality of the house). But it can mean, too, as it does in the Veneto, that there is a sizeable enough local demand to encourage wine-growers to go in for good wines, carefully made. (To say nothing of the German, Swiss and Austrian markets for the red wines of Garda.)

I was once a member of the jury at a Venice Film Festival, and at a grand party given by the city for the jurymen I found myself at the splendid buffet cheek by jowl with a French diplomatist. He demolished his *langouste* as greedily as I did, but when he came to his glass of Soave he sniffed it suspiciously, tasted it dubiously and then turned to me with,

"You know, they call a lot of things *vino* in Italy that we should never call *vin* in France." Politer to him than he was to his hosts, I forebore to say how much better this admirable, fresh, dry wine was than many a so-called Chablis or Pouilly-Fuissé that I had drunk, not only in English oyster-bars but in Paris restaurants that ought to have known better: the wines of the Veneto in general, and Soave in particular, are probably as consistent as any in Italy. (The growers can hardly be held responsible for what some of the Soho wine-merchants tell us is Valpolicella: I doubt if it was sold to them as that.) I have never had a Soave, it is true, to rank with a really distinguished white burgundy, but then I have never had one as nasty as some of the "Chablis" I have had in my time.

Wines of the Veneto

Arcugnano. Red and white wines of the Colli Berici (*q.v.*).

Arzignano. Dry red and white wines from near Vicenza. Light, unimportant table wines – the white is also known as Durello.

Barbarano. Red and white wines of the Colli Berici (*q.v.*).

Bardolino. Bright, fresh, clear red wine made from the Corvina and Negrara grape – for colour and body respectively, according to Mr Gerald Asher: with Molinara and Rondinella for brilliance and suppleness, all used together, as in Valpolicella and Valpantena (*qq.v.*). The Bardolino wines are grown on the eastern shores of Lake Garda, around the southward looking bay on which Garda and the charming village of Bardolino stand, as far south as Lazise, opposite the slender outline of Sirmione, where the soil produces rather lighter wines than do the heavier clays of the Valpolicella villages, farther inland. There are Italians who talk and write of Bardolino as being a wine worth ageing in bottle, as a wine to go with roast meats – Paolo Monelli claims that it is only with age that it loses a slight sweetness he finds in all the wines of this region – but my own preference is to drink it young (when it is often a little *frizzante*) and cool which is the way that most of it seems to be drunk locally. I have had a great fondness for this charming and refreshing wine ever since I found that Max Beerbohm used to take a glass of it every day at his villa in Rapallo at what a lesser mortal would have referred to as his teatime, and my affection for it was increased when I visited the village of Bardolino itself, a couple of years ago, on the day the vintage was celebrated, to see the peasant wine-growers trooping happily in to sell their fresh, young wine at the tasting-booths – threepence for an eighth of a litre, which is quite a substantial glass – along with salami sandwiches and crisply fried fresh-water sardines straight from the waters of Garda. A young priest officiated at the microphone, waxing more and more eloquent as they went on filling his glass.

It is certainly one of the most charming wines of Italy – which does not mean that it is a great wine, but charm, too, has its place at the table. 9·5°–11·5°. Good years: 1953, 1956. Exceptional: 1957. Protected by the association of Veronese growers, and shares with Valpolicella and Soave a neck-label showing the Roman arena at Verona (though there was news recently of an association being set up purely of Bardolino growers).

Breganze. On the southern foothills of the high country between Lake Garda and the Piave, near the towns of Breganze and Thiene (where there are remarkable Veronese frescoes in a Colleoni castle) they grow red and white wines of some interest, the whites (11°–12°) from a wide mixture of local grape varieties, dry and pleasantly fragrant, the reds from Negrara, and other local varieties, good light table wines not unlike the Lake Garda wines. 11°–12°.

Brendola Bianco. One of the wines of the Colli Berici (*q.v.*).

Cabernet. Grown here in the Veneto, as in the neighbouring provinces (see under the wines of the Alto Adige). Produces some very good red wines, notably in the hills around Vicenza (the Colli Vicentini), Breganze, Barbarano and San Dona di Piave. The Colfortin Rosso is especially highly thought of. 11°–13°. A Cabernet of the Valdobbiadene won a gold medal at the Ljubljana Exhibition in 1964.

Cabernet–Merlot. This classic combination, responsible for the great clarets, produces a lighter, but moderately claret-like wine in a small region towards the mouth of the Piave, almost at the Venetian lagoon, between San Dona di Piave and Portogruaro, near the Lido di Iesolo. Sometimes to be found in Venice and Iesolo restaurants, but production is small. 10·5°.

Cartizze. A sparkling Prosecco (*q.v.*) from Valdobbiadene (*q.v.*).

Colfortin Rosso. See under Cabernet.

Clinton. An American vine, grown near Padua, producing a light red wine with a marked bouquet, very low in alcohol (8°–10°) much appreciated locally, but perhaps chiefly for its lightness.

Colli di Asolo-Maser and Colli di Conegliano. White wines made from Prosecco, Verdiso and other grapes on the hills on either side of the Piave river, where it leaves the high country for the plains that stretch to the Gulf of Venice. Asolo and Conegliano are both charming small towns, the latter very much and very obviously a wine centre. The wines are fresh and pleasing when young, but are said to maderise very quickly: the Conegliano wines are said to be finer than those of Asolo. 10°–11°.

Colli Berici and Riviera Berici. Just south of Vicenza are the Berici hills where, around 1870, a number of French vines were introduced, among them Sauvignon and the white Pinot, which are blended with Italian varieties, and give some pleasant full white wines, with a touch of sweetness but also a hint of bitter almonds. 10°–12°. The red wines from Merlot, Molinara, Negrara and Raboso Veronese grapes are sometimes a little astringent, but can be good table wines. An association of growers has just been set up.

Colli Euganei. White wines from the hills to the west of Padua, made from Garganega, Prosecco and other grapes, with a certain amount of Riesling, both German and Italian, which gives lightness and delicacy to quite an agreeable local wine for fish dishes. 10°–11°. There is a Moscato Spumante from this area, too, sometimes known as Moscato dei Colli Euganei, sometimes as Moscato d'Arquà (8° upwards) and there are said to be some local red wines, too, dry, with a flavour of raspberries, one of them called Rosso del Venda, but I have found it little in evidence.

Colli di Valdobbiadene. Two types of white wine: a still dry and a sweetish *frizzante* – sometimes fully *spumante*, even – made chiefly from Prosecco grapes in the Piave valley, not far from the famous battlefield of Vittorio Veneto. The dry (11°) is drunk young, as a "wine of the year", when it is light and fresh, with a hint of bitterness in the after-taste; the other, though no stronger alcoholically, is a dessert wine. Most of the *spumante* comes from the small parish of Cartizze, in the Valdobbiadene, and take its name.

Colli Vicentini Centrali. Some authorities, and many of the locals, distinguish between the Colli Vicentini and the Colli Berici wines, but the distinction is slight geographically, and non-existent viticulturally. Here, I have classed all the wines worth mention as being of the Colli Berici, as they are in most Italian works of reference.

Colli Veronesi. General name given to the wide range of wines grown north and north-west of Verona, including such well-known growths as

Bardolino, Valpolicella and others. All such wines that are of any consequence are listed here under their more specific names.

Colline Trevigiane. Modest white wines, most of them from the
Prosecco grape, grown along the lower reaches of the Piave.

Colognola. A red and a pink wine are made near Soave, more famous
for its white, of the same mixture of grapes as the Colli Veronesi wines
(*q.v.*), such as Valpolicella, to which both the red and the pink Colognola
are quite similar, for most of the wines of this district are betwixt and
between, if rather nearer red than pink.

Costoza. One of the Colli Berici wines (*q.v.*). The white Costoza used to
be known as "the ladies' wine" – for no special reason that I can discover:
it is no more ladylike than any of the others. The red Costoza is rather
better than most of these local wines, and seems to me sometimes to have
something of a claret "nose".

Durello. See under Arzignano.

Fara Vicentino. A red wine very similar to those of Breganze (*q.v.*). 13°.

Fonzarso or Fonzaso. A red wine from near Bellino (where there is
very little wine-growing), made from a mixture of grapes that includes
Merlot, Barbera and a rare local variety called Nera Gentile di Fonzarso.
It is full-bodied and dry. 10°–12°. There is also a dry white Fonzarso that
is very hard to come by.

Friularo. Made south of Padua, inland from the picturesque fishing port
of Chioggia, from a grape that owes its name to having been introduced in
the seventeenth century from Friuli. A red wine, light in alcohol (10°) and
rather sharp in taste. Unlike most other red wines of the region, it ages
well, because of its acidity, and has many admirers. The Friularo from
Bagnoli is especially highly thought of.

Garganega di Gambellara, and Gambellara Rosso. White wine made
of Garganega grapes in the hills south of Vicenza that face those of Berici
across a small river valley. Of mainly local interest: one is told that at its
best it bears some resemblance to Soave (*q.v.*). But this may be when finer
wines are made locally by adding Sauvignon and Pinot Bianco to the
Garganega grape (though they are not used in Soave). The same district
produces a less important red wine, and also a Gambellara Passito, or *vin
santo*, in very small quantities, a very good dessert wine.

Malvasia di Nanto. A light, sweet dessert wine from near Vicenza, the
digestive properties of which, according to Cùnsolo, are so effective that
people take it in order to *fare il rutesin* – to belch.

Marzemino Trevigiano. An unimportant light red wine, made from the grape of the same name, in the same area as the whites of the Colline Trevigiane (*q.v.*) usually semi-sweet to sweet.

Merlot. Red wine from this noble red grape is made pretty well all over these parts of Italy – the Merlot is said to be fifth in quantity of the vines grown in the three Venetos. The Merlot of the Veneto itself, the region we deal with here, is neither so strong nor so full in flavour as that of the Trentino (*q.v.*).

Montegalda and Montelungo. Rather flavoury, dry, light red wines produced for drinking young in the hills between Padua and Vicenza. 11°–12°.

Orgiano Bianco. One of the wines of the Colli Berici (*q.v.*).

Prosecco. This is one of the most widely grown vines of the North of Italy, from the Oltrepo to the Friuli. In the Veneto it is the main grape for the white wines of the various hill districts already listed here. In the Conegliano district, along the Piave, some of the wines are known by its name rather than that of the district. There are sweet and dry, still and sparkling, versions, and the sparkling Prosecco Spumante di Conegliano is really quite good. 11°. A Prosecco of the region won a gold medal at Ljubljana in 1964, and the Prosecco wines of both Conegliano and Val-dobbiadene are protected and labelled by a local growers' association.

Raboso. This is the name of a local variety of grape, from which red wine is made pretty well all over the flatter middle part of the Veneto, and particularly between the Piave and Livenza rivers (when it is called the Raboso, or Rosso – a finer version – or Rubino del Piave (*q.v.*), and around Padua, where it is called the Raboso Veronese). These two main types differ a little in *cépage*, but both mix Merlot, Cabernet, the Italian Riesling and some of the local Tocai (*q.v.* under Friuli–Venezia Giulia) with the Raboso grape. With the exception of the Rubino, the Piave wines, especially, are roughish – it may be that the grape and the wine are so called because of this (*rabbioso* means furious, angry or froward), or perhaps because of a tumultuous fermentation – and although some people drink them young, like the wines of the Lakes, most Italian authorities I have consulted claim that the Raboso del Piave wines become unexpectedly round and mellow with bottle-age – some counsel putting them away for as much as ten years. The Veronese Raboso is another matter, for this is certainly pleasanter young, and therefore has less to gain by ageing: I have thought that this may be because it has less of the Raboso grape in the *cépage*, and more of the lighter varieties. 10°–12°. There are also sweet, semi-sparkling, versions of the Veronese.

Recioto Bianco or Recioto Soave. Sweet white wine made from Garganega and other grapes, largely around Soave, that have been specially picked (see below) and allowed to become semi-dried. 13°–14°.

Recioto. Red wine made of much the same *cépage* as Bardolino, Valpolicella and Valpantena, and from the same general area, as well as from the hills around Soave, save that only the "ears" of the bunches of grapes are gathered which have had more sun and more ripening than the others.* A fuller, heavier wine is the result – not, to every taste, as light or agreeable as the other red wines of the same districts. Indeed, I have found the so-called Recioto Amarone, which is held to be the best of its kind, at once harsh and flabby, although the wine I tasted had plenty of bottle-age. There is also a Recioto Nobile, a sweetish red sparkler that soon loses its bubble in the glass, but keeps a sharp prickle – quite an amusing wine, if no more than that. 13°–14°.

Rubino del Piave. Dry red wine, from the same district as the Raboso (*q.v.*), but better-bred and better cared for; I find it delicate by Italian standards, but one writer has described it as "peppery" – perhaps he means tasting of sweet peppers. What I have found myself is a hint of clove in the scent. 12°.

Soave. One of the best-known and, deservedly, one of the most highly regarded of the white wines of Italy, made largely of Garganega grapes, but with about twenty per cent Trebbiano, in the immediate vicinity of the picturesque walled town of Soave, at the southern edge of the hill country between Verona and Vicenza. Many Italian white wines are fermented on the skins, to give body and staying power, but the best Soave is made in the French way, which gives greater freshness and fragrance. Sometimes likened by Italian enthusiasts to Chablis, but it is not so delicate as Chablis at its best, though it is a firm, well-balanced wine, and less mawkish than Chablis at its worst, with an agreeable hint of floweriness in its bouquet. Should be drunk fairly young and very cool, when it goes extremely well with the fish-fries of neighbouring Venice – it is to be found in every Venice restaurant (though in pretty varying qualities). Protected, along with Bardolino and Valpolicella, by the local growers' association, and acknowledged bottles carry the Veronese neck-label. 10°–11°. Good years: 1946, 1948, 1953, 1954, 1955, 1956. Very good: 1952, 1957.

* Cf. "Note" under Trentino–Alto Adige.

Sona-Custoza. A light red wine, similar to Bardolino and Valpolicella (*qq.v.*) and grown just south of their districts, in the area to the west of Verona. Always drunk *"nell'annata"* – in its first year. 12°.

Terrematte. A Barbera (*q.v.* under Piedmont) grown at Montegalda, near Vicenza – rather more heady than its Piedmontese cousin, but a respectable table wine, produced only in very limited quantities.

Tocai. A little is grown at Lison, part of Portogruaro, near Venice, but see under Friuli–Venezia Giulia.

Torcolato. Golden dessert wine made from semi-dried Garganega and Durella grapes, mostly in the vicinity of Breganze, north of Vicenza. 14°–16°.

Ussolaro. A sweet *vin santo* made at Brendola, near Vicenza, from Ussalara grapes – a wine fast disappearing, and unknown to me.

Val d'Alpone, Val di Illasi, Val Mezzane, Val Squaranto and Val Tramignia. Red wines of the Colli Veronesi, not unlike those, better-known of Valpantena (*q.v.*).

Valpantena. Light red wine, very similar to Bardolino and Valpolicella (*qq.v.*), made of the same grapes, but in the valley that runs north from Verona, rather to the east of the districts where the others come from. It is said by experts to be the merest shade drier and more austere than they, but I confess that I find it hard to detect the difference from Valpolicella. 11·5°–12·5°.

Valpolicella. The best known, and the most popular abroad – in Germany, Britain and the United States – of all the wines of the region, and rightly so, for Valpolicella is a wine of considerable grace, with only a hint of underlying sweetness, suitable to drink with almost any dish, and for almost any climate. Ideally, though, it is a wine to drink cool, with light summery dishes: it is made of the same grapes as Bardolino and Valpantena (*qq.v.*), but grown in rather heavier soil, in hills away from the lakeside slopes where Bardolino is grown, and – probably because of the soil – very slightly fuller in flavour and deeper in colour.* This slightly greater fullness may be the reason why some of the better Valpolicellas lend themselves to ageing in bottle – more, at any rate, than the other two wines of the district – though even then they are not the wines I would choose myself for laying down. 11°–12°. Protected and labelled by the local

* According to Mr Gerald Asher it is the Corvina vine, particularly, that does well in the Valpolicella clay, and it is the Corvina that is the principal grape in both Valpolicella and Bardolino.

Plate VI Red and White

growers' association. Good years: 1945, 1947, 1949, 1950, 1956, 1959. Very good: 1946, 1948, 1952, 1953, 1955, 1957.

Verdiso. Dry white wine grown fairly widely around Treviso, from the grape of this name, to be drunk very cool and young. 9·5°–11°.

Vespaiolo. Light, sparkling, sweet but not too heavily luscious dessert wine grown near Breganze. 11·5–12·5°.

VII Bardolino, Lago di Garda
neto: vineyards on the Bertani estate

VIII Brolio estate, near Siena,
uscany: workers in the vineyards

Chapter 7

FRIULI–VENEZIA GIULIA

✾

THERE are Austro-Hungarian influences on the architecture and on the gastronomy of this north-eastern corner of Italy, and some of the vines nearest to Trieste grow in Yugoslav soil. Yet the wines of this frontier region owe more to France than to Austria, or to Yugoslavia – more than to Hungary, too, for the Tocai of the great plain of Friuli is not the Tokay of the great Hungarian plain. The Gamay, for instance, has been recently introduced, and does well, and the Cabernet of these parts makes a sound red wine.

There seems to be less parochial pride in the local wines here than in most of the other regions of Italy: many of the excellent fish restaurants of Trieste, for instance, are as likely to offer you a Soave from the Veneto, or a Verdicchio from the Marches, as they are a Tocai, which they profess themselves flattered to be asked for, yet often are unable to produce.

No other part of Italy is so modest about its own wines, but then this part of Italy – Trieste, at any rate – is like no other. The high-cheek-boned, snub-nosed market women, sitting behind their stalls under the Serbian Orthodox church, by the quay, with the church-Cyrillic letters on its façade, may be chattering and chaffering in Italian, but they look like Slavs, and in the Café Danubio, opposite, I have heard a bearded priest, who was speaking Italian, and reading an Italian newspaper, call for a *slivovitz* as his aperitif.

Trieste is in Italy now because the Triestini desired so intensely to be Italians, and yet at Miramare they put on every summer a *son et lumière* romanticisation of the life and death of Maximilian and his Carlotta; where else in Italy will you find them sentimentalising over a Habsburg, and in German? So perhaps it is fitting that the Hungarian goulash that has become acclimatised in Trieste as an Italian dish should be accompanied by a

Merlot, or a Cabernet, and the iota Triestina, which is an aromatic sort of sauerkraut, with a Riesling Renano from almost on the Yugoslav frontier.

The Wines of Friuli–Venezia Giulia

Borgogna Bianco, Borgogna Grigio and Borgogna Rosso. Red and white wines made in various parts of Friuli from the Pinot Bianco, Pinot Grigio and Pinot Nero grapes (under which names the wines themselves are sometimes found).

The *bianco* is a fairly light wine, both in texture and in colour, usually dry. 10°–13°. Quite a lot is exported, and there is a *spumante* version. The *grigio* is a more deeply coloured white wine, and is the same as the Rülander of the Alto Adige (*q.v.*). The *rosso* (the same as the Blauburgunder of the Alto Adige, just as the *bianco* is the Weissburgunder) is not so plentiful as the others. It is a reasonably smooth local table wine, perhaps a little more like French wines – like the commoner wines of Burgundy, say – than some Italian reds, but of no great distinction. 11°–12·5°.

The local growers' association of Friuli protects, and issues numbered heraldic neck-labels for, various of these wines under the names of Pinot Bianco, Pinot Grigio, Pinot Nero; Bianco and Rosso dei Colli Friulani, dei Colli Goriziani and others.

Cabernet. The Cabernet of the region is produced from a mixture of Cabernet Franc and Cabernet Sauvignon, and is a full big wine – much more so, whenever I have been able to compare them, than the Cabernet of the Alto Adige – and certainly not to be drunk young, when it is harsh and astringent. Veronelli recommends not less than three years in bottle, and says that it is at its best after eight. That of Buttrio is said to be especially good. The wine is protected and labelled by the local growers' association. 12°–13°.

Caneva or Bianco Misto di Caneva. Simple, dry, white table wine from near Udine, to be drunk very young. 10°–11°.

Collio or Collio Goriziano. White wine made from a mixture of Tocai Friulano, German and Italian Rieslings, and a number of other varieties, grown chiefly in the hills that encircle Gorizia. Similar to Caneva (above), but with rather more style. It is drunk young – "*nell'annata*" – when it has a fresh taste and a flowery bouquet: some experts claim to detect a slight taste of nutmeg. 11°. The Borgogna Rosso (above) produced in this district is also sometimes referred to as Collio Rosso.

Gamay. Imported quite recently from France, the Gamay does very well in the gently hilly country north-east of Udine, producing a clear, brilliant red wine, with an underlying sweetness, especially when young, becoming rather more austere when older, with a faint strawberry taste, and a high alcoholic content, which means that it will "travel" well and stand up to ageing, both in cask and in bottle.* There should be quite a future for this wine in Italy, where the climate and much of the countryside would seem to be suitable, and where many of the local red wines could well be improved upon. 13°–14°.

Malvasia del Collio and Malvasia di Ronchi. The first comes from near Gorizia, and the other (which is sometimes called Malvasia Bianca Friulana) from nearer the coast. The same wine, though – deep yellowish in colour, full in flavour, that goes well with the local richer dishes. 11·5°–12·5°. Protected and labelled by the local growers' association.

Merlot. Another French grape that is doing well in Friuli, though it is not such a recent innovation as the Gamay, for it is grown quite widely throughout Northern Italy, and has been for half a century or so. The Merlot of this region is not so distinguished as that of the Trentino – perhaps not so elegant, either, as that of the Veneto – and is a notably lighter wine than the Gamay. 12°. Protected by the local growers' association, which issues a heraldic neck-label.

Monfalcone. Red and white wines of some quality are produced in this district very near Trieste, the whites including Sauvignon, Tocai and Malvasia; the reds Cabernet and Merlot.

Piccolit or Picolit. This golden dessert wine, made from the Piccolit or Picolit grape, semi-dried, was once the great pride of Friuli, but the vine is vulnerable to the disease of "floral abortion", and many of the finest vineyards have been destroyed. Professor Giuseppe Dalmasso has been experimenting with crossing the Piccolit vine with the Tocai, Ribola, Verduzzo and others, and a certain amount of the wine is still produced from these immune hybrids, a certain amount from the small remnant of the original Piccolit stock. I do not share the view, expressed by some of its more perfervid Italian admirers, that Piccolit is a rival to Château d'Yquem, though it may reasonably be described as the Château d'Yquem of Italy,

* There is more than one Gamay in France, but none is regarded as a "noble" grape in Burgundy, though the Petit Gamay is considered as such in the Beaujolais.

which is very much another matter. Certainly, it has a finesse lacking in most of the other Italian dessert wines, and in Victorian times it was much admired at the Austrian, French and English courts. 12°–14°. Protected and labelled.

Prosecco Triestino. This is rather complicated. The Prosecco grape, which we have already come across in the Veneto, is named after the district of Trieste around the Miramare. But the Triestini call the grape not Prosecco but Glera, and the wine called Prosecco Triestino is named after the place, and *not* the grape, which is not highly regarded in its native district. The wine is, in fact, made from a mixture of Malvasia, Sauvignon and Garganella, as well as Prosecco; is sometimes known as Malvasia Triestina (a particularly good one is said to come from San Dorligo); and is appreciated to the extent that the Malvasia and the Sauvignon fragrance come through. It is a lightish, sweetish white wine, served with fruit. 12°–14°.

Raboso Rosato. Made from Verduzzo grapes (and so sometimes called Verduzzo di Ramandolo), semi-dried, grown in the foothills of the high mountains north of Udine, near Tarcento – a highly aromatic golden dessert wine, sweet but not intensely so, usually semi-sparkling, and a pleasant accompaniment, well chilled, to fresh fruit. 12°–13°. Protected and labelled by the local growers' association.

Refosco. Light, dry – even rather sharp – red wine, with a pretty violet tinge, made from a vine called Refosco dal Peduncolo Rosso, the Refosco with a red stalk. Varies a good deal in style and quality: there is a lighter and a darker, and a sweet Refosco made from the same grape, semi-dried. 11°–13°. Protected and labelled.

Ribolla Gialla. A very light, sweetish white wine, made from the grape of the same name, grown in the low country south-east of Udine. 9°–10°. There is also a fuller, sweeter variety, reaching 15°, and a Ribolla Nera that resembles the Refosco (*q.v.*).

Riesling. A good deal of Riesling Italico, and rather less Riesling Renano, is grown throughout the region. The Renano is to be preferred, though the Italico has the benefit of the protection and labelling of the local association.

Sauvignon. This grape, of French importation, is grown extensively throughout Friuli, as in other parts of Northern Italy, Here, it makes a white wine of some note, straw-yellow, with something of the Sauvignon fragrance we meet in the great Sauternes and the Loire wines, for instance, and an appetisingly bitter finish. (There are also semi-sweet versions.) Protected and labelled by the local association. 12°.

Terrano or Terrano del Carso. A vine common to Italy and Yugoslavia, for it is grown on both sides of the frontier north-east of Trieste, though in the Italian vineyards – I cannot speak of the Yugoslav – it is being replaced by other, presumably more prolific, varieties. So there is not a great deal to be found, and I doubt whether there is any outside Trieste. A pity, for it is a wine of some character: light red, with a flowery fragrance, but a clean and refreshing acidity, to be drunk young and cool, and very low in alcohol. 9°–9·5°.

Tocai. No connection at all with the Tokay of Hungary, though the Hungarians once tried in the Italian courts to obtain a ruling against the Italian use of the name. But it was established that this particular vine had been grown in Friuli, and known as such for centuries, the name deriving either from a Slav word meaning "here" (there are, of course, many Slavs in the area, and there used to be more in Habsburg times), indicating that this was "a wine of here" – a local wine – or perhaps from a village near Gorizia once called Tocai.

In any case, the Italian Tocai is very different from the Hungarian dessert wine – it is a dry, yellowish white wine, with a rather bitter undertaste, highly regarded in these parts, and justifiably so, as an accompaniment to the excellent fish dishes of this part of the Adriatic coast. Protected and labelled. 12°–15°.

Verduzzo. Golden-yellow wine, semi-sweet and sweet. 9°–11°. That of Ramandolo (*q.v.*) is fuller and stronger. Both the simple Verduzzo and that of Ramandolo are protected and labelled.

Chapter 8

EMILIA–ROMAGNA

※

THIS region is to Italy what Burgundy is to France – this is where the noblest dishes and the most famous cooks come from: there are more good restaurants in and around Bologna and Modena than in and around any other Italian cities of comparable size, just as Dijon and Lyons have more than any other French cities. This is the belly of Italy.

The cuisine of the region, usually referred to as Bolognese, though Modena is as distinguished a gastronomic centre, is rich and hearty, and the Romagnoli are noted for their size and their appetites. Rossini came from these parts (he was born in Pesaro, just over the regional border, in the Marches, but he made his home in Bologna for many years, and the Bolognesi regard him as a native son), and it is characteristic that a *garniture Rossini* involves truffles, *pâté de foie gras*, butter and Madeira. Italians from other regions criticise the *cucina Bolognesa* as being *ingrassamento*, fattening, but it is noticeable that they gladly patronise any restaurant in their own towns that offers Bolognese cooking, and strive to be able to afford a Bolognese cook. Usually, Italians are so proud of their own regions that they affect to despise every other, yet even the great Sabatini Restaurant in Florence, a temple of Tuscan gastronomy (to take only one example), boasts of the fact that not only is its *pasta* made freshly every day, in its own kitchens, but by a Bolognesa.

Yet the wines of Emilia–Romagna are not the robust, full-bodied wines one would expect in a region where the cooking and the eating are so whole-hearted, in the way that the wines of Burgundy go with the hearty Burgundian dishes. At its best, the white Albana, for instance, though it has its touch of sweetness, is far from being a big or a luscious wine, and most of the red wines of the region (the local Sangiovese is an exception) are on the lighter rather than the fuller side.

The red wine peculiar to Emilia–Romagna is peculiar indeed – Elizabeth

David has written of it that, "the most interesting and original of Italian wines . . . Lambrusco, is that oddity, a dry sparkling red wine which sounds so dubious and is in fact perfectly delicious". It sounds dubious only, of course, because we are not used to the idea that a dry red wine should sparkle. It is not at all dubious to the Bolognesi and, oddly enough, it seems to be Americans who react most vigorously against it: Schoonmaker has described it as being, "as nearly undrinkable as a well-known wine could be", and Samuel Chamberlain records having sent this sparkling red wine back at one of Bologna's most distinguished restaurants (and Bologna's distinguished restaurants are distinguished indeed), advising those of his readers who travel in these parts always to ask for a non-sparkling wine. Myself, I am with Elizabeth David and the Bolognesi in this matter, which is to be on the side of the angels.

The Wines of Emilia–Romagna

Albana, or Albana di Romagna. White wine produced throughout the region, from the grape of the same name, and especially around Forlì, and near the small town of Bertinoro,* between Forlì and Rimini. The road from Rimini to Bologna runs along the edge of the hills, and it is on the slopes just above the road that the vines flourish. This grape retains a certain amount of unfermentable sugar, so that Albana is, as Mr Charles Bode has put it, "definitely on the sweet side of the vaguely defined borderland that separates the clearly sweet wines from the perfectly dry ones". Yet it is light and fresh, far from being so sickly that one could not drink it with fish, though some Albana is rather sweeter than others, and there is also a fully sweet, luscious one, for dessert. Much drunk along the holiday coast from Rimini to Ravenna.† It is protected by the *consorzio* of the growers of the Romagna, which issues a neck-label showing a stylised white cock and bunch of grapes on a red ground. 12°–13°.

---

* The story goes that Bertinoro gets its name from a medieval princess's having been offered Albana here in a rough mug, and exclaiming, "It should be drunk in gold!" – *vorrei berti in oro* – Bertinoro.

† And it is the only white wine nominated as a speciality of the house by the three Bologna restaurants starred in the *Michelin Guide for Italy* – Pappagallo, Tre Vecchi and Cesarina.

Alionza. Local white wine, dry but full, notable only for the Bolognese phrase, "*al gd'a in di'alionza*" – "he's fond of his glass".

Barbera. A certain amount is grown near Bologna (Barbera di Maggio, or di Bologna) and near Parma (Barbera Langhirano). See under Piedmont.

Biancale di Rimini. A sound white wine from the grape and the place of the name – the grape being a species of Trebbiano.

Bosco Eliceo or Rosso del Bosco. Dry, rather sharp, deep-red wine made along the Adriatic coast from a grape called Uva d'Oro (although it is, in fact, a black grape) perhaps because of its prolific yield. All the better for a little bottle-age, when it becomes a full, mellow wine that goes well with meat dishes. 11°–12°.

Cagnina or Canina. A full-flavoured, dry *rosé* wine grown in small amounts in the Ravenna, Ferrara and Faenza districts. 8°–9°.

Castelfranco. Takes its name from a district round Modena, where a mixture of Montu, Albana, Trebbiano Romagnolo and Pinot Bianco grapes, grown together in the same vineyards, produces a dry white wine with a pleasing fragrance. 10·5°–12·5°.

Clinton. A little red wine is grown here from this American importation – see under Lombardy.

Correggio. See Lancellotta.

Fogarina. One of the frothy, alcoholically light, red wines of the district, made from the grape of the same name, growing on the banks of the Po, north of Parma. Almost violet in colour, and sometimes used to blend with the lighter wines of the district. To be drunk cool. 10°.

Fortana. Light-bodied red wine from various parts of the Parma district, from a grape of the same name that gives a half-sweet, half-dry, semi-sparkling, or *frizzante* wine, with only about 9° of alcohol. A rather finer sub-species of the Fortana grape, sometimes called Fortanina, or Fortanella, gives a lighter-looking, but rather stronger, sweeter wine that is the traditional partner of the *spalla* – shoulder of pork – of San Secondo. 10·5°.

Gutturnio. A clear, bright red wine, made from a mixture of seventy per cent Barbera, thirty per cent Bonarda grapes, in the district west and south of Piacenza, and intended to be drunk young, as a "wine of the year", "*nell'annata*". Dryish, with an underlying hint of sweetness, and usually – and very rightly – served cool. This is a particularly pleasing wine of its kind and class, and is likely to appeal to those who like young Beaujolais, and the Lake Garda wines. 11°.

Lambrusco. Quite the best known and most characteristic wine of the region – a dry red wine, with an evanescent sparkle, so that it pours out with a great deal of froth, which soon subsides, leaving not a bubble, as in champagne, but a pronounced prickle, as in the *vinho verde* of Portugal. This is strange to English eyes and palates, but Lambrusco is worth getting used to – it is fresh and clean and, as every writer on Italian wines observes, complementary to the rather rich dishes of the region. Every restaurant in Bologna offers it, and it is held to go especially well with the *zampone* – stuffed pig's foot – of Modena.

Lambrusco comes from the grape of the same name, grown throughout the region, and there are Lambruschi of Sorbara (which is to say of Modena) – this is considered the best* – of Castelvetro; of Fiorano; of Fabrico; of Correggio (or of Reggio Emilia); of Parma; of Salamino; of S. Croce; of Maestri and of Montericco; and a Lambrusco Scorza Amara – "the Lambrusco with a bitter skin", though I do not find it different from the others. I have also tasted a Lambrusco *amabile* – semi-sweet – but I found the sweetness less pleasing in a prickly red wine than I would have done in a white. Protected by the growers of the Romagna, the Lambrusco wines carry either the same label – a white cock and grapes – as Albana or, if made at one of the local co-operatives (those of Modena and Bologna having a *consorzio* of their own) with a label showing a man and a girl treading grapes – a method hardly surviving anywhere in Italy, and certainly not at the co-operatives. The Lambrusco of Parma seems to have a *consorzio* to itself. 10°–12°.

Lancellotta or Filtrato di Lancellotta. Clear red wine with a particularly strong bouquet, made from the grape of the same name, which varies a great deal in strength and style. Usually sweet, with a prickle, and much admired in Switzerland, though I cannot class it with the best Lambrusco. One of the better known varieties of this wine is Correggio.

Malvasia di Maiatico. A sweet white wine made from the Malvasia grape with about fifteen per cent of Moscato, light for its type, and pleasant with fruit or between meals, served very cold. 9.5°–11°.

Monterosso. It is the *monte* that is *rosso*, not the wine, which is white, from Belverdino, Santamaria and Trebbiano grapes, grown in the Piacenza

---

* Two restaurants in Modena – Fini and Oreste – are starred in the *Michelin Guide for Italy*. It is usual for starred restaurants to have the specialities of the house quoted in the *Guide*, and for at least two wines to be mentioned, but these restaurants each mention only the Lambrusco di Sorbara.

area, and meant to be drunk fresh, from the cask. Dry with a touch of sweetness, and very slightly *frizzante*. 10°–11°.

Montuni or Montu. A dry white wine, rather full and hard, from Castelfranco: Cùnsolo likes it better than I do.

Moscato di Torre Chiara. Here the proportions of the Malvasia di Maiatico are reversed – the eighty per cent or so of Moscato giving a richer, more luscious wine. 10°.

Pomposa Bianco. Dry white wine made from Trebbiano and Malvasia grapes, chiefly in the same area as the Bosco Eliceo (*q.v.*). 9·5°–11°.

Rossissimi del Reggiano. Extremely dark-red wines from the same area as the Lancellotta – much used for mixing, and for blending with white wines into cheap rosé.

Sangiovese Romagnolo; Sangiovese (or Sangioveto) dell'Ravennate; Sangiovese di Forlì. Red wine from the grape of Chianti and the great wines of Tuscany, widely grown throughout Emilia–Romagna. It has a great reputation, is protected by the local association, carrying the same label as the Albana (*q.v.*) and I must have been unlucky in never having met a really distinguished bottle – I have always found this a rather flabby, disappointing wine. But authorities whose opinions I must respect describe it as a full-bodied, serious red wine, well balanced and agreeable – both as a young wine, when it is said to have a fruity freshness, and when aged in bottle, after which its bouquet intensifies and the flavour mellows. Felice Cùnsolo describes it as being "livelier" than Lambrusco (not that it is *frizzante*: he means in character), and with more personality than Chianti, and I am sure that he has far more experience of the wine than I have. 11°–13°.

Sauvignon di Castel san Pietro. Similar to the Sauvignon of Friuli (*q.v.*) and grown only in one very small area near Bologna. A firm, dry wine, with a quite individual scent, and a flavour that some describe as "tarry". 11°–12°.

Scandiano Bianco. Both a still dry and a sweet sparkling white wine, each of very modest quality (though a local association has been formed to protect and label them) are made from local varieties of grape around Scandiano, near Reggio Emilia. 10°.

Tocai Rosato. Sweetish pink wine from the Tocai Rossa grape of Friuli (*q.v.*), grown near Piacenza.

Trebbianino. White wine, in a dry and a sweet version, made from Trebbiano and other grapes, near Piacenza. It is a "little Trebbiano" by name, indicating that it does not ask to be taken too seriously. One of the Vini del Piacentino (*q.v.*). 12°.

Trebbiano. In various parts of the region the white Trebbiano grape produces both common wine, to be drunk young, and a finer quality, aged in bottle, which goes well with fish, being dry – even rather acid – but with style and character. There is a small production, too, of a sweeter, *frizzante* wine. Although we have met it in other regions, the Trebbiano is presumably a native of Emilia–Romagna, taking its name from the Valley of the Trebbia, which cuts into the hills south of Piacenza, towards Bobbio, and this is where some of the best wines come from. There are also a Trebbiano di Forlì and a Trebbiano Ravennate. The Trebbiano di Romagna is protected and labelled by the local *consorzio*. 10°–11°.

Valtidone Bianco. Dry white wine, sometimes *frizzante*, from Trebbiano, Malvasia and Ortrugo grapes grown in the hills south-west of Piacenza, above the Trebbia valley, mentioned above. Not widely known, and not of any great distinction. 10°–11°.

Vien Tosc Rosso. Very light red wine grown rather high in the Apennines from a grape called Tosca, which may be closely related to the Sangiovese. Sharp and fresh, and low in alcohol. 8°–10°.

Vini del Piacentino. Generic name given to some of the wines grown nearest to Piacenza: Gutturnio; Monterosso; and Trebbianino (*qq.v.*).

Note: The tiny mountain republic of San Marino, a little enclave in Emilia–Romagna, also grows a Sangiovese, a dry Verdicchio (cf. that of the castelli di Jesi, to which it is inferior), and a sweet, sparkling Moscato Spumante that is particularly low in alcohol (only about 6°) and strong in bubble – just the thing for child-marriages.

Chapter 9

THE MARCHES

❦

THE hills of the Marches are more abrupt than those of Tuscany, the roads more winding, the cities smaller and less frequented by tourists. This is simple, peasant country, its cooking rough and savoury, and its wines the modest reds and whites that go with such a cuisine. With one exception – the Verdicchio of the Castelli di Jesi, a white wine that I am not alone in ranking with Soave as one of the best of all Italian white wines, though it is made to look at once more pretentious and more frivolous than it really is by the deplorably fancy bottles in which it is sold.

The Wines of the Marches

Bianchello. Rather light, dry white wine, made from the Bianchello grape near Pesaro, where it goes well with the Adriatic fish, as an alternative to the much more widely publicised Verdicchio dei Castelli di Jesi. Low in alcohol (10°), which normally means that a wine does not "travel" well, but quite a lot of this is exported satisfactorily to Switzerland. Sometimes called Bianchetto Pesarese; a better quality being called Bianchello del Metauro (the Metauro being the river that runs into the Adriatic just south of Pesaro), and protected and labelled by a local growers' association.

Colli Ameni. See Colli Piceni.

Colli Maceratesi. See Colli Piceni.

Cupramontana. Produces one of the best of the Verdicchio wines, and also a *spumante*, consumed locally.

Colli Piceni. At the southern end of the region, between Ancona and Ascoli, the hills come close to the coast, and grow a vast amount of rather modest red and white wine – variously referred to as Piceni dei Colli

Ripani, or Piceno Bianco or Rosso. They are all sorts – dry and sweet, red and white, still and sparkling – and none is remarkable. Other names are Montereale and Colli Maceratesi, both red and white, and there are a red and a pink from the Colli Ameni, near Ancona. At Cignoli, near Macerata, they make a *spumante* of the same grapes (mostly Vernaccia and Sangiovese) that has something of a local reputation.

Conero Rosso. Dry red wine, sometimes called Montepulciano del Conero, after the grape it is made from, chiefly around Ancona, though it is widespread throughout the region. Rather fruity, in taste and in scent – quite a pleasant modest local wine to drink in pleasant modest local restaurants. 11°–13°. A better quality of the same wine is more usually called Montepulciano Piceno.

Loro Piceno. A village near Macerata which makes a particularly fine Verdicchio (*q.v.*). It also produces a sweet *vin cotto* (*q.v.*) very strong and rich. 20°.

Montereale. See Colli Piceni.

Montesanto Rosso. Sound dry red wine, made from a mixture of Sangiovese with the locally prolific Montepulciano – rather more Sangiovese than Montepulciano, which gives it, to my mind, a little more distinction than most of the red wines of the region. 12°. There is also a red wine made of the Sangiovese only, and called Sangiovese Marchigiano, simply, very light in alcohol (10°), which at its best is delightful, drunk young. In good local restaurants, such as Cortigiano, in Urbino, it is served as a simple carafe wine – dry, but with the faintest underlying sweetness, and very refreshing.

Verdicchio dei Castelli di Jesi. This, of course, is the one really well-known wine of the Marches, widely sold on the holiday coast just to the north – from Cattolica to Rimini – and in Britain, too. The desperately fancy bottles and labels should not be allowed to put one off: it is a good, sound white wine, made chiefly from the Verdicchio grape, in the valley of the Esino river, on which Jesi stands, and which runs into the Adriatic north of Ancona. All the writers on the subject, English and Italian, seem to agree that this is a "delicate" wine, but that is not my experience, which is that it is full-flavoured, uncompromising in its hard austerity, with a bitter finish, though I understand that there is a *semi-secco* or *amabile* version, which has not come my way. The best Verdicchio is made like Chianti (*q.v*), by the *governo* system of inducing a secondary fermentation. Fairly high in alcoholic strength (12°–15°), which is why it travels well – I have enjoyed very good bottles in London, notably at the Tiberio restaurant. Protected by a local growers' association, each approved bottle carries a neck-label showing a heraldic lion. One of the best comes from Cupramontana. There is also a local *rosato* wine, rather full and bland, made by growers of the Verdicchio, but not protected, and also a Verdicchio di Matelica and a Verdicchio dei Colli del Nevola, similar in style to the Jesi, but not quite so consistent. An artificially made sparkling Verdicchio prompts the stern Nuova Enologica, the great encyclopaedia of Italian wines, to observe that if only Italy had an efficient wine law this couldn't happen. (It is fair to point out that the new wine law came into force in 1965.) Good years: 1945, 1946, 1949, 1950, 1951, 1953, 1956, 1957. Very good: 1947, 1954, 1955, 1960. Exceptional: 1958.

Vernaccia di Serrapetrona. Sweetish sparkling red wine made from the Vernaccia Rossa grape, and interesting to those who are interested in sparkling sweet red wines. 11·5°–13°.

Vin Cotto. In many parts of Italy, but especially in the Marches and in the Abruzzi, the peasant growers make a *vin cotto* ("cooked wine") by reducing must over the fire to two-fifths of its original volume, and then bringing it up to its original volume with uncooked must. After fermentation it is aged for two years and over, producing a sweet, rich, Malaga-like wine of about 20°.

Vin Santo. The Marches are famous for their *vin santo* (the final vowel of *vino* is dropped in conventional usage, as in *vin cotto*) – a sweet wine made from semi-dried grapes: some of the best comes from Urbino and Ripatransone.

Chapter 10

TUSCANY

❦

IN the time of Cyrus Redding, whose *A History and Description of Modern Wines* was published in 1833, the wine of Chianti came "principally from a creeping species of vine, *vite bassa*", and was little thought of. Luigi Barzini has told, in his endlessly fascinating book, *The Italians* (Hamish Hamilton, 1964), how it was a point of husbandly honour that brought Baron Bettino Ricasoli (who succeeded Cavour in 1861 as Prime Minister of the newly united Italy) to create the Chianti we know today, and a vastly profitable industry: it was

> . . . the case of a jealous and moral gentleman, who disliked being cuckolded, but managed to avoid it without harsh words and bloodshed. He was . . . a religious man, dedicated to politics and serious studies in his favourite field, agriculture. He was by no means handsome. In fact, he was extremely cross-eyed, but had a tall and lean figure, and carried himself with a military and proud bearing.
>
> One night, when he had been married only a few months, Bettino, who had been nicknamed *Barone di Ferro*, or Iron Baron (such unbending characters are not necessarily admired in Italy, where *souplesse* is prized above all; the sobriquet has a derisive quality it would not have elsewhere), took his young wife Anna Bonaccorsi to a ball in Florence. There the poor lady was briefly and perfunctorily courted by a young man, who danced with her a few times. The husband immediately told her: "We must leave, my dear." He escorted her to their waiting carriage, sat down next to her, and told the coachman: "To Brolio." Brolio was the family seat, a lonely and gloomy castle, lost in barren and sterile hills, where none of the Ricasoli had lived for ages. The couple rode in silence through the snow, until dawn, he in his black evening clothes, she shivering in her ball dress. They lived in Brolio for practically the rest of their lives.
>
> To while away the time he reconstructed the manor, which now looks as if it had been dreamed up by Sir Walter Scott or designed as a background for *Il Trovatore*. He also experimented with planting different qualities of new vines

and producing wines with improved processes. (One must have patience and a firm character for such pursuits. It takes approximately five years for a man to taste the first product of a new combination of grapes he has planted.) The Baron came across a pleasing mixture of black and white grapes, Sangiovese and Malvasia, and a way to make them ferment in two successive waves, which imparted a novel taste to the *cru*. The wine became popular, was copied by the vineyard owners of the region, the Chianti, and acquired, in the end, a worldwide fame. One of the best Chiantis is still the Ricasoli, of which the Brolio Castle is the choice and most expensive variety. Thus the Baron managed to preserve the sanctity of the family, his wife's name and his honour unblemished, to amass a fortune, and to enrich his neighbours, all at the same time.

Now there is a further revolution under way that is changing the very face of the Tuscan countryside, background to so many, and such familiar, paintings of the Italian renaissance. More and more in the past few years, and now at an increasing pace, new vineyards are being made, planted with trim rows of vines, many of them trained low as in France, and wide enough apart for a tractor to pass between them, where once the share-cropping peasant grew olive trees, alternating with vines that had been allowed to grow nearly as tall, trained up stakes or living trees, with either straggling wheat, or a grazing cow, also in the same field.

That was under the old Tuscan system of *mezzadria*, or share-cropping, under which the peasant took half the crop, his landlord the other half. The peasant needed wine, oil and wheat, or meat or milk, from each field for his subsistence, rather than half the profits (and the heavy risks) from one crop only.

Now, under a series of land reforms, *mezzadria* is doomed: every political party, from the Communists to the Christian Democrats, is pledged to its abolition. Not that it would have survived anyway: *mezzadria* or no *mezzadria*, the Tuscan peasant nowadays would be off in any case to sell souvenirs in Florence, or to make mackintoshes at Empoli – for what girl, these days, within bus ride of a town, will marry a man who tills the soil? (It is the same story everywhere: they told me in Germany that if it were not for the Spanish labour taking the place of the German countryman who has gone off to the oil refineries and the chemical plants, we would be hard put to it for many a famous hock.)

And so the landlord is having to rationalise his wine-growing, with properly planted vineyards, where a tractor can do the work of many men, uprooting olive trees to do so, for although the olive is a profitable crop, especially here in Tuscany, and needs little tending, the fruit has to be gathered later in the year, in November or December, when casual labour is more reluctant to work in the open than at vintage time, in September or October. On the whole, the Tuscan landscape looks none the worse, for a well-tended vineyard is a comely thing. But it looks *different*, for one used not to notice the vines here, and now one misses the olives – although some intelligent landowners are keeping a few olive trees scattered about in the new vineyards at points where they will not obstruct the tractors, as much for the look of the thing as for the oil. As one of them said to me: "There should always be grey as well as green in this countryside."

As for the wine, Chianti should be all the better for it, for it is already being more carefully grown and made than it used to be, and the new vine-yards will be easier to tend, to guard against pests and to irrigate. There is room here, too, for additional vineyards, as there is not in France. Which is all to the good, with demand rising all the time for sound wines at a reasonable price – a demand that Italy, the Chianti area of Tuscany par-ticularly, ought to be able to meet.

I have listed separately the wines of the Tuscan archipelago, which con-sists not only of the islands of Elba and Giglio but also of the mainland promontory of Argentario (where stands the increasingly popular resort of Porto Ercole), the wines of which are closely related to those of the islands. There is a *consorzio* in Portoferraio, the capital of Elba, but virtually all the wines of the archipelago come from small independent proprietors, and until more modern methods are established, as they have been, for instance, in the new Sardinian co-operatives, they will continue to be inconsistent. But wine looms large in the Elban economy, and many of the local growths have some merit. There is a great deal of iron in the soil of the island (long famous for its mines – hence the capital's name), and there is much in the wine, which gives it tonic qualities, as well as its characteristic tang. The wines from the east of the island are also rich in flavour and in sugar: those of the centre are noted for their deep and glowing colour; and in the west it is white wines that predominate. On the smaller neighbouring island of Giglio, table grapes are as important as wine-making.

The wines of the archipelago in general, and of Elba in particular, have their devoted admirers (I am fond of Elba myself, but I drink its wines with modified rapture): Paolo Monelli, author of *O.P., ossia Il Vero Bevitore*, upbraids Luigi Veronelli, author of *I Vini d'Italia*, for omitting from the seven hundred and odd wines listed in his book an Aleatico of Porto Ercole; the Riminese dell'Elba; three local wines of Orbetello (which is by Porto Ercole); and a clear Elban wine that he had once described, he says, as "more platinum than Jean Harlow". Well, only one of these very local, very modest, wines is listed here, and Monelli's own list is only two-thirds the length of the one he complains about.

The Wines of Tuscany

Arbia. Dry white wine grown on the banks of the Arbia river, in the open country noted for its sheep (and its *pecorino*, the sheep's milk cheese) that stretches almost to the very edge of the city of Siena; sometimes known as Val d'Arbia, sometimes Bianco Vergine della Val d'Arbia – "virgin' because it is made by fermenting the must without stalks or skins. Light and delicate in consequence: not found very far from its native place, probably because its delicacy makes it not a good traveller. There is a similar Bianco di Montalbuccio from very near by. Cortona Bianco, Bianco di Santa Margherita and Val di Chiana are similar. 10°–11°.

Artimino. Another name for the Chianti di Montalbana Pistoiese (see under Chianti).

Bianco di Montalbuccio. See under Arbia.

Bianco di Santa Margherita. See under Arbia.

Brolio. See under Chianti.

Brunello di Montalcino. The vineyards of a small Tuscan hill-town, south of Siena, grow one of the great red wines of Italy, made from the Brunello grape only, a variety of the noble Sangiovese grape that goes into Chianti, but without the other Chianti grapes. The Brunello grape by itself gives a stronger, fuller and more fragrant wine than Chianti; this wine would be entitled by Italian law and the rules of the local association to style itself "Chianti Colline Senesi", but sails proudly under its own colours, and does not always carry even the growers' association label.

Brunello is so "big" that it is aged in cask for five to six years before bottling, thus acquiring even more staying power, and is then kept in bottle for two years before being put on the market. I doubt whether it should be drunk for another ten years after that, for it enjoys – and deserves – a fantastic reputation for longevity: Luigi Veronelli gives it up to fifty years of bottle-age, and in 1963 the firm of Trimani, Rome's most notable wine-merchants, were offering the 1888 and 1889 Brunello di Montalcino at 40,000 lire (about £23) a bottle, the 1920 at 20,000 (£11 10s.) and the 1925 at 15,000 (about £9) – almost certainly Europe's oldest and most expensive table wine. Curiously enough, Felice Cùnsolo does not list its best vintage years. Whether Brunello ranks with the finest burgundies, as so many Italian enthusiasts claim, I cannot say – it is different, and I think nothing is gained but confusion and hurt feelings in trying to compare unlikes. I have no doubt at all that this is a great wine, in its own immensely full way, and the 1955 I have in my own cellar I propose to leave for twenty years.

The one really important grower of Brunello is Signor Biondi-Santi, and hardly any of his wine leaves Italy, for it would be extremely expensive abroad and would suffer the competition of fine French wines that might well be cheaper. (I am told that a very little finds its way to Switzerland.)

Experts recommend decanting Brunello as much as twenty-four hours before serving. 13°.

Candia. Sweetish to sweet red and white wines from the extreme north-west of Tuscany, near the Carrara mountains.

Capezzana Bianco. Semi-sweet white wine, almost entirely from Trebbiano grapes, grown near Florence. 11·5°–12·5°.

Carmignano, or Chianti di Montalbano. See under Chianti.

Castello di Meleto. See under Chianti.

Chianti. As already explained, it was Baron Bettino Ricasoli who, rather more than a century ago, hit upon the particular mixture of Sangiovese and other grapes that gives Chianti its particular style and fragrance.* Whether it was he, too, as Luigi Barzini supposes, who devised the *governo all'uso toscano* – the deliberately contrived secondary fermentation that gives freshness and sometimes a slight prickle to the young wine – seems more doubtful: I fancy that this is a practice that had been established in Tuscany much earlier.

* The classic proportion is: 70 per cent Sangiovese, 20 per cent Black Canaiolo, 10 per cent Malvasia and Trebbiano, but there are many variations. The Frescobaldi house, for instance, uses only 60 per cent Sangiovese, as much as 15 per cent Trebbiano and much less Malvasia.

The *governo* system, to put it simply, is that after the first fermentation is over, at about the end of the year, between three and ten per cent of a rich must from dried grapes is added to the racked wine, and this, to quote Mr Gerald Asher's notes, "uses up all residual sugar, and provokes an early malolactic fermentation to make the wine more supple" – a fermentation that lasts about another fifteen to twenty days. (Originally peculiar to Tuscany, this practice is now spreading to other Italian regions.) But it is most important to note that the *governo* system is for wines meant to be drunk young. The finest wines of the Chianti district are meant to be aged in bottle: they are not put into *fiaschi* and they are not made by the *governo* system.

Three things have combined to make Chianti the best known abroad of all Italian wines. It is grown in a big zone, so that there is a large amount of wine, of the same kind, entitled to the same name: other wines are produced in such small quantities that their names make no impact. Much of it has always been grown on big estates, many owned by old and noble families (the Ricasoli family itself being one of them), that could and can afford modern methods of viticulture, vinification and marketing. Thirdly, the wicker-covered *fiasco*, devised long ago as being easy and cheap to make, and at the same time ideally suited to wine made by the *governo* system (for it holds more wine offering less surface to the small amount of air contained than does an ordinary bottle, thus preserving the freshness and prickle of the young wine) caught the public's imagination all over the world as being the picturesque symbol of Italy. Never mind that the wicker nowadays is often replaced by plastic, or that the finest wines of the region are bottled not in *fiaschi* but in claret bottles – by now Chianti is the archetype of Italian wine, and firmly established.

As will be explained later, there are two – or even three – types of Chianti: wine to be drunk very young, straight from the vat; wine to be drunk almost as young, as soon as bottled; and wine to be aged – and aged very considerably. The young wines are fresh and fruity, often with a slight prickle – not actually resembling young Beaujolais, but the same *sort* of wine as young Beaujolais, and to be enjoyed in the same way. The older wines are full-bodied and fragrant, sometimes with a distinction (such as in the Brunello I have already mentioned) not necessarily like that of a fine burgundy but of the same order. It would be a pity if their reputation were to be spoiled by the amount of Chianti on the market that is indifferent because it was meant to be drunk young, and has not been. As will be seen, many growers bottle their finest Chiantis under other, special, names.

It is forty years since the Consorzio per la Difesa del Vino Tipico del Chianti was founded, and in 1932 it persuaded the Italian Government to delimit the area to which the name *Chianti classico* could be applied – a region of about a couple of hundred square miles of the gently hilly Tuscan countryside, stretching from just south of Florence to just north of Siena, corresponding to the country of the fourteenth-century League of Chianti.

But so much precisely similar wine, made from precisely similar grapes, in precisely the same way, is made in precisely the same sort of country, immediately adjacent, that there were many growers who felt, with some justice, that they had a right to call their wine Chianti, too – for how, under any other name, could it compete with a wine so well-known at home and abroad? All the *Chianti classico* growers could say was that well, such wines *might* be Chianti, but they were not *classico*. So the Government permitted wine made in the same way, in adjacent areas, to be called Chianti, but not *Chianti classico*.

So now there are the following wines of the district, all much of a muchness, all protected by growers' associations (not necessarily at daggers drawn, either: they often combine usefully), all with neck-labels. Some of these associations and labels are quite new.

Chianti Classico. Label shows black cockerel on gold ground. 12°–13°. Good years: 1945, 1950, 1958. Very good: 1947, 1949, 1952, 1955, 1957.

Chianti Colli Aretini. The neck-label shows a chimera. From the hills around Arezzo, to the east of the *zona classica*: harder and more acid than the others, and not often aged – it is generally drunk within the year, though Felice Cùnsolo does list 1951 and 1953 as its good and very good years, which suggests, though it is not certain, that they may have been regarded as worth keeping. 11°–13°.

Chianti dei Colli Empolesi. A newly formed group, its wines from around Empoli, the ancient hill-town twenty miles from Florence, on the road to Pisa. The wines are similar to those of the *zona classica*, though not, perhaps, so well balanced. One of them retains its own name of Dianella. The neck-label shows a bunch of grapes.

Chianti delle Colline d'Elsa. Another newly formed group, its wines coming from the Elsa valley, near Poggibonsi, and resembling the Senesi wines. The neck-label displays the Florentine lily in red on gold.

Chianti Colli Fiorentini. Also known as Chianti del Putto from the design of the neck-label, shared by the Chianti Rufina. Comes from the area immediately between Florence itself and the *zona classica*, the wine of which it closely resembles. 11·5°–13°. Good years: 1947, 1950, 1952, 1953, 1956, 1957. Very good: 1945, 1946, 1948, 1949, 1951, 1954, 1955, 1958.

Chianti Colline Pisane. The neck-label bears a centaur (it used to be the Leaning Tower). From the Pisan hills, and not highly regarded. 11°–12°.

Chianti Colli Senesi. From the district immediately to the south of the *zona classica*. The vines here are grown up living trees (maples and poplars, severely pollarded), and the wine they produce is not particularly consistent, though at its best it is true Chianti in style, but to be drunk young. The Association's neck-label shows Romulus and Remus and the she-wolf – badge of Siena as well as of Rome. 12°–13°.

Chianti Montalbano Pistoiese. The newly formed association has adopted a neck-label showing the towers of Montalbano. The district lies between Pistoia and Florence, and its wines are widely sold in Milan, Genoa and abroad, though they are not always consistent in quality. Good years: 1949, 1951, 1952, 1953, 1956, 1957. Very good: 1945, 1946, 1947, 1948, 1950, 1954, 1955, 1958.

Chianti Rufina. Sometimes rather fuller than other Chiantis (Nipozzano [*q.v.*], comes from this region). Some of the wines of the district that are meant to be drunk young are subjected to two *governo* processes, instead of the usual one. Carries the *putto* neck-label, along with the Chianti Fiorentino. 11·5°–14°. Good years: 1945, 1947, 1949, 1952, 1953, 1956, 1957. Very good: 1946, 1948, 1950, 1951, 1954, 1955, 1958.

As has already been explained, it is the wines meant to be drunk young that are put into *fiaschi* (so much for most of the Chianti we get in wicker-covered flasks in England, which has lost its freshness and has no right in a flask of this sort). The Chianti wines meant for ageing are made in a different way (without *governo*, that is) and are put into claret-shaped bottles. Many of the important houses use the word Chianti as only a secondary name for their finest wines, and anyone seeking the best wines of this area should look for:

Brolio Riserva. The best of the Ricasoli Chiantis, aged five years in wood before bottling. Mr Charles Bode recorded in 1956 having come across a 1923 Brolio at the Canelli Restaurant in Turin that, "was a sheer delight".

Castello di Meleto. Also a Ricasoli wine, and a cut above the ordinary Chianti, but not quite so full nor so fine as the Brolio. Along with the 1923 Brolio already mentioned, Mr Charles Bode found a 1937 Meleto, "equally good, with a distinct shade of onion-skin" – but I doubt whether it would have lasted so well as the Brolio.

Nipozzano. The claret-shaped bottle in which the Frescobaldi firm puts up its Nipozzano carries the *putto* neck-label of the Chianti dei Colli Fiorentini, to which it is entitled, but there is no mention of Chianti on the main label. Nipozzano is a fine, full wine, with the great power of ageing in bottle already observed in the Ricasoli wines and the Brunello di Montalcino: when I lunched at Nipozzano early in 1964 with the Marchese de' Frescobaldi and his brother, Piero, and was asked what year I should like to drink, I remembered the great range of old wines I had seen in the cellar, and asked for the year of my birth, 1908. It was superb – full, soft, majestic, with no sign of fading in the glass. When I exclaimed that it would be a rare French wine indeed that could match such longevity my hosts expressed gratification but no surprise – true, they said, they hadn't tasted the 1908 recently, but they had had the 1912 the other day, and it had been excellent.

Riserva Ducale. The best Chianti of the house of Ruffino (a family name: these wines are entitled to the *putto* label of the Fiorentino Chiantis, and should not be confused with those of Rufina, a place name).

Stravecchio Melini. The best Chianti of the Melini firm. It is interesting to note that although the Melini wines come from grapes grown in the *Chianti classico* area they are made and bottled just outside it, and by the strict rules of the association they are not entitled to the *classico* neck-label. They refuse to carry the *putto* label to which the position of the cellars and bottling plant entitles them, on the grounds that this would misrepresent the contents of the bottle, and although they cannot carry the *classico* neck-label, they do describe the wine as Chianti classico on the house-label.

Villa Antinori. The best red wine of the Antinori house, in the *zona classica*. (This firm deserves well of the English visitor: Italian courses are held in the beautiful Antinori Palace in the heart of Florence, where there is also a ground-floor "cantinetta", at which the Antinori wines can be tasted, very cheaply, by the glass, along with very good sandwiches and snacks.)

There is also a so-called "white Chianti", sometimes known as Bianco delle Colline del Chianti, sometimes rather vaingloriously as Chablis di Monte-paldi, produced in San Casciano Val di Pesa, near Florence, in the *zona classica*, made of the Trebbiano grape and others. It is dry and full-flavoured, but hardly as distinguished among Italian white wines as the best Chianti among the reds. Among the so-called white Chiantis one might include Arbia, Lacrima d'Arno, Trebbiano Toscano and others listed here under their own names.

Colle Salvetti. Deep red wine made near Leghorn, from the usual Chianti combination of grapes, very similar in style to the Chiantis of the Colline Pisane (*q.v.*) though sometimes *frizzante*. 12°.

Colline Lucchesi. Modest red and white wines from the olive-growing hills near Lucca, between Florence and the sea. The white, mainly from Trebbiano and other grapes, is dry and light. 12°. The red is sometimes *frizzante*, but dry. 13°. More distinguished wines from this district are the Montecarlo, red and white (*q.v.*).

Colline della Lunigiana Bianco. Dry, semi-sweet and sweet white wines from near Massa-Carrara, in the north-western corner of Tuscany. Lightish (10°–12°) and undistinguished.

Colline Sanminiatesi. Red wines are grown near Empoli on the other side of the river from the district where the Empolese Chianti comes from, but made from the same grapes in the same way. They are not in the same class as the best Chiantis, but their growers feel important enough to have formed an association to protect the "Vino Toscano Colline Sanminiatesi", with a label of its own, showing an old Barbarossa tower of the district destroyed in the war. 11·5°–12·5°.

Colline val di Nievole. Dry white wine from near the smart spa of Montecatini: often *frizzante*. 11°–13°.

Cortona. Dry white wine grown at Cortona, between Arezzo and Lake Trasimene, from a mixture of local grapes. 10·5°–12·5°. See under Arbia.

Dianella. See under the Chianti dei Colli Empolesi.

Follonica. Local red and white wine from the mainland opposite Elba, the white tending to be sweet and the red sweetish. 12·5°.

Lacrima d'Arno. Fancy name given to the white wines from the upper Arno, very like Arbia (*q.v.*).

Malvasia Toscana. Deep-amber dessert wine made in many parts of the region from semi-dried Malvasia grapes. 12°–14°.

Maremma. Similar to Follonica (*q.v.*).

Montalbuccio. Similar to Arbia (*q.v.*).

Montecarlo. Red and white wines of some interest from the hills around Lucca; there are two qualities of each – a *corrente* for local café use, and a *nobile*. The "noble" wines, both red and white, are full but dry (the red 13°, the white 12°–13°) and are, in effect, similar to German *auslese* wines, in that they are made of selected grapes – by the Chianti *governo* method, the white aged in cask for some three years, the red for as much as eight. To be found in the smart hotels and restaurants of Montecatini.

Montepescali and Monteregio. Both similar to Follonica (*q.v.*).

Moscadello di Montalcino. From the same hill-town as the fine Brunello (*q.v.*) comes a wine made from three parts of Moscatello grapes to one of Malvasia. This mixture gives a very light but sweet and fragrant wine, quite unlike any from other parts of Italy, though there are one or two similar Tuscan wines, in its combination of freshness and lusciousness. Drunk young and cold. 6°–8°. There is also a much heavier dessert wine, Moscadello Liquoroso, 15°–16°, and some confusion is being caused these days by a new tendency to call the heavy wine Moscadello, and to refer to the lighter wine, although this was the original Moscadello, as Moscadelletto – "little Moscadello".

Moscato di Subbiano. Similar to the Moscadello di Montalcino (see above) and made not far away, near Arezzo, though in small quantities, and not so consistent.

Pitigliano. Dry, but softish – flabby, even – white wine, from near Grosseto, of Trebbiano grapes, and made in the same way as the Umbrian Orvieto (*q.v.*). Sometimes I have fancied to find a faint lemon flavour. 11°–13°.

Pollera. Sweet red wine grown in the hills behind La Spezia, all consumed locally.

Pomino. Good red and white wines from the same area as Nipozzano (*q.v.* under Chianti). The white is made on the skins, which gives it more body than many white wines of the region. 11°–12°.

Rosatello Ruffino. A *rosé* wine made by one of the big Chianti houses from Sangiovese grapes, and with some of the Chianti style and fragrance. 11°–12°.

Scansano. Red wine, made largely of Sangiovese, though in these parts – in the hills inland from Grosseto – this grape is known as the Morellino. Quite like some of the neighbouring Chiantis, and worth looking for locally. 12°–13°.

Trebbiano Toscano. Similar to Arbia (*q.v.*).

Ugolino Bianco. Dry white wine, made fresh and prickly by applying the Chianti *governo* system to Trebbiano grapes (with a very small admixture of others, including the French Cabernet and Sauvignon). Comes from the coast on either side of Leghorn, and is drunk a great deal, usually very young – *nell'annata* – in the admirable local fish restaurants. Sometimes called Bianco del Littorale Livornese. 11°–12°.

Val di Chiana. A white "virgin" wine very like that of Arbia (*q.v.*), but from the Chiana river valley. Sometimes known and labelled as Valchiana. 11°–12°.

Val di Nievole. Red and white wines of the usual Tuscan grape varieties, of no especial merit, produced in the district around Montecatini.

Val d'Elsa, Bianco della. Rather better than average local dry white wine, made from the usual local white grapes, mainly Trebbiano, but with some finer additions – Traminer and Sémillon, for instance – in the better qualities. Comes from the same district as the red Chiantis of the Colline d'Elsa, and are unusual among Tuscan whites in being possibly as good of their kind as the reds. 11°–12°.

Vecchienna. Similar to Follonica (*q.v.*).

Vernaccia di san Gimignano. From the extremely picturesque (and extremely self-conscious) many-towered hill-town near Siena comes this white wine, made from the Vernaccia grape, treated in the same way as the "virgin" wine of Arbia and the Val di Chiana, and protected and labelled by the association that looks after the Chianti of the Colli Senesi and the Vin Nobile di Montepulciano, and to which the Brunello di Montalcino is entitled to belong. An important dry white wine that improves with a couple of years in bottle. 11°–13°. There is said to be a sweet version, too, which has not come my way, but of which Luigi Veronelli, expressing one of his extremely infrequent subjective judgments, says flatly, "I do not advise."

Vin Nobile di Montepulciano. A fine red wine, made of more or less the same *cépage* as the various Chiantis, but with rather more white grapes and not by the *governo* system, for this is a wine intended to be aged in bottle, and not to be drunk young from a *fiasco*. Comes from a pleasant small hill-town near Siena, very near and very like Montalcino, and very similar to that town's fine Brunello, though it is not known to live to quite such an age – perhaps because it is not made of the Brunello (which is to say the Sangiovese) grape only but has about twenty-five per cent of white grapes. But it is certainly a fine wine, especially after enough years in bottle (five upwards) for it to be showing its tawny tints, when it is big and flavoury, like a fine Hermitage, well balanced and smooth. Protected by the Senese association of growers, and carries the Senese she-wolf label. 12°–14°. There is also a sweet Montepulciano wine of small importance, and it should be noted that it is the *nobile* wine that is considered here, and that has its name protected – the local red wine called simply "Montepulciano" is an ordinary common wine.

Vin Santo. Quite a lot of this sweet, rich dessert wine is made throughout Tuscany as, indeed, it is throughout Italy. (See under the wines of the Trentino–Alto Adige.) Here, as elsewhere, it varies a great deal in quality: the best are said to come from the *zona classica* of Chianti, from the Val di Pesa (just south of Florence), and – very good indeed, but hard to find – from the Casentino hills to the east of Florence, along the curve of the Arno. Some is made by using one-third black and two-thirds white grapes, giving the partridge-eye colour from which it gets its name – Occhio di Pernice.

Wines of the islands of Elba and Giglio

Aleatico di Portoferraio. Dark, sweet, muscat-flavoured dessert wine, made in every part of Elba from the grape of the same name – a sort of dark Moscato – different in flavour and character, though not so much in scent, from the Moscato of the mainland and from Aleatico wines of other parts of Italy. Rich in iron, as is the soil it grows in, and said to be good, therefore, for invalids, especially those suffering from anaemia. 12°–15°.

Ansonica. Dry and semi-sweet white wines of only moderate importance and interest, grown on Giglio from the grape of the same name; also produced in the Argentario district of the mainland, and in a small part of Elba near Porto Azzurro. 13°–15°.

Elba Spumante. Dry and semi-sweet white sparkling wines are made on Elba from the local Procanico grape (a variety of Trebbiano) by the *cuve close* method – secondary fermentation in tanks, like Asti Spumante (*q.v.*). "Not for the educated palate," says the Italian wine encyclopaedia, and I agree: I suspect that many bottles find their way into the less reputable night-clubs of Europe, to be sold as champagne.

Moscato dell'Elba. Golden dessert wine, heavily scented, similar to Aleatico (*q.v.*) save in colour, and made from semi-dried Moscato grapes. 14°–15°. There is also a Moscato Spumante, usually rather more carefully made, and better in quality, than the drier Elba Spumante (*q.v.*).

Procanico. White wine made on Elba from a local variety of the Trebbiano grape. At its best, is quite the outstanding table wine of the island, red or white, and enthusiasts claim for it that it is of the same type, and class, as a Chablis (but there is Chablis and Chablis). Very good with the excellent local fish, and worth paying for the best quality. 12°–13°.

Riminese. A dry, full white wine made near Porto Ercole, on the mainland, from a grape said to have come originally from Rimini. Good with fish. 11°–13°.

Roselba. See Sangiovese, below.

Sangiovese or Sangioveto. The Elban red wine, made from the Sangiovese of the mainland and, at its best, not unlike the Tuscan Chiantis. That is when it is made of the Sangiovese grape only, but there is a lot of common red wine on the island, with little claim to the name of Sangiovese, though it assumes it, and less to its fame. Sometimes known as Roselba. 13°.

Chapter 11

UMBRIA

❧

ITALY is so diverse a country, and the Italian people themselves each so individual, that it is difficult to say of any place or any person that he, or it, is typically or characteristically Italian. Yet there is something of the *essence* of Italy in Umbria, one of the smallest regions, lying half-way between hip and toe of the long peninsula, and the only one entirely surrounded, so to speak, by Italy, for all others have either a coastline or a foreign frontier.

The Umbrian landscape has changed little since it served as model for the background of so many religious paintings of the fifteenth century:

> Behind the cross, or over the shoulder of a Saint Sebastian transfixed with arrows [writes Mr Michael Adams in his admirable book on the region] there opens out one of those Umbrian vistas, of meadows and cypress trees and hills swimming in the luminous distance, which appear so romantically improbable when you see them in captivity on the walls of some stuffy gallery, but which you recognise at every turn in the Umbria even of the twentieth century, so that you wonder at once how any artist could have captured so perfectly not merely the lineaments but the very essence and feeling of a landscape, and how the landscape could have preserved into our own day a beauty so pristine that the dew of the first day of creation seems to be still moist upon it.

One reason, alas, for that miraculous preservation is that although the system of *mezzadria* – share-cropping – is officially at an end, as we have seen in Tuscany, it is far from being so in practice. Much less so in Umbria than it is in more progressive, more prosperous Tuscany. Hence, indeed, the immensely heavy Communist vote in Umbria – some forty per cent as against just over twenty-five for Italy as a whole. (And even in Tuscany, in Siena, as I write these very words, in November 1964, I can look up from my desk and see a long procession of *contadini* from round about the town, dour-faced and sombrely dressed, in their go-to-town black trilbies and their thick stiff suits, winding its way into the Piazza Giacomo Matteotti, in front of the provincial Chamber of Commerce and Agriculture, carrying placards and banners demanding an end in practice, as well as in promise, to *mezzadria*; for payment in cash instead of in kind; and for the land to go to the people who work it.)

This is why there is no mention of the vine in that evocation by Michael Adams of the eternal Umbrian landscape; why Perugino did not paint it in his pictures; and why the twentieth-century visitor is nothing like so conscious of its presence here as he is in Piedmont, or Lombardy, or the Alto Adige, or in the newly organised and replanted great estates of the Chianti country: in most parts of Umbria, the vine still grows higgledy-piggledy with wheat and olive, and it is the olive trees which mark the landscape.

So Umbrian wine production is fairly modest, and only one of its wines has more than a local reputation. That, indeed, is well and widely known, and I suspect that more Orvieto, so called, finds its way into those characteristic squat *fiaschi*, flatter than those of Chianti, than the slopes of the fantastic hilltop city ever grew. But there is now an association in being to protect its good name, and to award neck-labels to flasks of the authentic wine, made in the right place and of the right grape.

Wines of Umbria

Alte Valle del Tevere. The country of the upper Tiber, north of Perugia, between Citta di Castello and Umbertide, produces a range of table wines, two-thirds of them red, one-third white (the reverse of what is the general Umbrian proportion), of modest quality, the reds chiefly made of the Sangiovese and Canaiolo of neighbouring Tuscany, and made in much the same way as Chianti; the whites of Trebbiano (the grape that makes its more famous neighbour, Orvieto), along with Pinot Bianco and a certain amount of Riesling, fairly recently introduced. Some of the white wines of this district are known as Tevere Bianco, and some by the name of the grape, Trebbiano. On the whole, both red and white wines of the Alte Valle del Tevere are simple picnic wines, and are not too heavy for summertime luncheons. 12°–14°.

Amelia. This district near Terni produces modest dry red and white table wines, to be drunk young. 10°–12°. Finer varieties are the Oro di Lugnago and the Rubino di Lugnago (*qq.v.*).

Bastia. The local wine of Assisi. (Bastia is a little township only a couple of miles away.) White, from Verdicchio as well as Trebbiano grapes; dry and quite unremarkable. 11°.

Canaiolo. See under Lazio.

Castiglione Teverina. A white wine from very near Orvieto, the wine of which it closely resembles.

Colli Perugini, Bianco and Rosso; Colline del Trasimeno, Bianco and Rosso. The hills around Perugia, and those around Lake Trasimene, grow a fair amount of common table wines. Those of any interest are listed here under their more specific names: those sold under generic names are the commonest.

Fontesegale, Bianco di and Rosso di. Among the rather better-quality wines of the Alte Valle del Tevere (*q.v.*). The red is said to improve with bottle-age. 12°.

Montecastelli, Bianco and Rosso. Also better-quality wines of the Alte Valle del Tevere.

Nebbiolo. A small amount of red wine, from the noble grape that makes the fine wines of Piedmont, is made near Gubbio, in the north-eastern corner of the region, and is quite good, though I have never known a bottle of the Umbrian Nebbiolo even to approach the majesty of a great Barolo, or the elegance of a Gattinara. 10°–11°.

Oro di Lugnago. Dry white table wine from near Terni, made of Trebbiano and Malvasia Toscana grapes. (See under Amelia.) 10°–12°.

Orvieto. The cathedral city of Orvieto heaves itself out of the Umbrian countryside on a great rocky bluff: "A strange dark mass like the bulk of an aircraft carrier out at sea," as Mr Michael Adams has described it. "The rock on which it stands is a volcanic deposit, left by some freakish cataclysm in the childhood of the world, a base of yellowish tufa whose almost vertical walls rise six hundred feet out of the plain." This great cliff is riddled with caves, in which for centuries past the wine of Orvieto has fermented and matured – a wine already famous in the fifteenth century (and certainly long before), for it is recorded that when Pinturicchio was working on his frescoes in Orvieto cathedral he had a special clause in his contract stipulating that he should be supplied with as much wine as he wanted of the grapes of Trebbiano, from which Orvieto is made to this day.*

* It was not unusual in those days for a painter's contract to include payment in food and

This was the Orvieto *abboccato* or *amabile* – semi-sweet; the Orvieto *secco*, though now perhaps more commercially important, is a relatively recent innovation. The *abboccato* is made by allowing the grapes to begin to rot *after* they have been picked (not on the vine, as with Sauternes, and the German *trockenbeerenauslesen*), developing what the Italians call *muffa nobile*, which means exactly the same as the French *pourriture noble* and the German *edelfäule*. This while the grapes lie in open casks in the tufa caves, before pressing. The curious thing is that this produces quite a light, delicate, only semi-sweet wine, nothing like so luscious or so cloying as the French and German wines already mentioned – not too sweet, indeed, to be drunk cool with one of the richer fish or chicken dishes, especially as a good example of the Orvieto *abboccato* will show quite a clean, fresh back-taste.

Both the dry and the semi-sweet Orvieto white wines are made of about sixty per cent Trebbiano grapes (sometimes here called Procanico, as on Elba), with twenty per cent Verdello, fifteen per cent Malvasia and five per cent of the small, sweet, scented Grechetto. Both wines are also kept for two years in cask before bottling. The dry Orvieto should be well balanced, with a pleasant flowery bouquet, and a slightly bitter after-taste: sometimes it can seem rather flat and lifeless, but at its best it is among the most delightful white wines of Italy. Both wines are bottled in the characteristic Orvieto *fiasco*, called *pulcianella*, squatter and bigger-bellied than that of Chianti,* and both are protected by the local Consorzio per la Difesa del Vino Tipico di Orvieto, which grants a numbered neck-label. Orvieto *secco*, 12°–14°; Orvieto *abboccato*, 11°–13°.

There is also a small amount of red Orvieto produced, made largely of Sangiovese grapes, like Chianti, and said to be kept for seven years in cask before bottling. Perhaps the best red Orvieto is, but I have never found one that is as distinguished in its own class as the white Orvieto is among the Italian whites. And there is an Orvieto Vino Santo; sweet, rich and luscious after five years in wood, of a deep topaz colour.

Panicale. Another of the red wines of the upper Tiber, usually drunk young, and consumed locally. 10°–12°.

---

wine as well as in cash: Signorelli, working on his "Last Judgment" in the cathedral at about the same time as Pinturicchio, was paid two measures of wine and two quintals of grain a month, as well as his fee and his lodging. It is Pinturicchio's stipulation that the wine should be of Trebbiano that is so interesting.

* But of smaller capacity: it holds three-quarters of a litre to the *fiasco*'s litre. There is a two-litre Orvieto *fiasco* called a *toscanello*.

Piegaro. Dry red wine, similar to Scacciadiavoli (*q.v.*).

Rubino di Lugnago. Dry red table wine, made from Sangiovese, Barbera and Pinot Nero grapes, rather better of its kind than the other wines of its district, around Terni. 11°–12°.

Sacrantino. A curious strong, sweet and heavily scented red wine grown in a very small area in the hilly district south of Assisi, near the villages of Montefalco, Giano Umbro and Gualdo Cattaneo – a sort of red Vino Santo, and hence perhaps its name, a diminutive of Sacro. There is an *amabile* (semi-sweet), and a *dolce* (sweet). 13°–15°.

Sangiustino. Another of the dry white wines of the upper Tiber, but from higher up the river than most, near the small town of San Giustino, north of Citta di Castello, with rather more flavour and fragrance than many others of the region, perhaps because both Malvasia and Riesling grapes are used, as well as the predominant Trebbiano. 9°–11°.

Scacciadiavoli. A full red wine, made from a mixture of Sangiovese and Barbera, with the Barbera predominant, and grown in the hill country south of Assisi. Strong (13°–14°) and heavy, with a great deal of tannic astringency when young. The name means, "drive the devil out", and it is interesting that it should come from the same region as the Sacrantino, and so near a city dedicated to two saints – Saint Francis and Saint Clare.

Tiferno. Modest red wine from the upper Tiber, often *frizzante* and drunk young. 11°.

Trebbiano Spoletino. From the grape that makes the white upper Tiber wines, and the Orvieto, but grown in the Terni area, in the south of the region, and said to be fuller than these others, and especially fragrant. 13°.

Vernaccia di Cannara. Sweet, deep-red wine made from a variety of Barbera, dried in the sun after picking, and with fermentation arrested.

Vin Santo. Like most parts of Italy, Umbria makes a sweet dessert *vino* or *vin santo*. This Vin Santo d'Umbria is one of the best, golden and heavily scented: the Greco di Todi, so called from the name of the grape and the district in which it is grown, has an especially high reputation.

Chapter 12

LAZIO

❧

ONLY a hundred years ago the Campagna stretched right into Rome itself and, as Mr Bernard Wall has recorded, vines grew around St John Lateran. Even now, the countryside presses close in on Rome, so that the hill-towns of only a dozen miles or so away, such as Frascati and Grottaferrata, are still separated from the capital by wheat-fields and vineyards, cypresses and chestnut groves.

As the Roman businessman is not a commuter, but lives in a block of flats in the smart suburb of Parioli, or in part of a more or less modernised *palazzo* in the heart of the city, the little towns themselves have kept their character, as places where country-folk live, and where the neighbouring farmers bring their fruit and their wine to market. Romans go there for the day, but not to live, and in a mere Sunday afternoon's drive can see the vineyards from which came the Frascati they drank for lunch or, on a rather longer excursion, taking a whole day off to bathe in Lake Bolsena, sixty miles away, those that yielded the Est! Est!! Est!!! of Montefiascone that they mean to have for dinner.

For there are two main areas of wine-growing in Lazio – the *castelli Romani*, or country of the Roman castles, in the Alban hills, and the area around Lake Bolsena, which would seem to be geographically part of the Orvieto district in Umbria, with which indeed it has close affinities. All three areas are volcanic: Orvieto, as we have seen, stands on a great bluff of tufa, and the lakes of the Alban hills, Nemi and Albano, are ancient craters, as is Bolsena. The wines do have a cousinly resemblance, deriving no doubt from the fact that they are all grown in volcanic soil, but the Est! Est!! Est!!! is more like the other wines of Lazio, the *castelli* wines, than it is like Orvieto, although Orvieto is so much nearer, for both groups of Lazio wines are made from a similar mixture of grapes.

The Wines of Lazio

Aleatico di Genzano. A wine from the district of the Castelli Romani (*q.v.*) though not classed as such, for the *castelli* wines are primarily light table wines, and this is a sweet dessert wine made from the Aleatico grape, served cold with fruit. 12°–15°.

Aleatico di Viterbo. Made from the same grape as the Aleatico di Genzano, but from the other wine-growing area of the region, near Lake Bolsena, and much fuller and more luscious. 14°–16°. Note that other Aleatico wines of this particular district have begun to be labelled "di Pitigliano" and "di Montefiascone".

Aleatico di Terracina. An Aleatico from the southern-facing coast between Terracina and Gaeta, more closely resembling the Viterbo than the Genzano. 14°–15°. An interesting variant here is the Aleatico Secco, a dry but extremely full and strong (16°–18°) wine made from the same grape, semi-dried, and more fully fermented out, and capable of immense ageing in bottle – up to twenty years or so.

Anagni, Bianco and Rosso. Local wines from the Frosinone area, the white (10·5°–12·5°) made from Romanesco, Bello Velletrano, Agostinella and Malvasia di Candia grapes, straw-yellow to gold in colour, usually dry, but sometimes slightly *abboccato* and sometimes, too, slightly harsh; the red (11°–13°) from Cesanese Commune and other grapes, and of very modest quality.

Aprilia, Bianco, Rosso and Rosato. The flat country between the hills of the Castelli Romani and the sea at Anzio was a battleground after the Anzio landings. Now it is wine-growing country, its marshes drained, producing white, red and pink wines. The white (11°–13°), from Trebbiano, Malvasia di Candia and Bellone grapes, trained along horizontal wires, from post to post, is a modest dry wine; the red (12°–13°), from Sangiovese, Merlot, Montepulciano and Ciliegiolo grapes, has rather more character, as local wines go. The *rosato* (12°–13°) is made from the same grapes as the red, taken earlier off the skins, and is rather full for a pink wine.

Barbera di Anagni. In the hill country rather to the east of the Castelli Romani, north of Frosinone, they grow a certain amount of Barbera grapes (see under Tuscany) from which they make a generous, full-bodied red table wine only to be found locally, but worth asking for in those parts, for big red wines are rare in this region. 13°–13·5°.

Canaiolo. Soft, light, sweet red wine from the grape of the same name, semi-dried, grown on the southern shores of Lake Bolsena, and pleasant to drink with fruit, or between meals. A similar wine is grown in Umbria, near Trevi.

Capena. One of the wines grown in the Colli Teverini. See under Monterotondo.

Castelli Romani. The district was delimited by law as long ago as 1933 – only wines produced in an area of about fifty square miles, in the Alban hills, south-east of Rome, can be described as *vini dei Castelli Romani*, though many of these wines, of course, give themselves a more specific name, of village or commune, or a co-operative brand name. Chiefly, they are white, and there are dry, semi-sweet and sweet versions, of which perhaps the sweet and semi-sweet are the most plentiful, though there is a growing demand for the dry. For the sweeter wines, the grapes are gathered late, when they are semi-dried on the vine, and may even be subject to the *muffa nobile* – the "noble rot" that gives the great French sweet wines their character, though these Roman wines are far less luscious. These semi-dried grapes are described as *infavata*, which seems not to be a dictionary word, but which I take to mean of the colour of cooked dried beans. The late gathering means that the weather is cold by the time fermentation is taking place: fermentation is slow, therefore, especially as the musts are *ingrottate* in the deep, cold caves that riddle the soft volcanic rock of the Alban hills.

The white wines are made from Bellone, Malvasia di Candia, Malvasia Gentile, Buonvino and – a recent importation into this area – the Trebbiano Toscano, and reach an alcoholic strength of 11°–14°. The dry *castelli* whites are firm, fresh wines, with plenty of body – quite enough, for instance, for them to be drunk with, and not be overwhelmed by, the savoury *pasta* dishes of Rome, such as *spaghetti carbonara* or *spaghetti matriciana*, or with the baby lamb, baby kid or sucking-pig that the Romans love so much. The semi-sweet (*abboccato*) wines are good of their kind, though it is not so easy to find suitable dishes to enjoy them with – it might be interesting to try them with a first course of *prosciutto e melone* or *prosciutto e fichi*: raw smoked ham with melon or figs, according to season. The really sweet (*dolce*) *castelli* wines are delicious with these fruits, or with peaches or pears after dinner.

Certain red wines, such as the sweet, dark Aleatico (*q.v.*) and the dry red Cesanese (*q.v.*) are grown in the Castelli Romani district, but are not regarded, or referred to, as *castelli* wines, a name normally reserved for the light white wines of the district.

Outstanding among the *vini dei Castelli Romani* are:

Cannellino. The sweet wine of Frascati (*q.v.*).

Colli Albani, Bianco dei. This is a narrower designation than *Castelli Romani*, and applies to the wines of the district in the Alban hills, more particularly around Albano Laziale, Ariccia and Castelgandolfo (where the Pope has his summer palace), all to the west of Lake Albano. The wine tends to be rather lighter than other wines of the district, perhaps because it is made mainly from Trebbiano and Malvasia, without some of the other grapes used in other communes, and I would choose it to go with fish, in preference to others, when opportunity offered: there is also, as usual, a sweet version, and there is a less important red wine – Rosso dei Colli Albani – made in the same parts.

Colli Lanuvi, or Lanuvio, Bianco dei. Similar white wines to the above, dry, semi-sweet and sweet, from the more southerly parts of the *castelli* area, some from near Genzano, between Lakes Albano and Nemi, but mostly from around Lanuvio, whence they derive their name, south of Lake Nemi. There is also a Rosso dei Colli Lanuvi.

Colonna. A white wine like the others, though rather deeper in colour than most, and lighter in alcohol, from the north-easternmost part of the Castelli district, towards Palestrina.

Cori. The red and white wines of Cori, in the group of hills (the Lepini) to the south of the Castelli, are very like the *castelli* wines, but tend to be stronger and drier.

Frascati. The most famous name among the *castelli* wines, partly because of the virtue of the wine itself; partly because of the charm of the country town, so near to Rome, yet with so much character of its own, and with such enchanting villas and gardens, and sweeping views over the Campagna. (Once, too, it gave its name to a notable London restaurant, now no longer with us, but well known to Victorian and Edwardian diners-out – a further help towards making the word familiar.)

A fragrant wine, dry, semi-sweet and sweet, the dry rather firmer – more masculine, as it were – in flavour than some other dry *castelli* wines, such as those of the Colli Albani. A good bottle of Frascati has a delightfully clear, golden colour, so much so that one writer swears that a lover of Frascati should be able to recognise his wine without tasting it – just by looking. Higher in alcoholic strength than most *castelli* wines, and suitable, therefore, for ageing in bottle.

The *consorzio* for the protection of Frascati was set up in 1949: there is a neck-label for authentic wines, which must come from a district limited to Frascati, Grottaferrata, Monteporzio Catone (where Cato came from) and a small outlying part of the city of Rome itself. The sweet Frascati is usually known as Cannellino, and regarded as the finest of all *castelli* wines, much drunk by the glass in Roman wine shops, mid-morning or mid-afternoon. A very small amount of red Frascati is produced, and is of no consequence. Good years: 1948, 1949. Very good: 1945, 1950, 1952, 1953, 1954, 1956, 1960. Exceptional: 1946.

Grottaferrata. One of the Frascati wines, and usually sold under that name.

Grottaferrata, Malvasia di. It is a long time since I tasted this wine. Only one Italian book on the wines of Italy lists it, and that only because the name has been made copyright: I never come across it these days in any Roman or *castelli* restaurant – not even in Grottaferrata itself. But a very small amount of this delightfully delicate dry white wine *is*, I am assured, still made, from Malvasia grapes, around the small town, and is to be enjoyed by fortunate guests in private houses: it is made on too small a scale, and with too much care, to be a commercial proposition.

Marino. Along the northern shores of Lake Albano, on terraces facing south across the waters of the lake, a higher proportion of Malvasia grapes is grown than is usual in the area, and the local white wine, though dry (there is less sweet wine made here than in other parts of the Castelli) is rather fuller and more spicily fragrant. In the little town of Marino itself, the priest leads a procession of thanksgiving to church at vintage time, and the fountain in the middle of the town plays wine for the day instead of water. There are said to be a Marino Rosato and a sparkling Spumante di Marino, both dry and semi-sweet. The red Marino, produced only in very small quantities, is really a Cesanese (*q.v.*).

Montecompatri. From the lower, northern slopes of the Alban hills, along the road to Palestrina – one of the lighter and drier *castelli* wines. 11·5°.

Velletri. Very similar to Montecompatri (above) – if anything, even lighter, in alcohol (11°), flavour, scent and colour, so that it sometimes seems insipid: it would certainly seem so if tasted against a good Frascati. This is perhaps the only corner of the Castelli where the red wine (see under Cesanese) has greater character than the white. Good years: 1948, 1956, 1960. Very good: 1945, 1950, 1952, 1953, 1954, 1958. Exceptional: 1946.

Castelbracciano. Sweet, golden wine from the shores of Lake Bracciano, a favourite week-end picnicking place for Romans. It is said to be exported, though I have never come across any save on its native shores – not even in Rome.

Castel san Giorgio, Bianco and Rosso. See under Maccarese.

Castiglione in Teverina. One of the few examples in Italy of a delimited zone stretching from one region into another. Castiglione is in Lazio, but hard by Orvieto, which is in Umbria, and its white wines are entitled to the appellation Orvieto (*q.v.* under Umbria).

Castrense, Bianco and Rosso. The caves that give their name to the township of Grotte di Castro are just on the north-west of Lake Bolsena, diagonally across from Montefiascone, where Est! Est!! Est!!! comes from. Around Castro they grow both red and white wines, the white from Greco, Romanesco and Malvasia grapes, both dry and semi-sweet, sometimes *frizzante*, and the red, of which rather more is produced, from Sangiovese (about sixty per cent), Canaiolo and Aleatico. Both are very light (9°–11°), and the red is said to resemble one of the lighter Chiantis.

Cecubo. The name is that of a wine that Cicero drank and Horace sang; but, as Cùnsolo observes, the soil may be the same, but are the vines? This is a very pale-red, almost *rosé*, wine made from a variety of local grapes, with a very strong fragrance, dry but soft and fairly full. It comes from near the coast, on either side of, and behind, Gaeta. 13°–14°. A local sweet red wine, made from semi-dried grapes, is fancifully known as Sorriso d'Italia.

Cerveteri, Bianco, Rosso and Rosato. Modest local table wines, red, white and *rosé*, from the coast on either side of Civitavecchia. 11°–13°.

Cervicione. See under Nettuno Bianco.

Cesanese. This local grape gives its name to most of the red wines of the region, including those of the Castelli Romani. The typical Cesanese

wine, whether described as Cesanese, simply, or dei Castelli Romani; d'Affile; d'Olevano; del Piglio; or di S. Vito; is a very deep red in colour, with a pronounced bouquet. There is a dry and a sweet Cesanese, and both are often *frizzante*; that of Piglio tends to be fuller and stronger than the others (13°–14°, as against 11°–13°).

Colli Cimini. Modest red and white wines, typical of the region – Sangiovese, Montepulciano and Canaiolo grapes for the reds; Trebbiano, Malvasia and others for the whites, along with a local grape called Sylvoz: 10°–12° for the whites, 12°–14° for the reds. Both reds and whites may be either dry or semi-sweet. More distinguished among them are the Vignanello, both red and white, and Ronciglione, white only.

Colli Etruschi, or Etruria, Bianco and Rosso. Wines precisely similar to the reds and whites of Castrense (*q.v.*) from the same grapes, and with the same character, but from the country of the ancient Etruscans, around Vetralla and Viterbo.

Est! Est!! Est!!! The story is all too often told, yet this list of Italian wines would be incomplete were it not told here yet again. In 1110, Bishop Johann Fugger was on his way from Augsburg to Rome for the coronation of the Emperor Henry V. A devoted amateur of wine, the bishop sent his major-domo, Martin, a day's journey ahead, with orders to write in chalk, on the door of any inn where the wine was good, the word "Est!". History does not relate how many inns on the long journey to Rome were so marked – only that in Montefiascone, the small hilltop town looking out over Lake Bolsena, sixty miles or so north of Rome, the wine was so good that major-domo Martin, beside himself in his enthusiasm, wrote "Est! Est!! Est!!!" on the door of the inn.

The good bishop got no farther. His retinue went on to Rome, but he and Martin stayed in Montefiascone, tasting and tippling, until the bishop tasted and tippled himself into his tomb,* still to be seen in the church of S. Flaviano, with Martin's inscription (Defuk being the Italian form of di Fugger):

> Est. Est. Propter Nimium
> Est Hic Jo. Defuk Dominus
> Meus Mortuus Est

("On account of too much Est Est Est my master Johannes di Fugger died

* Perhaps the first to justify the old Italian saying, *"Bere come un Tedesco"* – to drink like a German: i.e. heavily.

here.") Not, however, before the bishop had devised in his will that the town of Montefiascone should be his heir, on condition that every year, on the anniversary of his death, a barrel of the local wine should be poured over his grave. The custom obtained until the cardinal Barberigo, bishop of Montefiascone, ruled that instead of being spilled and wasted, the wine should go to the local seminary for the benefit of the young priests – where, as far as I know, it is enjoyed to this day.

A modest English footnote to the familiar story is that only a few years ago the wife of the then British ambassador to Rome, at a tasting of fine Italian wines, marked a particularly fine Barolo on her list with the words, "Best! Best!! Best!!!"

What about the wine itself? It is a light white wine, which can be dry (10°–12°) or semi-sweet (9°–10°), and sometimes slightly *frizzante*, made of Trebbiano, Rossetta, and Malvasia Toscana grapes – a mixture more like that of the *castelli Romani* wines than the much nearer Orvieto, though Est! Est!! Est!!! is sold in the flattish Orvieto *fiasco*.

The dry version is, indeed, quite like one of the lighter *castelli* wines – more like a Colli Albani than a Frascati. It is much drunk with the eels from Lake Bolsena, over which the picturesque but rather self-conscious little town enjoys splendid views, and I have drunk it with great pleasure as an accompaniment to a herb-flavoured roast chicken at the modest Dante restaurant, where they have an excellent carafe Est! Est!! Est!!! The sweeter version is very light and fragrant, and goes pleasantly with fruit. Both dry and sweet versions have always been highly popular wines in Rome, and the dialect poet, Belli, who flourished in the time of Dickens, wrote of the local wines:

> È bono bianco, è bono rosso e nero;
> de Genzano, d'Orvieto e Vignanello;
> ma l'este-este è un paradiso vero!

The same little town gives its name to a good vin santo (*q.v.* under Trentino–Alto Adige).

Falernum or Falerno. Disputes with a better-known wine of Capua (see under Campania) the dignity of descent from Horace's Falernian: made from Falanghina grapes, a dry white wine with a bitter finish, from around the bay of Gaeta. 12°–13°.

Fiorano Bianco. A white wine made in small quantities from Malvasia di Candia grapes grown in vineyards about ten miles from Rome, along the old Appian Way. Veronelli speaks highly of its delicate flinty taste, and advises it as an accompaniment to oysters, but it is hard to come by. 12°.

Maccarese, Bianco, Rosso and Rosato. From the area of drained marshland just along the coast from the Roman playgrounds between Fregene and Lido di Roma – one flies over the vineyards as one comes into or takes off from the new Leonardo da Vinci airport at Fiumicino. The white wine is made from the usual Trebbiano and Malvasia grapes, grown along horizontal wires, and is dry and light (10·5°–12°). The red and *rosé* are from Cesanese and other grapes and are also dry, light table wines (11°–12·5°). A better and rather fuller and stronger variety of each colour is the Castel San Giorgio. There is also a sweet, dessert Moscato di Maccarese.

Malvasia di Grottaferrata. See under Grottaferrata.

Mentana. One of the Colli Teverini wines: see under Monterotondo.

Monte Giove. A rather better than average local dry red wine, made from Cesanese grapes, grown in vineyards between Terracina and Monte Circeo, west of Gaeta, facing south over the sea, and on the edge of the Circeo National Park. Usually drunk young, locally, but worth asking at local restaurants for any with a few years of bottle-age, when the wine acquires a pleasing softness of taste, and a slightly flowery scent, some say of violets. 12°–14°.

Monteluci Rosso. A dry red wine, made chiefly from Olivella grapes, near Pontecorvo, within sight of Cassino. It is usually made after the stalks have been removed, so that the wine is lighter in texture and colour than some of the more run-of-the-mill local wines. Very small production. 13°–14°.

Monterotondo, Mentana, Morlupo, Capena. Wines, red and white, from communes of these names in the Colli Teverini – the low hills on either side of the Tiber north of Rome. The usual grapes of the district – Trebbiano and Malvasia for the whites: Sangiovese and others for the reds. More whites than reds, more sweetish than not, and none particularly remarkable. 11°–13°.

Morlupo. See above.

Moscato di Maccarese, Moscato di Terracina, Moscato di Viterbo. Sweet, rich, golden dessert wines made from Moscato grapes in the same district as the Maccarese table wines (*q.v.*) (14°–15°); on the coast west of Gaeta, and much lighter (10°–12°); and on the shores of Lake Bolsena, respectively.

Nettuno Bianco. A dry white table wine made from the same grapes as the *castelli* wines, but around Anzio and Nettuno. 12°–13°. Some of the better quality is called Cervicione, becoming better known in recent years, and much appreciated in Rome.

Olivella. This is a grape grown in the Pontecorvo district, usually in the Tuscan fashion – trained up living trees that have been heavily pollarded. It makes a light red table wine, not much known outside the immediate district. 11·5°–13°.

Ottonese. Local dry white wine made only from Buonvino grapes, in the steep hills around Palestrina. Drunk young, and all consumed locally, but rather highly spoken of by those who know it. 11°–12°.

Palestrina Bianco. Another local wine, from the same district as the above, but made of the same grapes as the *castelli Romani* wines, and with more body and less grace than the Ottonese.

Romagnano or Romanesco. Dry white wine made from Trebbiano and Malvasia grapes near Anagni, north of Frosinone. Listed only by Veronelli, who recommends it as a wine to go with fish. 12°–12·5°.

Ronciglione. One of the white wines of the Colli Cimini (*q.v.*).

Sabina. This is the country, in the Tiber valley north of Rome, where the Sabine women came from; a certain amount of local white wine is grown there, to be found under the name of such villages as Cantalupo in Sabina, Fara in Sabina and Montopoli in Sabina, and listed only in Veronelli.

Sanmichele, Rosso and Bianco. An experimental viticultural station near Cassino produces limited quantities of red wines from the French Cabernet, Pinot and Syrah grapes (some from Syrah alone); and whites from the Sémillon. Very good wines indeed, and of great interest to the future of Italian wine-growing, but not often met with.

Setino. This is the name of a wine that Caesar Augustus used to drink, and there is said to be some grown near Sezze, from which it takes its name, near Latina. I have never met it.

Sorriso d'Italia. See under Cecubo.

Torre Ercolana. A rather full, dry red wine, grown in the hills north-west of Frosinone. 13°–13·5°.

Vignanello. Red and white wines of the Colli Cimini (*q.v.*).

Vin Santo di Montefiascone. Rich dessert wine from the same district as Est! Est!! Est!!! (*q.v.*).

Zagarolo, Bianco and Rosso. From the hills around Palestrina – the white, usually semi-sweet, from Bellone grapes (here called Uva Pane –

bread-grape) as well as the usual *castelli* grapes, and the red from Cesanese and Buonvino rosso. Both red and white 11°–12°. Not much is produced, and it is sold on the Rome market usually rather more cheaply than the *castelli* wines, though I suspect that much of it reaches the consumer by way of carafes in small Roman restaurants under the nobler name.

Chapter 13

CAMPANIA

❦

THIS is the region which is dominated by Naples, a mixture of luxurious holiday resorts – Capri and Ischia; Ravello, Amalfi and Positano – and the grinding poverty of the narrow streets off the Via Roma, on the bare slopes of the Apennines, and in the fertile but overcrowded plains of volcanic soil.

Wine was grown in these parts in Roman times and, indeed, probably earlier still, for this was part of Magna Graecia, as the temples at Paestum bear witness, built by the Sybarites, Greek colonists whose wealth and luxurious tastes have given a word to the English language that may reasonably be applied to many of those who come holiday-making here, if not to the locals. There are few wines in the region that it would be unreasonably sybaritic to indulge in: much of the wine of Campania goes north for blending, and what remains is proper enough for holiday hotels, seldom more distinguished.

The Wines of Campania

Acinato or Alcinato. A *vino cotto* made in the Avellino area by cooking a must made of poor-quality grapes in the oven, or over the fire, with more grape juice added. Quite nasty.

Aglianichello. Sweetish red wine, made from Aglianico and other grapes, chiefly near Pozzuoli, on the promontory jutting out towards the islands of Procida and Ischia. Pleasant enough in the little holiday-resort restaurants of the district. 12°.

Aglianico. A grape that is widely grown in Southern Italy, and that we shall meet again in the Basilicata: it seems to do particularly well in volcanic

126

soil. It makes a good, robust red table wine, not unlike the Barbera of Piedmont (*q.v.*), sometimes rather astringent when young, which suggests that it might become a quite good wine with bottle-age, which it rarely gets much of. In Campania, it is grown a great deal around Salerno and inland towards the north, taking in Avellino and Benevento. The name is said to be a corruption of the word *ellenico*, and to indicate that the vine is a descendant of those introduced by the Greeks. 12°–13°. Some is sold as Avellino, from its place of origin: it tends to be lighter than the others, whereas Taurasi, which comes from the hills north-east of Avellino, is bigger altogether, and more of it than others is chosen to age in bottle.

Alburno. See Calore degli Alburni.

Asprinio or Asprino. This wine, which sounds like something in a chemist's shop, is a sharp, *frizzante* white wine, made from the grape of the same name, drunk young and cold, especially in Naples in the summer. It is a mere 8°–10°, and all authorities agree on its diuretic qualities.

Avellino. One of the Aglianico wines (*q.v.*).

Barano. One of the lighter white wines of Ischia (*q.v.*).

Biancolella. One of the lighter white wines of Ischia (*q.v.*).

Boscoreale. See under the wines of Vesuvio.

Buonopane. One of the white wines of Ischia (*q.v.*).

Calitto. One of the wines of Ischia (*q.v.*).

Calore degli Alburni. Dry, full red wine made from Aglianico, Strepparossa and Sangiovese grapes in the hills behind Salerno, with rather more breeding than the common Aglianico, and a particularly pleasing nose. 14°. Also called Alburno and Gelbison.

Campi Flegrei, Bianco, Rosso and Rosato. The white is made from Falanghina Verace, Falanghina Falsa, Soricella (or Cavalla), Biancolella and Forastera grapes, and is light, dry and rather sharp. 10°–12°. The red and the *rosé* are made from Aglianico, Piede di Palumbo, Tintore and other grapes, are sometimes sweetish, and used for blending as well as for local consumption. 11°–13°. Sometimes known as Procida or Monte di Procida, which is the district it comes from.

Capri, Bianco, Rosso and Rosato. "As famous as the island," writes one enthusiastic Italian of the white Capri wine,* but there is more Capri wine on sale than could ever be grown on Capri: much comes from the nearby mainland, and from Ischia and Procida. (Wine made from the same

---

* Even the sober La Nuova Enologia describes it as, "one of the best wines in the world", which really is stretching it a bit. It is not bad.

grapes – Greco and Fiano – on the Sorrentine peninsula, which is geologically identical with Capri, and on the neighbouring islands, is entitled to the name by Italian wine law, and quite reasonably so.) There are small peculiarities about the vinification – the must ferments on a paste made of some, only, of the skins. It is pale and dry, with a sort of burned aftertaste, and a fresh bouquet. Good years: 1945, 1946, 1956, 1957, 1958. Very good: 1947, 1950, 1955. Exceptional: 1953, 1960. The red and *rosé* wines of Capri and the neighbouring islands and peninsula are not so highly thought of: they are made from Aglianico, Tintore (or Guarnaccia) and Olivella grapes, and make reasonably good table wines. 11°–14°.

Casamicciola. One of the white wines of Ischia (*q.v.*).

Castellabate, Rosso and Rosato. Blending wines, red and *rosé*, from around Salerno, also used locally as common table wines: Moio della Civitella is one of the better ones. There is also a rich, dessert Liquoroso di Castellabate.

Cilento Alto and Cilento Basso. Just such wines as those of Castellabate (see above). It is said that they are much exported to give bouquet to some of the commoner wines of France and, of all unlikely places, Brazil.

Colli del Sannio, Bianco, Rosso and Rosato. Local red, white and *rosé* wines from around Benevento, in the mountainous middle of the region: the whites from Coda di Volpe, Greco and Trebbiano Toscano grapes, the reds and *rosés* from Aglianico, Piedirosso and Montonico rosso. All 11°–13°, and all rather sharp. There are also San Giorgio red, white and *rosé* wines, from a mountain town north of Benevento, in the same district and made from the same grapes, that have a touch more character about them: they seem to have had more ageing in wood before bottling than the others, and then longer in bottle.

Colli Sorrentini. Much of the wine grown on the Sorrentine peninsula qualifies, as we have seen, as Capri wine. But there are some local wines here, of modest pretensions, made of other grapes, and sold either under this general name or as: Colli Stabbiesi, Gragnano, Lettere and Corbara. They include reds and dry whites, some of the red being semi-sweet. 11°–13°.

Conca. A purplish red wine, rather sharp in flavour, made from a wide mixture of grapes, including Sangiovese, grown near Caserta, and frequently met with in the restaurants, where it will do the enquiring visitor no harm: indeed, it goes well with the richer dishes. 13°.

Corbara. One of the wines of the Colli Sorrentini (*q.v.*).

Epomeo. One of the wines of Ischia (*q.v.*).

Falerno, Bianco and Rosso. From the coastal plain north of Naples, named after Falernum, the capital of the Volsci,* and claims descent from the Falernian of classical times. The white wine, made these days from Falanghina grapes, is dry but full in flavour, the must being fermented on some of the dried skins, as with the Capri wines. 12°–13°. There is rather more red Falerno than white, made largely from Aglianico grapes, and similar to the wines described under that name. 12°–13°. There is also a sweet red Falerno that I have not come across, and some of the Falerno wines are sold under the name of Mondragone.

Fiaiano. One of the white wines of Ischia (*q.v.*).

Fiano. A light, frequently *frizzante* white wine, made from the grape of the same name, near Avellino. 11°–12°. There is also a pleasing Fiano Spumante, and a sweeter, non-sparkling version, for dessert drinking. Production is said to be declining.

Fontana-Serrara. One of the *bianchi superiori* of Ischia (*q.v.*).

Forastera. One of the wines of Ischia (*q.v.*).

Foria di Salerno. See under Irno Rosso.

Forio d'Ischia. One of the white wines of Ischia (*q.v.*).

Furore (or Gran Furore) Divina Costiera. Three wines enjoy this resounding title – an amber-white, rather strong in flavour; a lighter white, more delicate and often *frizzante*; and a rich, flavoury red. They come from, and are largely consumed in, the Amalfi peninsula (made from the grapes that hang so prettily from the pergolas around Amalfi and Positano), and are pleasant enough table wines. 12°–13°.

Gelbison. Another name for Calore degli Alburni (*q.v.*).

Giovi Rosso. From the immediate surroundings of Salerno – one of the better red table wines of the district, made from a mixture of Sangiovese with the local Aglianico and other grapes. 11°–13°.

Gragnano. One of the wines of the Colli Sorrentini (*q.v.*) – better than average, so that many mediocre wines of the district sail under its flag.

Greco di Tufo. *Tufo* means volcanic rock, but is also the name of a village between Benevento and Avellino, in the middle of the hilly district from which these dry and semi-sweet white wines come. Made from a grape called Greco di Vesuvio – very strongly scented, often *frizzante*, with a strong under-taste. 12°–13°.

* Not that Falernum was near here, but much closer to Rome: there is a Falerno grown in Lazio (*q.v.*) – not so well-known, but with perhaps a better claim to the name.

Irno, Bianco and Rosso. Light wines from the valley of the Irno, which runs into the sea at Salerno, the white made from a variety of grapes including Sanginella, after which it is sometimes named (11°–13°); the red from the usual mixture of Aglianico, Sangiovese and others (11°–14°). Among the better Irno reds are Foria di Salerno and Monte Iulio (which is said to have been a favourite of King Bomba's).

Ischia: Bianco, Bianco Superiore and Rosso. As we have seen, wines made on Ischia from the same grapes as those of Capri are entitled to the appellation "Capri". But Ischia has wines of its own, too, made of different grapes – the whites from Biancolella and Fontana – and they seem to me to have more individuality than those of Capri, even if they are not quite so publicised. There is a very light and delicate white, only 8°–10°, with a very pretty scent, to be drunk young, usually sold simply as Ischia Bianco; the Bianco superiore has more Binacolella grape to it, a little Forastera, and less of the others, and has more body and flavour (11°–13°). The reds are not quite so distinctive, but are pleasant enough local wines, made chiefly from Guarnaccia and Piede di Palumbo grapes, and drunk young (11°–13·5°). Among the reds the Calitto and the Epomeo are perhaps a cut above the others, and there is a dry, rather harsh, Tintone, made from the grape of that name. Some of the whites are made of one type of grape only, and are sold as Biancolella or Forastera, as the case may be, and there are many other local names. Good year: 1958. Very good: 1955, 1956, 1960.

Lacco Ameno. One of the white wines of Ischia (see above).

Lacrima Christi. Like Liebfraumilch, this is a wine that owes its fame to its name – as memorable and as evocative, and a good deal easier for the Englishman to pronounce. Alas, there is no association as yet to protect the name Lacrima Christi, and it will be some time before the new Italian wine law – in the absence of any association's rules to base itself upon, as it can with Chianti, for instance, or Barolo – will be able to delimit its zone of origin, or the grapes it must be made from. And so a good deal of so-called Lacrima Christi is simply the cheaper white wine of Vesuvio (*q.v.*).

Meanwhile, it is a matter of seeking out a reliable shipper or restaurant, for there is good Lacrima Christi to be had – the true Lacrima Christi being a white wine made from Coda di Volpe, Greco di Torre and Biancolella grapes in the district to the seaward side of Vesuvius, and also some of the eastern slopes: dry, delicate, with a hint of sweetness, like a German wine, or a dry white Bordeaux, but with a flowery fragrance peculiar to itself, and hard to define – of elder flowers and broom, suggests Bruno Bruni. It is a good wine to drink in the excellent fish restaurants of Naples, but it is rather headier than it seems, certainly more so than many an apparently comparable Rhine or Moselle wine. 12°–13°.

The sweet Lacrima Christi Liquoroso is made of the same grapes semi-dried, and comes from a rather wider area: the red and the *rosé* Lacrima Christi are not really true Lacrima Christi at all, but simply local *vins ordinaires* exploiting a famous name. They are often quite sound table wines, made of Aglianico, Piede di Palumbo, Soricella, Palombina and other grapes, but not really any more distinguished, or worth more money, than other modest red and pink wines of the area. They should really be called Vesuvio Rosso (*q.v.*) or Vesuvio Rosato.

Lettere. One of the wines of the Colli Sorrentini (*q.v.*).

Liquoroso di Castellabate. See under Castellabate.

Moio della Civitella. See under Castellabate.

Mondragone. One of the Falerno wines (*q.v.*).

Monte di Procida. Another name for Campi Flegrei (*q.v.*).

Monte Iulio. One of the light red wines from the valley of the Irno (*q.v.*).

Moscato di Baselice. A dessert Muscat wine rather lighter than those of other areas, from near Benevento. There is also a less-important Moscato di Ravello.

Pannarano and Partenio. Stout red mixing wines, not unusually heavy in alcohol as such wines go (11°–13°) but very hard, and showing a great deal of tannin, made from a mixture of grapes in which Aglianico predominates. They come from the Avellino–Benevento area, where they are also served as cheap table wines.

Pellagrello, Bianco, Rosso and Rosato. Rather pleasing light local table wines from near Caserta, where the white-wine grape, Coda di Volpe Bianca, is known as Pellagrello Bianco, and where a black grape, called simply Pellagrello, seems to be peculiar to the district. All three wines are faintly sweetish – the *rosato* perhaps the freshest and pleasantest of the three. 11°–13°.

Piedimonte. One of the light white wines – alcoholically, quite the lightest (7°–8°) – of Ischia (*q.v.*).

Procida, Bianco and Rosso. Other names for the red and white wines of Campi Flegrei (*q.v.*).

Ravello, Bianco, Rosso and Rosato. From the Sorrentine peninsula, west of Salerno, and much the same as the wines described under Colli

Sorrentini: pleasant enough light wines (11°–13°), with the *rosé* as a rule rather sweeter than the others, though there is also a quite sweet white, *frizzante*, that makes an agreeable dessert wine, and also a local Moscato. These wines are also sometimes known as Vini di Salerno. Good years: 1952, 1953, 1955. Very good: 1945, 1956, 1960.

Sanginella. The name of the grape from which the white Irno wines (*q.v.*) are made, and by which they are sometimes known.

San Giorgio. A full-flavoured white wine, a deepish gold in colour, with rather an acid under-taste, rather like the Greco di Tufo from near by, but with an even more noticeable fullness of flavour, especially at the finish. Made from Coda di Volpe and Fiano grapes, as well as the Greco. 12°.

Sangiovese. A certain amount of rather strong (14°), full red wine is made from the noble grape of Chianti in the Avellino area, but it has nothing like the charm or character of the better Tuscan wines. It is produced only in small quantities, probably more or less experimentally, and is hardly worth the trouble it takes to find.

Sele. Sometimes referred to as Alto Sele and Basso Sele, though there seems to be no discernible difference – red wines made from Aglianico and other grapes in the valley of the Sele river around Eboli (the last town, and pretty depressing it is, before the really deep South begins: "Christ Stopped at Eboli"). Mostly used for mixing, and sometimes called, when drunk locally as a table wine, Vino di Valva. 12°–13°.

Solopaca, Bianco, Rosso and Rosato. Wines from around Benevento – the dry whites made from Trebbiano and Malvasia, as well as the local Greco, which gives them more charm and fragrance than the Greco alone would afford (12°); the reds and *rosés* from the usual mixture of Aglianico and others, sometimes a little sharp, and drunk locally young and cool (11°–13°).

Sorrento. The red, white and *rosé* wines of Sorrento are the same as those described under Capri and under Colli Sorrentini, but they sometimes put on airs and call themselves Sorriso di Sorrento, which does nobody any harm, and lends a typical Neapolitan touch to many a *diner à deux* under an arbour, with a fiddler playing *"Torna a Sorrento"* over the lady's veal cutlet.

Sorriso d'Ischia. There is also a sweet, rich dessert wine from Ischia, with a laugh on its label, and nothing very serious in the bottle.

Taurasi. One of the Aglianico wines (*q.v.*).

Terzigno. One of the wines of Vesuvio (*q.v.*).

Tintone. See under Ischia.

Torre Gaia, Bianco, Rosso and Rosato. Precisely similar to the wines of Solopaca (*q.v.*).

Tramonti. A sweetish, local red wine, rather big in flavour and bouquet, made in the hills north of Amalfi, from Tintore, Strepparossa and Coda di Volpe grapes (10°–12°).

Valva, Vini di. Another name for the wines of Sele (*q.v.*).

Vesuvio, Bianco and Rosso. Pretty commonplace wines, red and white, from the slopes of the volcano: if they have anything about them at all (and sometimes when they haven't) they call themselves Lacrima Christi. Under their own colours, the white should be very light, but with a rather burnt under-taste (9°–12°). There is very little of it, for reasons that are all too obvious. The red is dry and sometimes *frizzante* (10°–11°). Boscoreale and Terzigno are among the better reds.

Vitulano, Bianco and Rosso. Mixing-wines from the wild country around Benevento, but when the red gets a chance of ageing it shows a certain touch of quality, thanks probably to the Sangiovese and Barbera grapes that are mixed with the predominant Aglianico. If frothy when poured out, it is young. 11°–13°.

Chapter 14

THE ABRUZZI AND MOLISE

❧

T HIS is the mountainous middle of Italy, culminating in the Gran Sasso d'Italia, ten thousand feet or so above sea-level – a rugged region in which bears roam nowadays in the National Park and in which it was not unknown during the Second World War for Indians of the Eighth Army, on night patrol, to die of exposure. The mountains crowd close to the sea, leaving only a narrow coastal plain, where much of the viticulture is for table grapes, though some wines are made for export to the north for blending, or for making into some of the cheaper *spumanti*. A few better wines are produced, however, notably as a result of the importation of nobler grapes from Tuscany, at about the beginning of the century, in an attempt at improvement.

The Wines of the Abruzzi and Molise

Abruzzo Bianco or Trebbiano. The white wine of the province, from the grape that it is sometimes named after, often rather sharp, but with a pleasant nose, and quite a good companion to the fish dishes of the coastal towns, sometimes with a slight prickle, and with a clean, fresh finish. 11°–13°.

Abruzzo Rosso or Montepulciano. A light red, almost *rosé*, wine, made from the Montepulciano grape, sometimes mixed with Sangiovese, produced throughout the region. It said to resemble the reds of the *Castelli romani*, which will not commend it to everyone, and cannot really be regarded as anything more important than a local *vin ordinaire*, not to be taken too seriously. Sometimes *frizzante*. One of the better ones is Giulianova. 12°–14°.

Cerasuolo. Light red, or *rosé*, wine, very similar to the Abruzzo Rosso (above), from the middle of the region, near the bigger towns of Pescara, Chieti and L'Aquila, and not at the northern or southern extremities. Like the Abruzzo, it is made from the Montepulciano grape, sometimes mixed with Sangiovese, and is taken early off the skins. Sometimes slightly sweet (*amabile*), sometimes sharpish. Usually seems to be drunk cool, like the light red wines of the Italian lakes, or a French rosé. 11°–13°.

Giulianova Bianco. A light white wine, made from Trebbiano grapes – to all intents and purposes the same as the Abruzzo Bianco, but the name applied only to the wines of the coast north of Pescara.

Giulianova Rosso. See under Abruzzo Rosso – it is the same wine, but from the coast north of Pescara.

Marsicano, Rosso and Rosato. Red and pink wines made of Montepulciano, Sangiovese, Ciliegiolo and other grapes in the district of Aquila – lighter in colour and in alcohol than Montepulciano, and fresh to the taste when drunk young, as becomes them. 10°–12°.

Moscato del Pescarese. A sweet Moscato wine from near the coast, not so good as others.

Peligno Bianco. Perhaps the best, and best known, of the Abruzzo Bianco wines (*q.v.*). From Pratola Peligna, near Aquila.

Torre de' Passeri. A village in the district from which come both Cerasuolo and the Abruzzo Rosso or Montepulciano, which are therefore sometimes known as Rossi di Torre de' Passeri.

Chapter 15

APULIA, THE BASILICATA
AND CALABRIA

ORE wine is grown in Apulia than in any other region of Italy –
in an average year, as much as in Piedmont and Lombardy put
together, or as in Tuscany and the Veneto combined. It is the
great economic staple of the region. But there are no Apulian wines in the
same class as any of the fine wines of these four regions: the strong sunshine, in addition to, in some parts, the heavy soil, produces strong,
coarse wines, the reds used for blending and the whites as a base for vermouth. Sweet unfermented grape juice for soft drinks (and for export to
countries that make wine of sorts from it) is also produced. No great body
of tourists from abroad, or of holiday-makers from the northern cities,
reaches this region to demand good wine in the hotels and the restaurants,
and there is little in the way of a well-to-do local middle class, so that
there is little inducement to the grower to plant nobler vines or to produce
wines that will tie up capital while they age.

The same is true of the Basilicata, though production here is as low as
it is high in Apulia, for this is a bare, wild countryside of mountains and
high moorland, handsome but unprofitable (Potenza, the biggest town, the
size of Leamington Spa, is 2,500 feet up, surrounded by higher country
still, and bitterly cold in winter). Only here and there are vineyards to be
seen, the straggling vines supported on tripods of cane, from the feathery
clumps that grow alongside: most of such vineyards are around the foot
and on the lower slopes of the extinct volcano Vulture – yet another of the
Italian volcanoes, dead and alive, in the soil of which vines thrive.

Good wines could be produced in these three southernmost regions of
Italy – Calabria, the toe of the peninsula, is the third – if more money were
forthcoming to provide better care for the vines, modern machinery in the

wineries, and up-to-date methods of marketing. As it is, their wines are unknown in other parts of Italy, except as blending wines, let alone abroad, and they are not all that highly thought of on their home ground. This part of Italy is nearer to Africa than it is to Switzerland, and not only geographically: there is an African look about the towns, and about much of the countryside and many of the people. So, too, the wines, which are not unlike those of Algeria and of the vineyards in Libya which were, in fact, planted and cared for by people who came from these very regions in Mussolini's time. In Calabria, particularly, the wines are all the coarser for the vines being trained close to the ground, absorbing additional heat from the soil.

The wines are listed here separately, in their respective regions.

The Wines of Apulia

Aleatico. The rich, dark-red, sweet dessert wine, found in many parts of Italy, and made from the grape of the same name, is probably more frequent in Apulia than elsewhere, and is made here by taking the must off the skins of semi-dried grapes rather quickly (the colour is fairly fully taken up, but this may explain why the Apulian Aleatico has pale orange tints to it that seem to be lacking in others), and then arresting fermentation by the addition of spirits, which is not done in every part of Italy, and is probably the reason for its being stronger than most (14°–17°). As it is grown so widely throughout the region, it has many local names – that of Brindisi is said to be the finest.

Asprinio. See under Capo di Leuca.

Avertrana. A variety of Manduria (*q.v.*).

Barbera Leccese. The Barbera grape of the north is grown in limited quantities around the little baroque city of Lecce, where it makes a much bigger, stronger red wine (15°–16°) than it does in Piedmont, and with nothing like the distinction, but interesting to meet, down here in the heel of Italy, where they drink it young and – rather surprisingly – cooled.

Barletta. A coarse, red, mixing wine from the east coast, made chiefly from Troia grapes.

Borraccio. See under Capo di Leuca.

Brindisino or Brindisi. One of the wines of Salento (*q.v.*).

Capo di Leuca. Wines are grown widely in the very bottom of the heel of Italy, from a wide mixture of local grapes. The Parasini is a pale red, dry and *frizzante*, and is said to have a tarry taste; the Borraccio is paler still, and more delicate; the Asprinio is white, semi-sweet, *frizzante*, and rather like a Moscato to the nose. (All about 14°–16°.)

Carasino. See under Tarantino.

Casarino. One of the wines of Salento (*q.v.*).

Castel Acquaro. One of the wines of Salento (*q.v.*).

Castel del Monte, Bianco, Rosso and Rosato. From between Barletta and Bari, but inland, where the Bombino Bianco grape produces a fresh white wine with, usually, a pronounced prickle, and rather light (11°–12°) for the region, and where red and *rosé* wines of only moderate interest are made from local varieties of grape. Rather better wines, more carefully made, come from the local co-operative, and are marketed under the name Rivera. Good years (for the Rivera wines): 1946, 1948, 1956, 1957, 1960. Very good: 1953, 1958. Exceptional: 1951.

Castellana and Conversano. Two townships in the hills above Monopoli, which is on the east coast, south of Bari, where some white, red and *rosé* wines are grown. One Italian writer, having described them as being of "distinct quality", winds up by saying that the red and the pink, "can aspire to the honour of being bottled" – which indicates what they are: very modest local wines indeed, usually drunk young, *nell'annata* and from the cask, and also used for mixing with their betters. The red is probably the best of the three.

Cerasuolo delle Murge. A cherry-red wine from near Bari, the best quality coming from around the small town of Bitonto, made from a black grape called Primativo (*q.v.*) and a variety of white grapes, drunk young and all consumed locally. 12°–14°.

Cinque Rose. See under Salento.

Colatamburo. A dry white wine from near Bari, pale with a marked bouquet and rather strong. 14°.

Conversano. See under Catellana, above.

Copertina. One of the wines of Salento (*q.v.*).

Galatina. One of the wines of Salento (*q.v.*).

Gallipoli. One of the wines of Salento (*q.v.*).

Grottaglie. One of the Tarantino wines (*q.v.*).

Lacrima di Gallipoli. A dry *rosé* wine from the Gallipoli peninsula – inside the heel, so to speak, of Italy – and also to be found around Lecce.

It has a fine nose, and I seem to see in it the nearest Apulian approach to what one describes as "elegance" in French wines. Sometimes known as Lacrima del Salento. 14°.

Lacrima di Corato. Similar to the above, but from near Bari.

Lecce, Rosato di. See under Salento.

Locorotondo, Bianco di. An almost colourless white wine, made in enormous quantities around Bari, from Verdea, Alessano and Buonvino grapes, in varying proportions, with the skins and pips removed, to produce a neutral base for vermouth, for which it is largely used. Veronelli says that it deserves a better fate, as he has drunk a good bottle of it with the local fish – being luckier than me. It is true, though, that rather better qualities than the wine exported to the Turin vermouth factories are to be met with locally under various names, such as those of the grapes (Verdea di Albarello), or of local communes (Martina Franca, and San Carlo).

Malvasia di Brindisi, or di Puglia. Dry (or semi-sweet) and sweet wines made from Malvasia grapes, the dry and semi-sweet being pleasant table wines, though not so fine as the Malvasias of Friuli and elsewhere; the sweet made from semi-dried grapes, and a very ordinary dessert wine. 12°–14°.

Manduria. This – if the Italian wine-writers are to be believed – is one of the most curious wines of Italy, perhaps of the whole wine-growing world. It is made of the Primitivo grape, in the flat country east of Taranto, and when young – as usually consumed – it is a frothy, naturally semi-sparkling red wine (18°) with a heavy bouquet, very rich in flavour, and much used for mixing. This is the only form in which I have come across it, but many authorities maintain that in two years it becomes like Aleatico, in four like Barolo, and in seven like Marsala. But very little is produced; I have never seen it outside its own immediate district; and opportunity for research into this phenomenon is limited. Meanwhile, I suspend my disbelief.

Martina Franca. See under Locorotondo.

Massafra. One of the Tarantino wines (*q.v.*).

Melisano. One of the wines of Salento (*q.v.*).

Mesagne. One of the wines of Salento (*q.v.*).

Moscato di Puglia. One of the strongest (15°–17°) of the rich, sweet dessert wines found pretty well all over Italy, though not so fine as some – certainly not in the same class as that of Siracusa, which has both more depth and greater subtlety of flavour. But a good, smooth after-dinner wine – among the better examples being the Moscato del Salento and the Moscato di Trani. The latter is produced in very small quantities, and is probably the better, especially the particular Moscato di Trani produced at the experimental station at Barletta. There is also a Moscato d'Amburgo, which I do not know.

Nero del Brindisino. See under Salento.

Ostuni Bianco. A very uninteresting dry white wine from where the hills begin, north of Brindisi, made of Impigno, Francavidda, Verdea, Fiano and other grapes. 11·5°–13°.

Ottavianella. The name of a grape from which a pink wine is made in the same district as the Ostuni Bianco, 12°–13°.

Parasani. A red wine of Capo di Leuca (*q.v.*).

Passito di Novoli. A very strong, amber-coloured *passito* dessert wine, from Novoli, near Lecce.

Primativo or Primitivo. The latter is the proper Italian form; Primativo is the way that the Pugliesi spell and pronounce the word, which in these parts means not "primitive", but *primaticcio* – early. For here is another of the wine curiosities of the region: the grapes and bunches of grapes that receive the most sun ripen and are gathered in August – the earliest vintage in Europe, and in good time for the young wine to be sent to fortify the weaker wines of the north, of the same vintage. Then comes the second vintage – of the grapes that had been shaded by foliage, and these give a fine red wine that ages as well as a good Tuscan or Piedmontese wine: I have heard tell of fifty-five-year-old bottles of Primativo. So this second wine is of some importance, big and full-flavoured, and well worth looking out for in the Taranto area: Primativo di Manduria, Primativo del Tarantino and Primativo di Gioia del Colle are names it goes under.

Primofiore. One of the wines of the Salento (*q.v.*).

Rivera. See under Castel del Monte.

Salento or Salentino, Rosso and Rosato. An enormous range of red and *rosé* wines are grown all over the flattish country of the heel of Italy, in the triangle formed by Taranto, Brindisi and the southernmost cape, Capo S. Maria di Leuca. Among the grapes are Negro Amaro, Malvasia Nera, Malvasia Bianca and others, including the Primativo mentioned above. They are mostly wines for export to the north or abroad as mixers and strengtheners, and have no especial character or distinction – not even much consistency, with strengths ranging from 12° to 15°, colours from the palest pink to the deepest red, tastes from dry to semi-sweet, and quality from fairly good to downright nasty. Such examples as are offered locally as table wines do tend to be better than those shipped elsewhere as fortifiers: they include some dozen that are included in this list, all with references to this entry: the best is possibly the red Castel Acquaro, from Mesagne, near Brindisi, a single-establishment wine that is produced in small quantities and given a chance to age in bottle, which I have found rather more refined than one may normally hope for in these parts.

The pink wine is sometimes known as Rosato di Lecce, and there is a *consorzio* to protect the Rosato del Salento. There are also a Vecchio Bianco and a Vecchio Rosso di Salento, both strong, sweet dessert wines (16°–18°), not to be compared with such other dessert wines of the region as the Aleatico and the Moscato.

San Carlo. See under Locorotondo.

San Pietro Vernotico. One of the wines of Salento (*q.v.*).

San Severo. A rather coarse white wine produced in considerable quantities in the Foggia plain. It is said once to have been an Austrian favourite, but it has dwindled now into being exported chiefly as a base for vermouth. It is made from Bombino Bianco and other grapes, and some of the better qualities are kept as table wines, among which I have heard the white Torre Giulia and the white Torre Quarto well-spoken of. 11·5°–13°.

Santo Stefano. A very much smaller quantity of sharpish, dry red wine (12°–13°) comes from the same region as the white San Severo, made from Montepulciano, Lagrima, Alicante, Uva di Troia and other grapes, and not exported, but consumed locally. As with the whites, the Torre Giulia and Torre Quarto labels indicate a touch of quality, but I cannot recommend the dessert Torre Quarto, fortified, and the fermentation arrested, by the addition of neutral spirits, and very strong.

Sava. A variety of Manduria (*q.v.*).

Squinzano. One of the wines of Salento (*q.v.*).

Tarantino. Strong, coarse, red wines for blending and for even less dignified industrial purposes are made from Primativo grapes around Taranto. Those retained for local consumption may be drunk with mild enjoyment by hardened travellers.

Torre Giulia and Torre Quarto, Bianchi and Rossi. For the reds see under Santo Stefano, and for the whites under San Severo.

Trani. This is the name by which the Milanesi – the length of Italy away – describe the Apulian wines, such as the rough open wines they drink in their wine-bars: hence the Milanese slang word *"tranatt"* for a hardened drinker.

Troia. The name of a common grape, so called after the village of Troia, near Foggia, and from which a strong mixing wine is made.

Verdea or Verdeca. See under Locorotondo: sometimes *frizzante*.

Vecchio Salento, Bianco and Rosso. See under Salento.

Zagarese. A strong, sweet Malaga-like, or Marsala-like, dessert wine (15°–18°) made from the grape of the same name in the Bari–Brindisi–Lecce area. Very plentiful before the phylloxera, but since then a lot of the vineyards that once produced it have gone over to strong blending wines for export, and Zagarese is now hard to find outside the little farms that grow it for their own table: an old bottle is worth tasting.

The Wines of the Basilicata

Aglianico del Vulture. Around, and on the lower slopes of the extinct volcano, Vulture, there grows the Aglianico grape, recording in its very name – a form of *ellenico* – that this was once part of Magna Graecia. The dry Aglianico del Vulture, with a few years of bottle-age, is one of the best red wines of Southern Italy – so much less well off than the North for good table wines. My impression is that it is capable of considerable improvement in bottle over many years, like such wines of the North as Barolo and Brunello, but I have been unable to find any Aglianico old enough to prove my theory. At its best, it is full, rounded, and well balanced, and goes well with the richer meat dishes of the region. 12°–14°. There is also a sparkling Aglianico Mussante.

Aglianico di Matera. A very similar wine to the above, made from the same grape, grown in the vicinity of Matera, much nearer the coast, and sometimes called Val Bradano Rosso, from the valley of the river near which Matera stands. 12°–14°.

Asprinio or Asprino. This medicinal-sounding wine is so called not because of any analgesic qualities (though it is said to be diuretic), but after the grape of the same name, which makes a dry but *frizzante* white wine, grown in the Potenza area, and said to be good with oysters. Light in alcohol, but stout enough to travel, for a lot is sold to Naples, where the locals drink it between meals as an aperitif, or café drink.

Malvasia, Malvasia di Vulture. Naturally sparkling, sweet golden wine from the Malvasia grape, which is grown widely throughout the region: the best is said to be that of Rapolla, near Melfi. Enthusiasts claim to detect in it the scent of almond blossom. 10°–12°.

Moscato. Another sweet sparkling wine, deservedly less well-known than those of the North, but pleasant enough, drunk cool, here in the sun-baked deep south of Italy, especially as it is fairly light in alcohol. 10°–12°.

The Wines of Calabria

Arghilla Rosato. A strong, rich and rough *rosé* wine made from Malvasia and Alicante grapes in a district of the name at the very edge of the town of Reggio di Calabria. It is listed in none of the reference books, but I have found it much in evidence in the local wine bars and restaurants. 14°–17°.

Attafi Greco, Attafi Rosso and Attafi Mantonaco. The name of Attafi is mysterious to me, as it seems to be the name neither of a place nor of a grape. These wines come from near Reggio di Calabria: the red is a strong (14°) table wine made from Alicante and other grapes, coarse and heavy. The other two are rich, sweet dessert wines, made from the Greco and Mantonaco grapes respectively. 18°.

Balbino. A strong white wine, in both dry and sweet versions, though the sweet is much more frequent and better known, made from a grape of the same name in the mountainous Altomonte district, near Cosenza. It is sometimes known as Balbino d'Altomonte. 15°–16°.

Cafaro. A red wine, fairly light for this part of Italy (12°–15°), made from Magliocco, Greco Rosso, Greco Bianco, Montonico and other grapes in the district of Cafari, which is part of the small town of Nicotera on the Gulf of Gioia. Dry or semi-sweet, some is kept by local families to acquire age in bottle, but a good deal finds its way north to cut and stretch lighter wines. The same wine grown in the next commune takes that commune's name, Limbadi.

Cerasolo (or Cerasuolo) di Scilla, di Palmi. As the name denotes, a cherry-red wine, from Scilla, on the Straits of Messina (the Scylla of Scylla and Charybdis), and also from a little farther north, near Palmi. Other well-known names are Favagreca, Ieracare and Paci. Made from a wide mixture of grape varieties, rather sweet and fairly light. 12°–14°.

Cirò. North of Crotone, on the ball, so to speak, of the Italian foot are Ciro and Melissa, around which grapes have been grown, and wine made, since the time of the ancient Greeks. (The *cremissa* given to athletes returning victorious from the Olympic Games is said to have come from here.) Now the district produces a big, robust red wine, from Gaglioppo and Piedilungo grapes, drunk locally as a table wine, and also sold to the North. A local variety is known as Collina di Crotone. There is a *rosé* (Cirò Rosa) and a sweet red wine (13°–15°). The white Cirò is made from the Greco Bianco grape, grown *ad alberello* – as "a little tree", close to the ground, that is – and is one of the best table wines of the region, with a marked bouquet and a full, flowery, but dry taste (12°–13·5°). Good years: 1945, 1947, 1949, 1950, 1951, 1954, 1956, 1957. Very good: 1960.

Collina di Crotone. See under Cirò, above.

Coticchietto. See under Greco Rosso.

Donna Camilla. A dry, rather sharp, fragrant red wine (there is also a *rosé*), from near Gioia, on the west coast. 12°–13°.

Donnici. A dry, red table wine, made from Montonico grapes, in the hilly country around Costenza. Deep red in colour, with orange tints, and rather full in flavour. 12°–14°.

Favagreca. One of the Vini di Scilla: see under Cerasolo.

Frascineto. Precisely similar to, and from the same grape and district as, Lacrima di Castrovillari (*q.v.*).

Gioia, Bianco, Rosso and Rosato. The district wines from the shores of the Gulf of Gioia, north of Reggio, where they are the commonest table wines. The white is made from Malvasia grapes only, and is dry, almost bitter. 13°. The red is very coarse and common, from a mixture of local grapes, and the *rosato* very pale indeed, almost amber in colour, and alcoholically the strongest. Better varieties have a neck-label awarded by a consortium set up by the provincial government, but even these are not remarkable.

Greco di Gerace. A really distinguished dessert wine, made in the hills around Gerace, just inland from Locri, on the east coast of the toe of Italy. The grape, Greco di Gerace, is not to be confused with the white and red Greco grapes (see below). Little of the real stuff – a deep amber in colour, rich in flavour, and smelling deliciously of orange blossom, 16°–17° – reaches the market,* though it is much in demand: the local small farmers grow a few modest rows of the Greco di Gerace between those of the

* Though there is a commercial brand of some repute: Greco Rizziconi.

Plate XIII Vineyards near As
Campania

more common grapes used for table wines, and keep the wine they make from it to celebrate births, baptisms, weddings and, no doubt, funerals.

Greco Rosso, Greco Rosso di Pontegrande, or Coticchietto. A cherry-red wine, from the mountainous district near Catanzaro, made from Greco Nero, Greco Bianco, Nerellone and Nerello grapes. Harsh when young, but seldom found with any bottle-age. Sometimes called Coticchietto, after a small commune in the district that has the reputation of producing better wine than its neighbours – enquiring outsiders find it hard to discern the distinction. 13°.

Ieracare. One of the Vini di Scilla: see under Cerasolo.

Lacrima di Castrovillari. Dry red wine from the Lagrima grape, grown in the Cosenza district, said to be worth keeping in bottle for a year or so. 14°.

Lametino. A dry white wine with a full, rather madeira-ish taste.

Limbadi Rosso. A precisely similar wine to Cafaro (*q.v.*).

Magliocco or Magliocco di Calabria. A big red wine, from the Magliocco, Marsigliana and other grapes, grown widely around the region, and especially near Nicastro (after which it is sometimes called Nicastro Rosso. It is also known as Sambiase, and there are local varieties known as San Sidero and Rossano). Extremely deep in colour and high in alcoholic strength (14°); a great deal is sent north for blending.

Malvasia di Catanzaro. A strong, sweet wine made from the white Malvasia grape, grown in rows between those of commoner vines, in the plains of Cirò and Sambiase and on the hills around Catanzaro. 16°.

Mirto. A strong (16°–17°) red wine with amber tints, aged locally in bottle for as much as fifteen years – when it is still coarse.

Montonico. Another strong, sweet dessert wine, from the grape of the same name, grown in much the same areas as the Greco di Gerace, which it closely resembles, and under which name I suspect it is sometimes sold. 16°.

Moscato. As elsewhere, a good deal of sweet dessert wine is made in Calabria from the Moscato grape: according to locality, it is known here as Moscato di Cosenza, di Frascineto, di Reggio Calabria and di Saracena – this last variety being said to differ slightly from the others, as being made from a slightly different *cèpage* which gives a little less sweetness and more character. 15°–16°.

Nicastro Bianco. Semi-sweet and fragrant white wine, made from Malvasia, Greco Bianco and other grapes around Nicastro (better known for its red Magliocco) on the hills facing the Gulf of St Eufemia, or Nicastro. Probably the lightest table wine of the region. 11°.

Paci. One of the Vini di Scilla: see under Cerasolo.

Palizzi and Pellaro. Full red wines, made from Nerello grapes in the very tip of the toe of Italy, and largely sent north for blending. 13°–16°. Drinking it locally, I have found the Pellaro very sharp and bitter under a superficial sweetness.

Pollino. More general name for the robust red wines of which Lacrima di Castrovillari (*q.v.*) is an example.

Provilaro. A dry white wine, of some delicacy as Calabrian white wines go, from south of Cosenza. 13°.

Rogliano Rosso. Another name for Savuto (*q.v.*).

Rossano. See under Magliocco.

Rubino. A common red wine of Reggio di Calabria, very strong and very deep in colour. 14°–15°.

Sambiase. See under Magliocco.

San Sidero. See under Magliocco.

Savuto. From the same area as Provilaro, but red, made from Magliocco (known here as Arvino), Greco Nero and Greco Bianco grapes. A full-bodied, hearty wine, sometimes rather frothy when poured, but not as a rule *frizzante*. 13°. Was well-known enough before the phylloxera, which struck here in 1870, to have been exported to the United States (no doubt because of the number of immigrants there from this poverty-stricken part of Italy), but now little known outside its own area.

Scilla, Vini di. See under Cerasolo.

Sila, Rosso della. Red table wine from the district of the same name, near Cosenza.

Trasfigurato di Seminara. Veronelli records a curious wine from Seminara, near Reggio, which is smoked in jars. I have never come across it, and cannot imagine what it must taste like.

Verbicaro, Rosso di. A dry, big red wine from near Cosenza. 14°.

Chapter 16

SICILY

❧

As poor as the southern region of the mainland, and even more over-populated, Sicily presents a more luxurious face to the visitor than does Calabria, with its forbidding mountains and thick forests, the Basilicata with its bleak moorlands, or Apulia's drab villages, in the mountains or by the shore. What is not mountain in Sicily is taken up by vineyards and orchards and olive groves, dates and figs and pomegranates, especially in the country around Marsala, at the flat western end of the island, and in the Conca d'Oro or "golden shell" of rich countryside around Palermo.

The Greeks were in Sicily nearly three thousand years ago – in the eighth century B.C. – and it is certain that wine was being grown there at that time. According to Critias, the Athenian tyrant who was writing some four centuries later, Sicily was already then legendary as birthplace of the art of good living, and the Sicilian Greeks as the inventors of kottabos, the game of tossing the last drops of wine in a glass with a flick of the wrist into a vase across the room. Archestratus, a Sicilian Greek, who wrote a book on gastronomy in epic hexameters was, according to Mr Warner Allen, the Brillat-Savarin of Aristotle's time.

Nowadays, Sicily is neither so distinguished as to set the style in eating and drinking, nor so carefree as to play games with heeltaps. The vivid chapter on "The Vine Harvest" in Mr Gavin Maxwell's *The Ten Pains of Death* reflects something of the bitterness of the Sicilian peasant who sees the shops selling wine at ten times the price he was paid for it by the big wholesale dealers who, with the large-scale cultivators, now have a grip on the Sicilian wine trade. Most of the wines of Sicily are made in big commercial wineries, and those peasants who have any land at all, or the use of any (all too many are both landless and jobless, hiring themselves out to the big growers at vintage time), move their modest vineyards every twenty years or so, and sell either the grapes or the wine they have made from them to the big firms.

Eventually, no doubt, the spread of co-operatives will do something to provide a better life for the peasant grower, as well as raise the standards of quality of Sicilian wines, most of which, at present, are coarse and heavy, used largely for blending, although the dessert wines of the island, of course, have a special place among the wines of Italy; there are, in fact, some few pleasant enough table wines to be found in the island, but they do not get exported even to the mainland, let alone abroad.

The Wines of Sicily

Adrano. A red wine from the foot of Etna, very similar to Biancavilla (*q.v.*).

Akracas Bianco. The un-Italian name derives from the old Greek name for Agrigento, on the south coast, around which they grow Catarratto Lucido, Insolia and other grapes, which make a dry white wine, much used on the mainland for blending, but here as a table wine, which takes on something of a Marsala flavour when it has any bottle-age – or so the locals say, though to many palates it will seem simply to have become maderised. 12°–15°.

A.L.A. The initials stand for Antico Liquor Vino Amarascato, a curiosity of the island, which one could be inclined to omit from a book about wines, as being a liqueur, save that all the reference books include it, where they exclude such other after-dinner digestives as Strega, Sambuco and the like. This oddity is said – like so much else Sicilian – to date from Graeco-Roman times, and is made by allowing sweet, semi-dried black grapes to ferment in casks made of cherry-wood, the scent and flavour of which are imparted to the resultant heavy sweet wine, which is drunk in these parts both as an aperitif and as a liqueur. 19°.

Albanello di Siracusa. From the grape and the district of the same names. There is a dry and a sweet Albanello: the dry I have found to be full and flavoury – more suitable as an aperitif than as a table wine; it has a bitter and appetising finish. Some experts detect a flavour as of Marsala about it, especially as it is aged in wood for eight or ten years, and reaches a strength of 17°–18°. Veronelli does not recommend the sweet Albanello, made of semi-dried grapes, though other Italian experts regard it as the more important of the two.

Alcamo. A dry white wine from Alcamo and the district around the Gulf of Castellamare, made from Catarratto Lucido, Grecanico, Damaschino and other local grapes. Soft and lacking in acidity; a great deal of it is used as a basis for vermouth, both locally and on the mainland. 12°–15°. A local variety is sometimes known as Segesta Bianco, from the Roman city near by, and there is a new *consorzio* of growers who aim to improve quality and award labels.

Ambrato di Comiso. Heavy, dry white wine, reaching as much as 18°, deep amber in colour, made from Catarratto, Calabrese, Damaschino and other grapes in the south-east of the island, near Ragusa. In deference to changing tastes, the growers are now trying to produce a wine lighter both in taste and alcoholic strength, though soil and sun are against them.

Aragona-Canicatti. A dry, full, fairly strong, cherry-red wine, with pretty tawny lights in it, made around Agrigento, by taking the must off the skins fairly early, as for a *rosé*; but then adding a concentration of sweet must to give more body and alcoholic strength. Drunk as an aperitif, it is said to resemble Marsala – but so is every strong aperitif wine in Sicily. 13°.

Barcellona. See under Capo Rosso.

Bazia. A red wine from the north-east of the island: see under Capo.

Belice Bianco. A dry, heavy wine, made from Catarratto Comune, Catarratto Lucido and other grapes in the south of the island, some used as a basis for Marsala, some sold as table wines. A new growers' association is beginning to watch quality. 11°–15°.

Biancavilla. A full, deep-red wine, with a powerful bouquet and a bitter after-taste, deriving a great deal of its character from the volcanic soil at the foot of Etna, where it comes from. Adrano and Ragalna are similar wines, though not quite so well known. (Adrano and Biancavilla are twin townships, south-west of Etna, and Ragalna is a smaller village near by.) Made from Nerello, Montellato, Spagnolo and Vernaccia Rossa grapes (12°–14°). A good, sound table wine that is said to acquire greater distinction with bottle-age.

Bianchi Carta. Strong, dry white wines (17°–18°) grown from a wide variety of common local grapes around Castellamare del Golfo, west of Palermo, in the north-west corner of the island, and exported for blending, though a lighter local wine of much the same breed, and no particular merit, is drunk as a table wine and known as Bianco di Castellamare.

Bosco dell'Etna. A red wine from those slopes of Etna that descend towards Catania; see under Etna.

Capo Bianco, Capo Rosso. Wines from the north-east corner of Sicily, opposite the Lipari Islands. The white is made from Catarratto Bianco, Chasselas Doré and Panse Precoce grapes, light, dry and fairly delicate as Sicilian wines go (12°–12·5°) and to be drunk young and very cool, when it goes well with the local shellfish. The red is lightish in shade, often between a red and a *rosé*, made from Nerello Cappuccio, Mascalese, Nero d'Avola, Nocera and, in some cases, some Sangiovese and Barbera grapes, but stronger and fuller than its colour would suggest. One of the better local red wines of the island, but rather astringent when very young, as it is too often served. 13°–15°. Very similar wines from the same district are Milazzo, both white and red (the red sometimes known as Barcellona) – the red tends to be stronger and coarser (13°–17°) than the Capo Rosso – and Furnari and Bazia, which are not quite so rough, and sometimes fuller in colour.

Cerasuolo. Wines with this name – which means cherry-red – come from Vittoria, Isola and Floridia, in the south-east corner of the island. They get their colour from a mixture of black and white grapes, chiefly Frappato (hence the alternative name of Frappato di Vittoria), Calabrese, Grosso-nero, and Albanello, fermented very quickly. These are generous, full-bodied wines that mature quickly, with a herby, fruity scent, and go well with rich dishes. The Vittoria is probably the finest of the group (13°–14°); the Floridia the heaviest and headiest (15°–17°) and better used for blending.

Ciclopi, Bianco, Rosso and Rosato. See under Etna.

Corvo di Casteldaccia, Bianco and Rosso. From near Palermo, the white made from Catarratto and Insolia grapes, dry, rather pale, and with not a great deal of character, but the red, to my mind, one of the best in the island (not so like a claret as the locals would wish to think, and often say, but more like one of the red wines of the Loire), made from Perricone and Catanese grapes, clear, light and dry, and credited by some writers with all sorts of medicinal qualities. It needs a couple of years in bottle. White: 12°–14°. Red: 13°–14·5°. One of the whites is also called Corvo Colomba Platino, which means platinum-blonde dove-raven, a phrase much harder to swallow than the wine. (The name Corvo comes from a complicated local legend involving a hermit; a noisy raven; the big stick the locals gave the hermit to beat the bird away with; and the vine that sprang from the stick.)

Eloro, Bianco, Rosso and Rosato. Eloro was the old name for the river Tellaro, which flows through the plain of Noto to the sea at the south-east corner of Sicily: hence the name of these rather coarse red, white and *rosé* wines – the whites made from Grillo, Catarratto and Albanello grapes (13°–14·5°), the reds and the *rosés* from Calabrese, Nerello d'Avola and Nerello Mascalese (13°–15°).

Etna, Bianco and Rosso. The lower and some of the middle slopes of Etna are covered with vineyards, producing red and white wines of moderate quality and with various names. Generally speaking, the whites are made from Carricante, Catarratto Comune, Catarratto Lucido, Minnella and Insolia grapes, and are dry and a little *frizzante*. They are much more plentiful than the reds. 12°–13·5°. The reds are made from Nerello Mascalese and Nocera grapes, and are rather astringent and light-bodied. 12°–14°. The wines from the middle slopes (Etnei di Mezza Montagna) grown at a height of about two thousand feet, tend to be finer than the others – such district names as Linguaglossa and Sant'Alfio are worth looking for – but in general the reds are for export as mixing wines, or even as "industrial wines", in which latter case they go abroad (notably to Germany) to be made into brandies and vermouths, and it is permitted, as they will not bear Italian names of origin, to add neutral alcohol to them. (Indeed, the Germans require so high a strength as to make this necessary.) Among the individual Etna wines are Ciclopi, Ragabo, Biancavilla, Ragalna (these four being among the better reds), Sparviero, Trecastagni, Villagrande, Mascali, Randazzo and Solichiata. Good years: 1953, 1958, 1961.

Etna Madera. A sort of poor man's Marsala, from the coast east of Etna, fortified with alcohol. 16°–17°.

Faro. One of Sicily's better red wines, made from Nerello Cappuccio, Nerello Mascalese, Nocera and other grapes, near Messina: said to have been imported a great deal by the French at the height of the phylloxera crisis and still exported to the United States and elsewhere. Matured two years in cask before bottling, it is dry and rather pale in colour: I have always found it flat and disappointing at the finish, but quite an acceptable table wine. 13°–14°. Good years: 1945, 1948, 1949, 1950, 1953, 1954, 1956, 1959, 1960. Very good: 1946, 1952.

Fontana Murata, Bianco, Rosso and Cerasuolo. See under Valledolmo.

Francofonte. A heavy red mixing wine, the only claim to distinction of which is that it is quaffed by Turiddu in *Cavalleria Rusticana*.

Frappato di Vittoria. One of the main Sicilian Cerasuolo wines (*q.v.*).

Furnari (or Bazia). See under Capo.

Garitta. See under Maniaci.

Goccia d'Oro. See under Moscato.

Lacrima d'Aretusa. Sweet wine from Moscatellone and Zibibbo grapes, grown in various districts around Syracuse.

Leonforte, Bianco and Rosso. The white (12°–14·5°) made from Catarratto, Minella and Carricante grapes, is dry and rich in flavour; the red, from Nerello Mascalese, and Nocera rather more coarse (13°–15°). They come from the mountainous middle of the island, between Leonforte and Enna.

Malvasia di Lipari, Malvasia di Milazzo. Quite one of the best – perhaps the best – of the sweet golden dessert Malvasia wines found all over Italy is that called "di Lipari", though in fact most of it comes from the other islands in the little Aeolian group: Stromboli and Salina. It is rich and luscious, much prettier to the nose than one would think from the enthusiastic Cùnsolo, who describes its scent as being "a marvellous mixture of broom, fennel and liquorice". Good years: 1945, 1948, 1949, 1950, 1953, 1954, 1956, 1959, 1960. Very good: 1946, 1952.

Not perhaps quite so fine, but well above the national average, is the Malvasia di Milazzo, from the Sicilian promontory that juts out towards the Aeolian Islands. Both the Lipari and the Milazzo come from a Malvasia grape that is said to differ slightly from the mainland variety, pressed when semi-dried, and the fermentation arrested by the addition of spirits. The maturing and bottling (after three years in cask) takes place in Messina and Naples, where production is now commercialised. 14°–16°.

Mamertino. Named after the Mamertini, a tribe that inhabited the north-eastern corner of Sicily some centuries before Christ, this was a wine known to the Romans and referred to by Martial, Pliny and others. Made from Catarratto, Insolia and Pedro Ximenes, the grape of Southern Spain that adds sweetness to dessert sherries, there are both dryish and very sweet types, but most of it is drunk on the spot, semi-sweet, by the people who grow it. 15°–17°. Good and very good years as for Malvasia di Lipari.

Maniaci and Garitta. Red wines from the shores of Lake Garitta, not so coarse and heavy as many local Sicilian wines. 13°–14°.

Marsala. This rich fabrication is Sicily's most famous wine, for which the British may well take some credit, for it was John Woodhouse, a Liverpool merchant who, visiting Sicily about 1760, realised that the wines of the extreme western end of the island, grown in the dry, iron-bearing soil, under the blazing sun, between Trapani and Marsala, had strong affinities with the basic wines from which port, sherry and madeira were made, and set up, with his sons, the Marsala firm of Woodhouse, soon to be joined in rivalry with such others as Inghams and Whittakers. The name of Marsala was soon well known because Nelson victualled his fleet here, and had dealings with Woodhouse (though it was probably ordinary table wine that he took aboard for his men), and although it is rather out of fashion in England nowadays as an aperitif or a dessert wine, in Regency and Victorian times it rivalled Madeira. The world was again reminded of its name in 1860, when Garibaldi landed with his Thousand at Marsala, with British men-o'-war offshore to protect what by this time were substantial British interests, though there is no historical foundation for the pleasing legend that a bombardment by Bourbon ships was stopped because of representations that British property – the Woodhouse and Ingham factories – was being, or was in danger of being, damaged.*

Like sherry and port, Marsala is a fortified wine, and it bears some resemblance to madeira in that one, at any rate, of its constituent parts is cooked, or heated. Marsala is made by adding to the dry – even harsh – fragrant white wine of the district,† in the proportion of six parts to every hundred, a mixture of one-quarter wine brandy and three-quarters of a much sweeter wine of the area made from semi-dried grapes. Then a third component is added, also six parts to every hundred of the original "straight" wine – a young, unfermented grape juice that has been slowly heated until it has become thick, sweet and caramelly, in colour, texture and flavour.

The mixture rests in cask for anything from four months to five years, taking on a deep-brown colour, with the original dry white wine giving a dry under-taste to the general sweetness – a sweetness that slowly diminishes with age. (Many of the finer Marsalas are made on the same *solera*

* There is a detailed account of how the British ships came to be present, and the part they played, in the late G. M. Trevelyan's *Garibaldi and The Thousand* (London, 1909), Chapter XIII.
† Made from Grillo, Catarratto, Insolia and Damaschino grapes, and reaching a strength of 14°–16°.

system as sherry, so that a date such as 1840, or 1870, indicates only the oldest wine in the blend. But age is to be prized in a Marsala.)

By laws of 1931 and 1950, the zone in which Marsala is produced has been strictly delimited, and the grades of wine have been defined as follows:

Marsala Fine (sometimes labelled "I.P." or "Italia Particolare") must be aged at least four months, and reach 17° of alcohol and 5° of sugar;

Marsala Superiore (sometimes labelled "L.P.", "S.O.M." – for "Superior Old Marsala", or "G.D." – for "Garibaldi Dolce", in honour of the landing of the Thousand), must be aged at least two years, and have 18° alcohol and – if a sweet Marsala, for there are drier types – 10° sugar;

Marsala Vergine. This is the original wine, without the additions, but aged, often by the *solera* system. Must be at least five years old and old and reach 18° alcohol; and

Marsala Speciale. These are the special types, such as Marsala Uovo, Marsala Crema and Marsala Mandorla – thickened, sweetened and flavoured: 18° alcohol and 10° sugar.

Marsala is not to everyone's taste – it is not to mine – but it is an important dessert wine, with one particular virtue: it does not deteriorate after the bottle has been opened, so that one can be sure in any Italian café or restaurant of having a glass of Marsala in decent condition. Blended with egg yolks, it makes one of the best of all after-dinner sweets, *zabaglione*, the bottled commercial version of which, Marsala Uovo (or all'Uovo) tastes simply like toffee and is nothing like so nice, though I have no doubt that it is wholesome.

Virtually all the production of Marsala is in the hands of big companies, both those with the English names already mentioned and other, Italian, foundations, of which Florio is probably the most distinguished, as its wines seem to be the most highly thought of. The leading firms are now joined in a *Consorzio per la Tutela del Vino Marsala*, and all bottles of the real thing should bear a numbered neck-label showing the outline of the island of Sicily in red.

Mascali. See under Etna.

Menfi. Very little of this dry white wine is consumed as a table wine: most is used in the making of Marsala, as the district from which it comes, on the south-western coast of the island, lies just within the delimited Marsala area.

Mezza Montagna dell'Etna (Vino di). See under Etna.

Mila, Bianco di. An extremely light, rather acid, white wine, a rare thing in these parts (9°–10°) from the Etna district, without a great deal of interest, and used to lighten some of the coarser Sicilian wines.

Milazzo, Bianco and Rosso. See under Capo.

Monreale. Both Marsala (*q.v.*) and Partinico Bianco (*q.v.*) are produced here, and sometimes take the name – also a very strong but pale white table wine.

Moscato. Good sweet wines are made in various parts of Sicily, as elsewhere, from the Moscato grape, semi-dried, that of Siracusa being the finest – and the most difficult to find. Others are from Chiaramonte, Comiso, Note, Pantelleria, Segesta, Vittoria and Zucco. (This last is also known as Goccia d'Oro.) The Moscato of Pantelleria, which is protected by a *consorzio*, is made not from the true Moscato but from a variant called Zibibbo, which is said to have been brought to the island by the Arabs, the word meaning "raisin", or dried grape.

Naccarella. Another golden dessert wine, also – like the finest Moscato – from Syracuse, made from a small local grape that is allowed to be attacked on the vine by the "noble rot" that makes the great Sauternes. 18°.

Ombra. A cherry-red dry wine, made on the outskirts of Catania from Nerello, Mascalese, Carricante and Vesparo grapes, fairly light in flavour and texture, unlike the Cerasuolo wines (*q.v.*) in that it is taken earlier off the skins, and is meant to be drunk young. 12·5°–13·5°.

Pachino Rosso. A heavy red wine made from Calabrese and Negro d'Avola grapes in the Syracuse district, and meant largely for export as a blending wine, though some small growers age it for family use by a sort of *solera* system, called here the *botte madre* or "mother-cask" system, by which is produced what is claimed to be a very fine table wine, though it has never come my way. 14°–17°.

Partinico Bianco. Made from local varieties of grape between Trapani and Palermo, around the Gulf of Castellamare, and included among the "virgin" Marsalas. Also drunk in its own right, chilled, as an excellent dry aperitif or, young, as a table wine. 16°.

Passito di Linguaglossa, Passito di Misilmeri, Passolato di Trapani. Sweet golden wines made from semi-dried (*passito*) grapes in the various districts named. See under Piedmont.

Piana di Catania, Vini della. Mixing wines made very harsh and strong, in the Catanian plain, by keeping the must on the skins for at least twenty-four hours – a method known locally as *scrudazzato*.

Piana di Mascali, Vini della. Wines somewhat similar to the above, but more frequently used locally as table wines, from the narrow strip between Etna and the sea, north of Catania.

Pollio. Another name for the Moscato di Siracusa (*q.v.*).

Porto Casteldaccia. They say now that the little town of Casteldaccia (the Corvo wine of which we have already listed: see above) once had a port, and that this sweet dessert wine owes its name not to any deliberate attempt to imitate the wine of Oporto, but because wines destined for Genoa used to lie in cask on the quay of the *porto*, acquiring flavour and character under the Sicilian sun. Personally, I doubt this tale, for there is also a so-called "Sherry Stravecchio di Casteldaccia": this is a town the wines of which aim to please by adopting the names of their betters.

Ragabò. One of the wines of Etna (*q.v.*).

Ragalna. Red and white wines of Etna (*q.v.*).

Randazzo. One of the wines of Etna (*q.v.*).

Ribollito di Marsala. Called "re-boiled" because fermented with the stalks. A dry red wine, very full and big, with a taste like that of a young Manduria (*q.v.* under Apulia). 12°–14°.

San Salvador. A deep-red, dry wine, made from Catarratto and Morello grapes near Catania, and aged in wood for three years before bottling, to produce a sound, full-bodied table wine of some modest distinction and, according to Veronelli, considerable therapeutic properties. But the same seems to be said in Sicily of any drinkable red wine. 13°–14°.

Scoglitti. A heavy red mixing wine, from near Vittoria, once distinguished above its present apparent merits as having been imported by the Bordelais at the time of the phylloxera.

Segesta Bianco. A variety of Alcamo (*q.v.*).

Sherry Stravecchio di Casteldaccia. See under Porto di Casteldaccia.

Sicilia Liquoroso. General name for the rich sugary wines produced pretty well all over the island as a basis for dessert wines, aperitifs of various kinds, and for blending, both in Sicily and on the mainland.

Siculiana. Made from Calabrese, Nerello, Insolia and Catarratto grapes in the coastal area west of Agrigento, on the south coast. A red wine, lightish in colour, but big enough in body to be used on the mainland as a mixing wine, though Sicilians like it as a table wine. 14°.

Solichiata. One of the wines of Etna (*q.v.*).

Sparviero. One of the wines of Etna (*q.v.*).

Taormina. Not all the wines offered as "local" in the smart hotels and tourists' restaurants of Taormina come from around the fancy little town itself – many are the cheapest Etna wines. But there *is* produced, on the nearest Etna slopes, a very good dry, fragrant white wine, from Catarratto, Grillo, Insolia, Minnella Bianca, Damaschina and Carricante grapes, admirable with fish, to the amount of only about 50,000 bottles a year – nothing like enough for the total number of visitors, and nothing like so many as claim the name. 12°–12·5°.

Terreforti, Rosso delle. A powerful red wine, made in the Catanian plain, drunk young locally as a table wine, and also exported for blending. 14°–16°.

Tintone or Tintore. A similar wine to the above, not so strong, but of a particularly intense red, which is also useful in blending or, as they say, "as a corrective".

Trecastagni. See under Etna: the wine is drunk in vast quantities on every 10th of May, the day of the local Saint Alfio.

Val d'Anapo, Rosso (or Rubino) and Bianco (or Ambra). From the Anapo valley, inland from Syracuse. The white is made from Catarratto and Insolia grapes, and is deep gold in colour and quite uncompromisingly dry. 12°–13°. The red, very clear in colour and also very dry and light, is made from the same grapes, along with Nero d'Avola and Calabrese. 12°–13°. Sometimes served rather too young, when they have a rather astringent finish, but with a mere year or two in bottle are among the pleasantest of the island's table wines.

Val di Lupo, Bianco, Rosso and Rosato. From the same area as Leonforte (*q.v.*), but wines of a greater delicacy, for the white, which is dry and elegant, has Trebbiano, Malvasia Toscana and Pinot Grigio grapes in its *cépage*, as well as those of Leonforte; the red and the *rosé* also have Sangiovese, the red Val di Lupo being particularly soft, though dry, and an admirable table wine. 11·5°–12°.

Valledolmo and Vallelunga. Two names for the same wines, white and red, the Valledolmo from near Palermo, the other from the middle of the island, but both made from the same grapes – the white from Catarratto and Insolia grapes, producing a dry, rather full, golden wine of 12°–13°; the red from Perricone and other grapes, not particularly full for a Sicilian red, but rather light and dry. 12°–13°. Fontana Murata is another name for very similar red and white wines.

Villagrande, Bianco and Rosso. Among the wines of Etna (*q.v.*).

Vittoria. Another name for Scoglitti (*q.v.*).

Zucco. Another name for Corvo di Casteldaccia (*q.v.*).

Chapter 17

SARDINIA

✼

"NOT a bit like Italy." The theme recurs throughout D. H. Lawrence's peevish yet frequently perceptive *Sea and Sardinia*: Cagliari, the capital, is "strange and rather wonderful, not a bit like Italy"; the countryside, "is very different from Italian landscapes . . . much wider, much more ordinary, not up-and-down at all, but running away into the distance. Unremarkable ridges of moor-like hills running away, perhaps to a bunch of dramatic peaks on the south-west. This gives a sense of space, which is so lacking in Italy . . . like liberty itself, after the peaky confinement of Sicily."

As with the cities and the countryside, so with the people and the wines. The people, as Mr Alan Ross has observed,* displaying "none of the superficial gaiety of the Italians, none of their malleability or lightness of heart. They are courteous, generous, but essentially reserved." And the wines are strangely individual: dry wines drunk as dessert wines, sweet wines drunk as aperitifs, and table wines "powerful of impact and dark in colour", in Mr Iain Crawford's summing-up:† the whites almost *rosé*, and reds that truly deserve to be called, as they are, *vini neri*, black wines. Many of them are stronger than the 14° that the British Customs and Excise decrees as the upper limit of alcoholic strength for table wines: were they to be imported, they would pay as high a duty as port or sherry. Mention of sherry reminds one of the strangest Sardinian wine of all, Vernaccia, uncannily like a sherry, though made without any of the elaborate processes that a true sherry demands – an unfortified aperitif wine that may well have a great future as Sardinia develops.

The island is changing fast – faster, perhaps, than any other part of Italy. A post-war Italo-American campaign, backed by the Rockefeller

* In his *South to Sardinia* (London, 1960).
† In "Giustamente Alcoolico", article in *Wine* magazine, March–April 1964.

Foundation, cleared the island of malarial mosquitoes, and this made it possible to open the island to tourists. Already, there are night clubs, and an airport, and new hotels, and millionaires' beaches in the north-east corner of the island, providing new markets for the island's wines, and new inducements to make them more carefully and market them more skilfully.

All the more so because with the stricter application of the new Italian wine laws there will be at any rate a slightly diminished demand from the mainland for strong, coarse Sardinian wines of high alcoholic strength as "cutting" wines: such wines will have to be taught their manners (ageing can mellow wine as it mellows men) so as to be able to enter the more sophisticated society brought to Sardinia by the tourist trade.

It is all the easier for this to happen because of the amazing growth of the co-operative system in Sardinia in the past few years. Much of the money that both the central Government in Rome and the regional Government in Cagliari have put into Sardinian agriculture has wisely been spent on new co-operative wineries with new equipment – about eighty per cent of the island's wine now comes from co-operatives, and the extra money they earn for the growers may well, as the next stage, go towards replanning the older vineyards and replanting them with newer and perhaps better-bred vines.

The Wines of Sardinia

Anghelu Ruju. The curious name is that of one of Sardinia's strange prehistoric townships, near Alghero, in the north-west of the island, near which a strong, sweet, red dessert wine is made in small quantities from the Cannonau grape, dried in the sun for a week after picking, and with stalks removed. Not so much like port as the local people fondly imagine but somewhere between a ruby port and an Aleatico in style – with a little of the distinction of the port, and less of the fragrance of the Aleatico. 19°.

Arbaia. A rather finer variety of Gallura (*q.v.*).

Barbera Sarda. The Barbera grape of Piedmont was introduced into Sardinia in the last century and is grown fairly widely in the south of the island, around Cagliari, where it makes a good red table wine, though rather coarser than those of the north of Italy – perhaps because of the

Plate XVI Orvieto, U

greater heat and stronger sunshine, the heat intensified by the Sardinian method of growing vines *ad alberello*, close to the ground, from which the heat is reflected on to the vines. 13°–15°.

Campidano di Cagliari. A simple local red table wine, from the Campidano plain, which stretches north-north-west from Cagliari, made from Cannonau, Bovali, Girò and Monica grapes, light in colour and drunk young. The name is fairly general, and some of the wines are called Sandalyon, Parteollese and Marmilla: the Sandalyon in my experience being very pale, with tawny tints, dry but with an underlying blandness – a pleasant table wine. 12°–14°.

Castelsardo. Similar to the red wine of Sorso (*q.v.*).

Cannonau. The Cannonau grape is widely grown throughout the island, and dry, sweet and semi-sweet red and *rosé* wines are made from it. (Note that the so-called Cannonau Bianco di Jerzu, or Ogliastra Bianco, is in fact a *rosé* wine.) The sweeter varieties make pleasant light dessert wines (about 15°–16°); the dry Cannonau is fairly commonplace, though I have drunk in the mountains a 1958 Perla Rubia, which is one of the "white" Cannonaus of Jerzu, a pale pink with orange tints, that was a table wine of considerable character, but strong (16°) for midday drinking. (It fortunately lacked what the enthusiastic Cùnsolo found to praise in the dry Cannonau: "a scent of roses; a taste of bitter almonds; and an under-taste of chocolate".)

Capo Ferrato. One of the outward and visible signs of the rehabilitation of Sardinia, partly due to the regional Government, partly to money from Rome, is the sweep of newly planted vineyards in many parts of the island. Near Capo Ferrato, in the south-eastern corner, are those of the *Ente di Trasformazione Fondiaria Agraria della Sardegna* (EFTAS), where they grow a good strong red table wine, largely from Cannonau grapes, dry but mellow, heavy enough to suit the local game. 15°–17°.

Capo Giglio. One of the wines of the Nurra (*q.v.*).

Dorato di Sorso. An almost orange-coloured wine made from Cannonau grapes grown near Sorso, the great wine-growing centre near Sassari; light but strong, bitter-sweet, and drunk as an aperitif or a dessert wine. 16° and over.

Dorgali, Rosso and Rosato. Dry red and *rosé* wines from near Dorgali, in the middle of the east coast, from Cannonau and other grapes, and said to be perhaps the strongest table wines of Italy (the *rosé* not quite so strong). Authorities differ as to their alcoholic strength: I have seen it put as low as 14·5°, which makes nonsense of the boast, but as high as 19°. Certainly not fine wines.

Embarcador. An attempt to fabricate a sort of port, by mixing various wines or musts – some, I am told, from Portugal itself – at Alghero. Not to be recommended. 20°–22°.

Fior di Romangia. A dry, deep-pink table wine that I have drunk in Cagliari, but that is not recorded in any of the reference books. Cf. Lagosta.

Gallura. A dry red table wine, with a bitter finish, made from a mixture of Cannonau and other grapes in the Sassari area; rather light for a Sardinian wine, and more advisable, therefore, than most for midday meals in high summer. 11°–13°.

Girò. A very pretty, topaz-coloured lightish dessert wine made from the Girò grape, similar to Monica and Nasco (*qq.v.*). 16°–17°.

Ierzu or Jerzu. See under Cannonau.

I Piani. Among the better red wines of the Nurra (*q.v.*).

Lagosta. A dry – even tart – white table wine from Alghero, made from a mixture of grapes that includes Vermentino – possibly a brand name, as it is not recorded in the reference books.

Logudoro. Wines very similar to the Gallura wines (*q.v.*), but rather lighter and sweeter, from south of Sassari and the Lago del Coghinas. 11°–13°.

Malvasia di Bosa; Malvasia di Cagliari. Made from Malvasia grapes in various parts of the island, but chiefly in the two named: an aperitif or dessert wine, according to individual fancy – it smells sweeter than its taste, which is almost that of a medium sherry, an amontillado or an oloroso, not luscious, but not wholly dry. The bouquet is pleasantly flowery. The Malvasia of Bosa has the more intense colour of the two named here, and a rather fuller flavour. 17°.

Mamuntanas. One of the better red wines of the Nurra (*q.v.*).

Mandrolisai. A good red table wine, from one of the newly established co-operatives in the very middle of the island, in the district from which it takes its name. Made from Cannonau grapes and the recently introduced Dolcetto of Piedmont (not, as is sometimes stated, Nebbiolo), it is a clear brilliant red, with a pleasant bouquet, and a firm, dry finish. 12°–13°.

Maristella. One of the better white wines of the Nurra (*q.v.*).

Marmilla. One of the wines of Campidano (*q.v.*).

Mògoro, Bianco, Rosso and Rosato. All are dry – even rather acid – table wines, from the north-western end of the Campidano, almost at the middle of the west coast: the whites (11°–13°) from Nuragus, Vernaccia and other grapes; the others from Cagnulari, Monica and Greco Nero. 12°–14°. The same wines are sometimes called Terralba, according to which end of the district they come from.

Monica. A sweet dessert wine made from the Monica grape, similar to Girò, but much redder: not unlike the Spanish Malaga. 15°–18°.

Moscato or Moscato Sardo. Sweet dessert wines are made in various parts of the island from the Moscatello grape – that of Gallura (or Tempio) being perhaps the richest and finest. There is also a Moscato Spumante. The Moscato of Campidano has a pleasant musky scent. 15°–16°.

Nasco. Another of the island's lightish golden dessert wines, of the same type as the Monica and the Girò, but made from the Nasco grape. It has a quite charming orange blossom bouquet, and the faintly bitter under-taste to the sweetness makes it perhaps the most interesting of its type. 15°–17°.

Ninfeo. A white dessert wine, sweeter, stronger and more scented than the other Nurra wines.

Nuraghe Majore. One of the better white wines of the Nurra (*q.v.*).

Nuragus. This is the name of what is economically the most important grape of Sardinia (opinions differ as to whether there is any etymological connection with the *Nuraghi*, the island's curious little stone houses). It is grown pretty well everywhere, but especially in the Campidano, and makes a simple, almost neutral, dry white wine much used not only as the local carafe wine – it goes pleasantly enough with fish – but to export for blending with the mainland wines, and as a basis for vermouth and sparkling wines. 11°–14°.

Nuoro. Virtually the same wine as the red Dorgali (*q.v.*).

Nurra, Bianco and Rosso. The north-western horn of the island is called the Nurra, a great wine-growing area. The whites are made from Vermentino, Torbato and the recently introduced Tocai Friulano grapes, and are dry with a fruity smell and a full flavour – used locally as common table wines drunk young, and for export (12°–14°). The reds are rather heavier and of no great distinction (13°–14°), though there are some finer varieties sold under more specific names: I Piani, Mamuntanas and S. Maria la Palma. The better whites include Nuraghe Maggiore, Maristella and Capo Giglio.

Ogliastra Bianco. See under Cannonau.

Ogliastra Rosso and Rosato. Only slightly more deeply coloured versions of the above.

Oliena. A big, full-flavoured, almost bitter, red wine from the middle-east of the island, made from Cannonau, Monica and other grapes, which one Italian wine writer says has a tarry after-taste, and another says tastes of bitter chocolate. D'Annunzio praised it highly: it is, in fact, a good robust wine, to be drunk with rich dishes, and at dinner rather than at luncheon, preferably in the place where, like Jorrocks, one not only dines but sleeps – it reaches a strength of 18°. There is also a sweeter, dessert version, with the lusciousness of the Monica (*q.v.*) coming through.

Parteollese. One of the red wines of the Campidano (*q.v.*): there is also a *rosato*.

Perla Rubia. A particularly fine example of the Cannonau wines (*q.v.*).

Sandalyon. One of the wines from the Campidano (*q.v.*).

Sangiovese Sardo, or di Arborea. An acclimatisation vineyard in Arborea, by the reclaimed marshland and salt-pans of Terralba, has had considerable success for the past thirty years or so with the noble Sangiovese of Chianti, producing an admirable red table wine not unworthy of its parentage. It is surprising that this grape has not been planted more extensively in Sardinia, but it may well be that it is not so prolific and not, therefore, so profitable, as the local varieties. Also, it will be a long time before a Sardinian Sangiovese can command the same price on the mainland or abroad as that of Tuscany. But it is worth seeking out when visiting Sardinia – a sound red table wine, with more than just a hint of the Chianti fragrance and flavour, but rather stronger and fuller, as one would expect from a sunnier, hotter climate. 13°–14°.

Santa Maria la Palma. One of the better red wines of the Nurra (*q.v.*).

Sardinian Gold. One of the brand names, now protected, of a Vernaccia (*q.v.*) from one of the island's most important co-operatives.

Sardus Pater. A deep-red, strong (16°) and very fragrant dry table wine, made chiefly from Caregnano grapes, in the little island of Sant'Antioco, just off the south-west of Sardinia. There is also a less strong *rosato*.

Semidano. A dry white wine from the Campidano area, made from local grapes, but rather like a drier version of the Malvasia of the district.

Sorso, Rosso di. The district north of Sassari grows a variety of red wines from a mixture of grapes – wines that vary according to whether the Cannonau or the Cagnulari predominates, the one making a pleasant local table wine, the other, stronger and darker, being exported for blending.

The wine of Castelsardo, hard by, is said to be more delicate, and of better quality. 13°–14°.

Sorso, Dorato di. See under Dorato di Sorso.

Terralba. The same wines as those of Mògoro (*q.v.*).

Torbato di Alghero. This local variety of grape, grown only around Alghero, produces three types of wine:

Torbato Secco. A dry aperitif, though some drink it as a table wine. 14°.

Torbato Extra. A medium-sweet aperitif or dessert wine. 15°.

Torbato Passito. Made from the semi-dried grape, and very sweet. 18°.

Without being *like* sherry, these wines can be regarded as similar in style to sherry, and as corresponding to a very light fino or manzanilla; a sweetish amontillado or oloroso; and a cream or golden sherry, respectively. If one does not expect too much of them, they are very agreeable, and show an individual character.

Torrevecchia. One of the few wines to come from salty, marshy country – that of Marceddi at Faro di Capo Frasca, which juts into the sea near Terralba. It is made from a wide variety of grapes, including some Barbera and Sangiovese, as well as local varieties, and is a heavily scented, full, dry red wine, sometimes frothy and *frizzante*. 12°–14°.

Trebbiano Sardo or Trebbiano di Arborea. Another of the mainland grapes being successfully acclimatised at Arborea, like the Sangiovese (*q.v.*). It makes a light, fresh table wine: see under Emilia–Romagna and elsewhere.

Vermentino, or Vermentino di Gallura. An amber-coloured white wine, so dry and with such a bitter finish that it makes an admirable sherry-type aperitif, like Vernaccia (see below), though it is also drunk locally as a table wine. From the Vermentino grape, grown chiefly in the Gallura district, in the extreme north of the island. 14°. There is also a Vermentino Spumante, semi-sweet, known usually simply as Gallura Spumante.

Vernaccia. A curiosity of the island, and by far its best-known wine – a very dry, appetisingly bitter aperitif, made from the Vernaccia grape, with something of the style and character of a natural, unfortified sherry. The Sardinians drink it after, as well as before, meals: there are Vernaccia wines described as being di Nuoro, di Siniscola, and di Oristano (the branded Sardinian Gold – *q.v.* – from near Oristano). Good year: 1956. Very good: 1954, 1955, 1957, 1960. Exceptional: 1958, 1959.

Vin Cotto. A certain amount is made in Sardinia: see under Marches.

THE ITALIAN WINE LAW OF 1963

DECREE OF THE PRESIDENT OF THE REPUBLIC.
12th July 1963, No. 930.
Regulations to protect the sources of musts and wines.

THE PRESIDENT OF THE REPUBLIC

Reference: Art. 87 of the Constitution.

Reference: Act of Parliament of 3rd February 1963, No. 116, by which the Government was delegated to issue regulations for the protection of the denominations of the sources of musts and wines. Heard by the Council of Ministers.

Proposed by the Minister of Agriculture and Forestry, in conjunction with the Ministers for External Affairs, Justice, Finance, the Treasury, Industry and Commerce, and Foreign Trade.

IT WAS DECREED:
I
OF THE DENOMINATIONS OF ORIGIN

Art. 1. By the denomination of the origin of wines, is meant the geographical name, and geographical qualification of the particular production zone – accompanied or not by the name of the vines, or other indications adopted to specify the wines originating in these areas – when the characteristics of the wines are essentially dependent on the vines and natural conditions of the place.

The production zone (under the preceding paragraph) may include, in addition to the territory indicated in the respective denomination of source, the immediate neighbouring territories, provided that they possess similar natural conditions, and, at the date of this decree coming into force, that they have been producing wine for at least ten years, and marketing it under the same name. The wine must have the same physical, chemical and organic characteristics, be produced from grapes of the traditional vines of the zone and be made by the methods adopted in that zone.

Art. 2. There will be three denominations describing the origin of wines:

(*a*) "*Semplice*" – (unblended)

(*b*) "*Controllata*" – (controlled)

(*c*) "*Controllata e garantita*" – (controlled or tested and guaranteed).

Art. 3. The denomination of *semplice* will apply to wines made from grapes of the traditional vines of the particular production zone, processed according to the local methods and coming from vineyards true and constant to the zone.

The boundaries of each zone are decreed by the Minister of Agriculture and Forestry, in conjunction with the Minister of Industry and Commerce. In the absence of a ministerial decree defining the boundary, the production zone will constitute the established limits of the Commune of the whole territory which refers to the name or geographical qualification assumed as the denomination of origin of that wine.

Art. 4. The denominations of *controllata* origins are reserved for those wines which answer to the conditions and established qualifications laid down for each one in the relevant production controls.

The denominations of *controllata e garantita* origins are reserved for wines of particular reputation and worth – the manner of their presentation will be shown in the following Art. 7. Wines which qualify for this denomination must answer to the conditions and established qualifications laid down for each one in the relevant production controls.

The recognition of the denominations of *controllata* or *controllata e garantite* origins, and the delimitation of the respective zones of production, will come into effect simultaneously with the approved regulations of production, on a decree of the President of the Republic, on the proposal of the Minister for Agriculture and Forestry, in conjunction with the Minister for Industry and Commerce, on the previous advice of the National Committee (see Art. 17).

The above-mentioned decree will determine the date of the enforcement of the rules concerning the control of production, and, when necessary, will define and decide any temporary regulations. The decree will be published in the *Gazzetta Ufficiale*.

The adoption of denominations of *controllata* and *controllata e garantite* origins will not be permitted for wines which are, either totally or in part, a direct product of hybrid vines.

Art. 5. Among the production controls shown in Art. 4, the following are to be established:

(*a*) The name of the origin of the wine.

(*b*) The boundaries of the grape-producing zone. This zone will comprise the territories which have already been admitted by the decree issued by the Minister of Agriculture and Forestry in execution of the Act of 10th July 1930, No. 1164.

(*c*) The conditions of production. (The natural characteristics of the land, the vine stocks, the planting routines and cultivation of the vine plants, the maximum allowed production of grapes per hectare,* preparation methods, including those for "special" wines, corrective practices which may mean the inclusion of grapes, musts or wines of other production zones when necessary, though these additions must be limited to the agreed corrections.)

(*d*) The maximum *resa* (residue) to be allowed in musts or in wine.

(*e*) The physical, chemical and organic characteristics present in the wine, including the minimum degree of natural alcoholic strength.

(*f*) Methods of production conditions, and eventual territorial limits, regarding the making of wine from grapes grown outside the production zone – always observing the traditional customs and methods of the zone itself – and also regarding the preparation of *liquorosi* and *spumanti* wines, including those coming from outside the designated production zone.

The following are the prescribed disciplinary measures for production:

(1) A progressive increase in the ratios grape–must–wine, with the aim of achieving a higher level of production.

(2) Arrangements and regulations concerning the type and capacity of containers, also their relative characteristic appearance for the retail sale of the wines, plus a guaranteed indication of the year of production.

(3) Regulations concerning the use of indications other than those of the denomination of origin, together with the labelling indications established in Art. 16 (*a*) of this decree.

(4) Wine-tasting during the stages of bottling, to be confined to wines of *controllata e garantita* origin, to determine the characteristics.

(5) The use of the additional specification *classico* to the denominations of *controllata* and *controllata e garantite* sources, for products from the oldest wine-producing zones, when these production zones also consist of

* A hectare is approximately two-and-a-half acres.

other territories. With regard to the denomination of "Chianti", such a specification will be exclusively granted to products from the zone of "Chianti cassico", defined in the Ministerial decree of 31st July 1932.

By decree of the President of the Republic, on the proposal of the Minister of Agriculture and Forestry, in conjunction with the Minister of Industry and Commerce, the Minister of Finance and the Minister for Foreign Trade and in recognition of the particular requirements of the foreign markets, consent will be given for wines, including the *speciali* wines, to be made by methods differing from the rules for production laid down, and likewise, the minimum degree of alcoholic strength of the said wine may differ from the same rules.

The rules of production will take into account the methods adopted locally, when they are constant and true, and when the granting of permission for them will help to improve the qualitative characteristics responsible for the marketing of these denominations.

Art. 6. Requests for recognition, for wines from denominations of *controllata* and *controllata e garantita* origin must be presented by the interested parties to the Inspector's office, at the appropriate territorial Department of Agriculture. They will be advised by the Inspector, and after publication in the Record of Legal Announcements of the Province, the requests, together with the opinions and considerations of the Regional Committee for Agriculture, will be forwarded to the Minister of Agriculture and Forestry. (Much will depend on the advice of the regional Committee for Agriculture. Ref. Art. 5 of the Presidential decree of 10th June 1955, No. 987, which has been considered, together with Art. 3 of the law of 2nd June 1961, No. 454, by technicians particularly qualified and expert in the problems of agricultural development, appointed by Organisations of Economics operating in the region.)

All requests must be accompanied by the following documents, in triplicate:

(*a*) An illustrative report giving evidence in support of the local use of the denomination of the origin of the wine in question, with all documents which may help to confirm the contents of this report. In the illustrative report, documentary evidence of the regions proposing the introduction of any neighbouring territory into the zone of production indicated by the official denomination of origin, must be included.

(*b*) Precise indications of the position of the zone (to be clearly marked on a map with the scale of 1:25,000) where the grapes for the wine will be grown, with notes on the boundaries of the ground and the geological nature of the soil.

(*c*) Indications of the average annual production of the wine seeking recognition.

(*d*) Indications of the vines from which the grapes contributing to the making of the traditional product are harvested and the proportions of the various grapes in the final product.

(*e*) Indications of the maximum and minimum percentages of grapes, musts or wines to be brought in from other sources, for the eventual adjustments necessary to the manufacture of the finished product.

(*f*) Indications of the principal physical, chemical and organic characteristics of the wine, including the natural alcoholic strength of the product.

In addition to the documents listed above, requests for recognition under the denomination *Controllata e garantita* must be accompanied by a separate document declaring the approval of the following:

(*a*) Wine producers responsible for at least thirty per cent of the total quantity of wine produced in the zone, when the request concerns origins of *spumanti* or *liquorosi* wines.

(*b*) Not less than twenty per cent of the wine growers, responsible for at least twenty per cent of the total production from vineyards registered in the "Albo" (see Art. 10), when the request concerns wines not already dealt with in the above paragraph.

The wine producers and growers referred to under the previous headings (*a*) and (*b*) must state expressly that they are prepared to agree to the regulations laid down in the following Art. 7.

The above provisos apply also when the request is to transfer a wine already in the denomination off *controllata* origin, to the denomination *controllata e garantita*.

The request, with the relative documents, will be put before the Minister of Agriculture and Forestry and the National Committee (see Art. 17), and the decision reached will be announced within ninety days of receipt of the request.

Art. 7. Wine from a *controllata e garantita* denomination of origin must be presented to the consumer in bottles or other vessels, with a capacity not exceeding five litres, bearing the indications set down in Art. 16 of this decree, and sealed by the bottling firms, with a State countersign applied in such a manner as to eliminate any possibility of the contents of the bottle being tampered with, without the countersign being broken.

The countersign, or trade mark, besides bearing the emblem of the State, will have the words "Minister of Agriculture and Forestry", the denomination of *controllata e garantita* origin, and the name of the wine. The countersigns will be in series, each with an identification number.

By decree of the President of the Republic, on the proposal of the Minister of Agriculture and Forestry, in conjunction with the Ministers of Industry, Commerce and Finance, any other characteristics of these seals will be established, including the methods of fabrication, the uses and controls thereof. The price of each seal may not exceed 3 lire per litre. By the same decree, the organisations responsible for distributing these countersigns (seals) will be announced. The proceeds from the sale of all seals will go to the State.

Art. 8. As from the date when the decree on the recognition of denominations comes into force (Ref. Art. 4) the denominations of *controllata* and *controllata e garantita* origins may not be applied to any wines which do not conform to the regulations and standards laid down in this decree.

From the same date, qualifications of wines bearing the denominations of *controllate* or *controllate e garantite* origins, in any way differing from those expressly consented to in the decree of recognition, will be forbidden.

However, this prohibition does not extend to the use of precise geographical localisation on the label, e.g. the name of the farm, estate, Commune or village.

Although, even before the passing of this present decree, it has never been considered as taking the place of the denomination of origin, the use of geographical localisation, including the address of the Company, cellar or farm, etc., may be included on the label, on condition that the print used for these indications does not exceed three millimetres in height by two in width, and in no case exceeds one quarter of the height or width of the print used to display the denomination of the product, and the registered company or firm of the manufacturer, merchant or the firm responsible for the bottling of the wine.

The recognition of a denomination of *controllata* origin, excludes the possibility of wines bearing that label being confused with wines of *semplice* origin, just as the recognition of a denomination of wines of *controllata e garantita* origin prevents the possibility of these wines being mistaken for wines of *controllata* or *semplice* origin.

Art. 9. Thus, the regulations laid down on labelling, vessels, packing and presentation, price lists, and documents of sale of each of the three denominations, are to certify conformity between each wine and the denomination it appropriates.

II

THE REGISTER OF VINEYARDS, DECLARATIONS AND PRODUCTION CONTROLS

Art. 10. In the production zones of wines of the denomination of origin *controllata* or *controllata e garantita* the ground set aside for the production of these wines *must* be recorded in a public register which is lodged at each Chamber of Commerce, Industry and Agriculture.

This is arranged through the Commune on a declaration from the manager or other competent person. At the same time a declaration must be made to the Inspector's office for Agriculture of the Province concerned, attesting that the land to be registered answers to the conditions laid down for the production of these wines. Where there are societies (see Art. 21), the Inspector for Agriculture of the Province may avail himself of their assistance in assessing the validity of the declaration.

This declaration must be made within six months of the planting of the vine stocks. For vines already existing at the date of this decree coming into force, the declaration must be made within six months of that date.

A declaration must also be made, through the Commune, within sixty days, of any variation of the consistency of the registered land, or any modification of the systems of cultivation.

The agents responsible for the prevention of fraudulent practices during the preparation or trading of Agricultural products, including the societies mentioned in Art. 21, on discovering the existence of any variations or modifications which have not been declared will inform the Agricultural Inspector's office of the Province, who, after assessing the validity of these changes will make the necessary alterations in the Register of vineyards.

Art. 11. Persons wishing to put their wine on the market as *controllata* or *controllata e garantita* must make a declaration to the appropriate Chamber of Commerce, through the Commune, within ten days of the end of the vintage of the quantity of grapes produced. If the grapes have already been sold, the name and address of the purchaser must be supplied as well as the vineyard from which the grapes were gathered.

Once the declaration has been made, the manager will receive from the Chamber of Commerce through the Commune a receipt for the amount declared. In this receipt the following details will be indicated:

(*a*) The quantity of grapes and the corresponding denomination of origin.

(*b*) The location of the vineyard producing the grapes and their destination.

(*c*) The name and address of the producer, and in the case of the grapes having been sold already, the name and address of the purchaser, or party for whom they were purchased.

(*d*) The date of the presentation of the declaration.

This declaration of production (which concerns also the by-product remaining after the wines have been made), confirms the ruling of the Presidential decree of 14th December 1961, No. 1315. As distinct from other products, the quantity of wine rated as *controllata* and *controllata e garantita* must be declared, specifying for each of these wines the corresponding denomination, the quantity of grapes used in the preparation of that wine, the limits set down in the declaration of the quantity of grapes produced, and the relevant receipt referring to these quantities.

Art. 12. The manager, or persons responsible for the sale of the declared grapes must transfer to the purchaser – after filling in the necessary details in the space provided for this purpose – the receipt of the production declaration, or fraction of that receipt, to enable the purchaser to register the grapes in a *magazzino di carico e scarico* as will be shown in the following Article.

Art. 13. All manufacturers or merchants of wines with the denominations of source *controllata* or *controllata e garantita* must establish a register of *magazzino di carico e scarico*, to contain details of stocks produced or acquired as stated in the production declarations, together with the relevant receipts, and also the stock sold, together with the receipt of sale.

At the moment wine retailers are not obliged to keep a register of *carico e scarico* provided that they do not prepare or bottle the above wines, but they must, however, retain the receipts for the wines bought for three years.

Producers of *spumanti* and *liquorosi* wines with the denomination of source *controllata* or *controllata e garantita* must also keep:

(*a*) A register of production for the products prepared by them.

(*b*) A register of the raw materials to be used in the making of these wines.

Art. 14. The following rules to be observed will be published by decree of the President of the Republic on the proposal of the Minister of Agriculture and Forestry, in agreement with the Ministers of Industry and Commerce and Finance:

(*a*) For the establishment of a register of the lands mentioned in Art. 10, with the relevant formalities to be observed in the declarations to be registered, and any variations.

(*b*) For the declaration of production, and the obtaining of a receipt (see Art. 11).

(*c*) For the establishing of registers (see Art. 13).

Art. 15. For any product not stored in containers specified in Art. 16, the wine-growers – either singly or in association – the manufacturers and the merchants must, for bulk sale of the wine, state clearly the correct registered name or firm and the locality from which the wine comes, as well as the name of the firm responsible for the bottling of the wine when this takes place outside the locality. The above statements must appear in indelible characters on the containers of wines to be put on the market under the denominations of origin *controllata* or *controllata e garantita*, or on the labels of these containers as well as on all receipts and transport documents. Persons marketing products already bottled and bearing a seal are exempted from these obligations.

Art. 16. On the bottles, or other containers with a capacity not exceeding five litres containing wines marketed as *controllate* or *controllate e garantite*, or on the labels of these containers, the following indications must be clearly stated in indelible characters:

(*a*) The denomination of origin under which the wine is put on the market, and immediately underneath, the words "denomination of origin *controllata*" or "denomination of origin *controllata e garantita*".

(*b*) The quantity of wine effectively contained in the bottle or other container, to be marked *contenuto netto litri* . . . (nett. content in litres . . .).

(*c*) The name and surname, or firm, and the locality of the producer's establishment. If not responsible for the bottling of the wine, then the name of the firm employed to bottle the wine must be given.

(*d*) The words "wine bottled by the producer", or "wine bottled in the production zone" or equivalent indications depending on whether the wine was bottled by the producer or by a third party, inside or outside the production zone.

Whoever is responsible for the bottling of the wine is also responsible for the regularity of the product bottled, and the veracity of the indications on the label or on the container.

III

THE INSTITUTION OF A NATIONAL COMMITTEE FOR THE PROTECTION OF THE DENOMINATIONS OF ORIGIN

Art. 17. A National Committee has been set up for the protection of the denominations of origin of wines.

The rules of the organisation and the functions of this Committee will be established by decree from the President of the Republic on the proposal of the Minister of Agriculture and Forestry in agreement with the Minister of Industry and Commerce.

The members of this Committee will be nominated by decree of the Minister of Agriculture and Forestry in agreement with the Minister of Industry and Commerce, and will consist of:

Two Civil Servants from the Ministry of Agriculture and Forestry.

One Civil Servant from the Ministry of Industry and Commerce.

One Civil Servant from the Ministry of Foreign Trade.

One Civil Servant from the National Institute for Foreign Trade.

Two members chosen from six submitted by the Academy of Vines and Wines.

Two experts in the field of Viticulture and Oenology.

Two members selected from four submitted by the Association *Enotecnici Italiani* and the National Order of Wine Tasting.

Three members selected from six submitted by the Syndicate of Farmers, one from northern Italy, one from central Italy and one from southern Italy.

Three members selected from six submitted by the Syndicate of Cultivators, one from northern Italy, one from central Italy and one from southern Italy.

Three members selected from the six submitted by the Syndicate of Growers, one from northern Italy, one from central Italy and one from southern Italy.

Two members of the "Cantine Sociali" and the Co-operative Agricultural Producers.

One member drawn from three submitted by the Syndicate of Industrial Wine-growers.

One member drawn from three submitted by the Syndicate of Wine-growers and Wholesale Dealers.

One member drawn from three submitted by the Syndicate of Wine-growers for Export.

One member particularly qualified in the production of *vini speciali* selected from four submitted by the Syndicate of Competent Organisations.

One member drawn from three submitted by the Organisation of Mediators and Representatives of Wines.

One member drawn from three submitted by the National Union of Consumers.

The President of the Committee is nominated by decree of the Minister of Agriculture and Forestry in agreement with the Minister of Industry and Commerce.

Art. 18. The National Committee:

(*a*) Must express its considered opinion concerning Arts. 4 and 6, formulating and proposing to the Minister of Agriculture and Forestry regulations of production for wines of the denomination of origin *controllata* or *controllata e garantita*.

(*b*) Use its own initiative in promoting the recognition of denomination of origin either *controllata* or *controllata e garantita* where these have not been requested by the parties concerned, or by the competent Chambers of Commerce, Industry and Agriculture, on the advice of the regional committee for Agriculture.

(*c*) Collaborate with the competent State agents to ensure that this decree and the relative production regulations for the denomination of origin *controllata* or *controllata e garantita* are observed.

(*d*) Intervene in Italy and abroad to protect the denominations *controllata* or *controllata e garantita* according to the laws and international treaties. To this end the Committee may avail itself of assistance from the voluntary Societies mentioned in Art. 21.

(*e*) Use its initiative in matters of propaganda and methods of study in order to obtain higher production and wider publicity for the products in this decree.

(*f*) Carry out the commissions entrusted to their charge by competent authorities, to achieve a satisfactory functioning of this decree.

The decisions reached by the Committee on paragraphs (*a*) and (*b*) of this Article must be published in the *Gazzetta Ufficiale* of the Republic for possible petitions and counter-deductions on the part of the interested parties. These petitions must be presented to the Minister of Agriculture and Forestry within sixty days of the date of publication.

Art. 19. The National Committee has the authority to carry out all the investigations it considers necessary, including discussions with the interested parties. Any technical advice required will be provided by the consultants.

With reference to the proposals concerning the production regulations of wines with the denomination *controllata* or *controllata e garantita* the Committee may seek advice from the territorial Chamber of Commerce.

Art. 20. The decisions reached by the Committee must be communicated to the Ministries of Agriculture and Forestry, Industry and Commerce, and Foreign Trade within fifteen days of their being adopted.

IV

THE VOLUNTARY SOCIETIES

Art. 21. The Minister of Agriculture and Forestry, in agreement with the Minister of Industry and Commerce, on the advice of the Committee (see Art. 17), by a decree to be published in the *Gazzetta Ufficiale* of the Republic, announce that the Voluntary Societies for the protection of wines of the denominations of origin *controllata* or *controllata e garantita* may have the authority to act in a supervisory capacity. Their duties will be to ensure that the rules laid down in this decree are observed, including the production regulations. They may have the authority to take a civil part in penal prosecutions, and may distribute the State Countersigns mentioned in

Art. 7 to members of their own Society. Supervision may be exercised on the part of each Society only by members of that Society.

The power to act in a supervisory capacity may be conferred only on such Societies as:

(*a*) Include enough members to represent not less than thirty per cent of the wine producers of the zone, and when dealing with the denominations of origin regarding *spumanti* or *liquorosi* wines not less than thirty per cent of the production.

(*b*) In connection with wines other than those mentioned in paragraph (*a*) of this Article, include enough members to represent not less than twenty per cent of the wine producers of the zone, and not less than twenty per cent of the total area of vineyards – registered in the register (see Art. 10) – regarding the corresponding denomination of origin.

(*c*) Do not admit indiscriminately into the Society viticulturists, either singly or in association, with industrial or commercial interests.

(*d*) Guarantee an effective and impartial treatment of the supervisory duties.

To Civil Servants of these voluntary Societies is given the recognised qualification of Agent to the Judiciary Police Force in accordance with the Royal decree of 15th October 1925, No. 2033, converted into the law of 18th March 1926, No. 562, with its successive modifications and integrations. These may be limited to the parts concerning the supervision of the use of a denomination, for the protection of which these Societies are appointed.

The authority of the Ministry of Agriculture and Forestry and other public Administrations must be accepted as final.

Art. 22. The responsibilities of supervising, as shown in the preceding Article, may be given to one Society, also for additional wines provided these are covered by the same denomination of origin either *controllata* or *controllata e garantita*.

The Societies entrusted with these responsibilities come under supervision from the Ministry of Agriculture and Forestry.

Any modifications of the statute of the Societies must be approved by the Minister of Agriculture and Forestry, in agreement with the Minister of Industry and Commerce.

Art. 23. Requests for the position of supervising the production and trade of a wine with the denomination of origin *controllata* or *controllata e garantita* must be published in the *Foglio* of legal announcements of the Province, by the interested Society. It must then be put forward by a legal representative of the Society, for consideration by the Minister of Agriculture and Forestry, accompanied by the following documents:

(1) A list of the members of the Society, plus a certificate from the competent Chambers of Commerce, Industry and Agriculture proving that these agree with the regulations set down in paragraphs (*a*) and (*b*) of Article 21.

(2) An authentic copy of the Articles of Association and the Statute of the Society.

(3) A report of the technical and administrative aspects of the Society, and its Balance Sheet.

Three copies of the request and the documents indicated above must be forwarded to the Ministry of Agriculture and Forestry, and one copy to the Ministry of Industry and Commerce.

Art. 24. The Administrative Councils of the Societies, to whom the responsibilities set down in Art. 21 have been entrusted, are liable to have this office terminated by decree of the Minister of Agriculture and Forestry, in agreement with the Minister of Industry and Commerce, when, after a warning to observe the obligations laid down in the legislations, rules and statutes, the Council persists in breaking the rules. This may also happen in the case of insufficient action being taken by a Society, or other circumstances underlining any irregularity necessitating the cancellation of the appointment.

By the same decree the Administration is given to a Government official who must, within three months of taking over the administration, call an assembly of the members in order to nominate a new Administrative Council.

In more serious cases, especially when the supervising has not been done impartially, the revocation of the recognition of that Society may be arranged by decree of the Minister of Agriculture and Forestry, in agreement with the Minister of Industry and Commerce.

This may also be done in cases where the membership of a Society falls below the limits established in the third paragraph of Art. 21.

V

MEASURES FOR THE PREVENTION OF FRAUD AND UNFAIR COMPETITION

Art. 25. All agents, including those from the Societies mentioned in Art. 21 are responsible for guarding against fraudulent activities during the preparation and in the marketing of agricultural products. They must be given free entry to all premises where musts or wines are produced or stored, where they are entitled to verify the declarations of production (Ref. Art. 11), check for any irregularities in the registers (Ref. Art. 13) and take samples of musts or wines.

These verifications may not be obstructed by the owners or persons in charge of the wines, who are obliged to declare to the agents the quantities of musts or wines stored in the casks, barrels or wine jars.

As a result of inspection, the containers must be marked – in indelible characters at least 10 centimetres high – with the respective capacity and quantity, to within four per cent, that may be contained in each vessel.

Art. 26. Any person producing, selling or in any way dealing commercially with the products mentioned in this decree, wherever these products are found must, on request, supply samples to officials or agents to whom authority has been given.

These samples must be taken away by the officials and agents indicated above. For each inspection at least five samples must be taken, of which two will be consigned to the producer or merchant.

Concerning the withdrawal of samples, the analysing of them, and all other activities considered necessary for the execution of this decree, reference should be made to the Royal decree of 15th October 1925, No. 2033, converted into the law of 18th March 1926, No. 526, the relative regulations approved by Royal decree on 1st July 1926, and their successive modifications and integrations.

Art. 27. Whosoever produces, puts on the market, or in any way distributes for consumption with the denomination of origin *semplice* wines which do not qualify (see Art. 3) for the use of this denomination, shall be suspended for up to six months, or fined between 10,000 and 50,000 lire for each hectolitre* or fraction of a hectolitre.

* A hectolitre is approximately 22 gallons.

Art. 28. Whosoever produces, sells, puts on the market, or in any way distributes for consumption with the denomination of origin *controllata* or *controllata e garantita* wines which do not qualify for the use of these denominations, shall be suspended for up to one year and fined between 20,000 and 100,000 lire for each hectolitre or fraction of a hectolitre. Should the infraction of the rules concern only the labelling of the bottles, then there shall be no suspension, and the fine will be reduced to one quarter.

Art. 29. Whosoever forges or alters the countersigns mentioned in Art. 7, or introduces them into State territory, or buys, holds, transfers to others or in any way uses countersigns which have been forged or altered, is liable to be suspended for six months to three years, and fined between 10,000 and 200,000 lire.

Art. 30. The measures laid down in Arts. 27 and 28 do not apply to merchants selling, putting on the market or in any way distributing for consumption wines with the denominations *semplice*, *controllata* or *controllata e garantita* unless the merchant knows of any infringement of the rules or the original products showing signs of alteration.

Art. 31. Whosoever uses the denominations of origin *controllata* or *controllata e garantita* for wines not qualified for the use of these denominations, and uses as a prefix the words *tipo*, *gusto*, *uso*, *sistema*, etc., or in any way deforms that denomination by the use of indications, illustrations or signs liable to mislead the buyer, will be suspended for up to two months, and fined up to 200,000 lire.

The same penalty applies when the altered wording or denomination is placed on the covers or wrappers, on any commercial papers, or published in any way.

Art. 32. Whosoever adopts the denominations of origin *controllata* or *controllata e garantita* for the "firm" or "company", and uses them in this way will be fined between 20,000 and 200,000 lire.

These measures will apply after one year from the date of the decree of the recognition of the denomination of origin coming into operation.

For the companies already existing at the date of the publication of this decree, the Ministers of Agriculture and Forestry, Industry and Commerce have the authority, when advised by the National Committee, to allow the continuation of the utilising of old denominations or firms on the labels in anticipation of approval.

Art. 33. Whosoever omits to present the declarations laid down in the second or fourth paragraphs of Art. 10, will be fined between 5,000 and 30,000 lire for each hectare or fraction of 1 hectare which should have been declared, with a maximum fine of 100,000 lire.

Art. 34. With regard to the declarations laid down in Art. 10, whosoever declares a quantity of grapes or wine greater than that produced is liable to a fine of between 2,000 and 10,000 lire for each quintal or fraction of 1 quintal in excess.

Art. 35. Whosoever writes, or is responsible for the writing of false statements in the registers prescribed in Art. 13, will be suspended for up to six months or fined up to 200,000 lire.

Art. 36. Whosoever violates the regulations laid down in Art. 15 and 16 will be fined between 10,000 and 200,000 lire, unless whatever takes place constitutes a more serious crime.

Art. 37. Whosoever impedes the carrying out of investigations to verify certain facts (see Art. 25), refuses to reveal a declaration (see the second paragraph of Art. 25), or makes an inaccurate declaration, will be fined between 20,000 and 300,000 lire.

Art. 38. The penalty for each of the offences listed in this decree necessarily means the publication of the sentences in two of the publications with the highest circulation in the region, one being a daily newspaper and the other a technical journal.

In particularly grave cases the products may be confiscated, and the establishment, cellar or store be closed for up to twelve months.

Art. 39. In commercial transactions, advertising and any publicity of the wine itself, after 180 days from the date of the publication of the production regulations for each wine it will be forbidden to:

(*a*) Qualify as *classico* a wine for which this qualification has not been recognised by a Ministerial decree in accordance with the law of 10th July 1930, No. 1164, or by a decree from the President of the Republic (Ref. Art. 4 of this decree).

(*b*) Use such terms as *disciplinato, regolamentato, controllato, garantito, delimitato*, etc., when describing the denomination of a wine or its respective territory. The denominations of wines which will be recognised are clearly stated in this decree, with their relative production regulations (Ref. Art. 4).

The violation of such regulations, e.g. (*a*) of this Article, carries the penalty of a fine between 10,000 and 50,000 lire for each quintal or fraction of 1 quintal of the product which has been sold or is held in custody.

VI

FINAL REGULATIONS

Art. 40. The rules of this decree apply also to musts.

Art. 41. The rules of this decree apply also to the wines *Moscato Passito di Pantelleria* and *Marsala* when they are not a contradiction of the law of 4th November 1950, No. 1068, or the law of 4th November 1950, No. 1069, the relative regulations of which were approved by the President of the Republic on 20th October 1961 by decree No. 1644.

Art. 42. Where not specifically stated to the contrary, all regulations in opposition to this decree are hereby repealed.

This present decree, stamped with the State seal, will be placed in the Official Collection of the laws and decrees of the Italian Republic. It is the duty of all persons to whom it may concern to observe this decree and ensure that it is observed by others.

Dated in Rome, 12th July 1963.

Registrato alla Corte dei conte, 13th July 1963.

Act of the Government, registered No. 171, foglio No. 127.

ITALIAN WINE-PRODUCTION

(in hecto-

Region	1967
PIEMONTE	7,063,000
VALLE D'AOSTA	55,000
LIGURIA	442,000
LOMBARDIA	2,940,000
TRENTINO-ALTO ADIGE	1,303,000
VENETO	9,982,000
FRIULI VENEZIA GIULIA	920,000
EMILIA-ROMAGNA	8,579,000
MARCHE	2,725,000
TOSCANA	4,092,000
UMBRIA	857,000
LAZIO	5,005,000
CAMPANIA	3,322,000
ABRUZZI E MOLISE	2,634,000
PUGLIA	12,666,000
LUCANIA	620,000
CALABRIA	1,242,000
SICILIA	8,992,000
SARDEGNA	1,586,000
Total	75,025,000

2

BY REGIONS 1967-1970

litres)

1968	1969	1970
5,659,000	5,172,000	5,186,000
51,000	57,000	41,000
369,000	355,000	461,000
2,263,000	2,157,000	2,340,000
1,099,000	1,117,000	1,454,000
8,567,000	9,512,000	9,494,000
925,000	837,000	1,097,000
5,140,000	8,824,000	10,763,000
2,238,000	2,308,000	2,359,000
3,856,000	3,862,000	4,263,000
831,000	644,000	823,000
4,746	4,980,000	4,761,000
3,309,000	3,186,000	3,084,000
2,177,000	2,562,000	2,252,000
11,037,000	12,203,000	11,104,000
642,000	636,000	521,000
1,169,000	1,139,000	947,000
9,315,000	9,886,000	6,069,000
1,844,000	2,033,000	1,855,000
65,237,000	71,470,000	68,874,000

Appendix 3

PRINCIPAL FOREIGN MARKETS FOR
ITALIAN WINES: 1969-1971

(in hectolitres)

	1969	*1970*	*1971*
AUSTRALIA	6,333	6,939	7,113
AUSTRIA	80,479	65,623	70,797
BELGIUM AND LUXEMBOURG	72,050	62,829	106,582
CANADA	23,224	22,651	37,446
CZECHOSLOVAKIA	1,087	1,266	895
DENMARK	2,173	2,341	1,836
EIRE	404	524	706
FINLAND	3,472	4,997	3,147
FRANCE	86,702	1,751,731	4,344,745
GREAT BRITAIN	43,944	49,161	65,705
HOLLAND	56,021	91,846	87,764
JAPAN	1,220	1,348	1,276
NORWAY	817	888	716
SWEDEN	12,563	16,490	15,011
SWITZERLAND	479,046	486,371	515,511
USA	139,374	171,560	224,043
USSR	18	629	259
VENEZUELA	3,778	4,674	5,158
WEST GERMANY	1,485,003	2,233,633	3,095,944

BIBLIOGRAPHY

ALLEN, H. Warner. *A History of Wine*, London, 1961

BODE, Charles. *Wines of Italy*, London, 1956

BRUNI, Bruno. *Vini Italiani*, Bologna, 1964

CAPONE, Roberto. *Vini Tipici e Pregiati d'Italia*, Florence, 1963

CAVAZZANA, Giuseppe. *Itinerario Gastronomico ed Enologico d'Italia*, Milan, 1950

CHAMBERLAIN, Samuel. *Italian Bouquet*, New York, 1958

CÙNSOLO, Felice. *Dizionario del Gourmet*, Milan, 1961

DAVID, Elizabeth. *Italian Food*, London, 1954

DETTORI, Renato G. *Italian Wines and Liqueurs*, Rome, 1953

GAROGLIO, P. Giovanni. *La Nuova Enologia*, 3rd Edition, Florence, 1965

HENDERSON, Alexander. *The History of Ancient and Modern Wines*, London, 1824

MARRISON, L. W. *Wines and Spirits*, London, revised edition, 1963

MINISTERO dell' AGRICOLTURA. *Principali Vitigni da Vino Coltivati in Italia* (Rome, in course of publication, 2 vols. so far in print).

MONELLI, Paolo. *O. P. ossia Il Vero Bevitore*, Milan, 1963

PENZER, N. M. *The Book of the Wine-label*, London, 1947

REDDING, Cyrus. *A History and Description of Modern Wines*, London, 1833 (third edition, with additions and corrections, 1860).*

SCHOONMAKER and MARVEL. *The Complete Wine Book*, New York, 1938

SELTMAN, Charles. *Wine in the Ancient World*, London, 1957

SHAND, Morton. *A Book of Other Wines than French*, London, 1929

SICHEL, Allan. *The Penguin Book of Wines*, London, 1965

SIMON, André. *The History of the Wine Trade in England*, London, 1905/6, 3 vols. (reissued 1965)

VERONELLI, Luigi. *I Vini d'Italia*, Rome, 1961. (The edition in English, published in Italy in 1964, is considerably abridged.)

WALL, Bernard. *Italian Life and Landscape*, 2 vols. London, 1950

YOUNGER, William. *Gods, Men and Wine*, London, 1966

* Third edition consulted by the Author.

GLOSSARY

ABBOCCATO. Sweet, or sweetish. (But not luscious.)

ALL'ANNATA. "Of the year" – of a young wine, drunk in the year after the vintage

AMABILE. Sweet, or sweetish. (But not luscious.)

AMARO. Bitter, but sometimes used of a dry wine

BIANCO. White

CERASUOLO. Cherry-red, *rosé*

DOLCE. Richly sweet

FRIZZANTE. Semi-sparkling, prickly. Cf. the French *pétillant* and the German *spritzig*

MUFFA NOBILE. "Noble rot", permitted to attack grapes from which certain luscious dessert wines are to be made. Cf. the French *pourriture noble*, in Sauternes, and the German *edelfäule*.

MUSSANTE. Sparkling

NERO. Black; sometimes used of a red wine

PASSITO. Semi-dried – of grapes thus treated to make sweet wine; and the wine thus made.

ROSATO. Pink, *rosé*

ROSSO. Red

SECCO. Dry

SPUMANTE. Frothy – hence sparkling

INDEX OF PRINCIPAL WINES

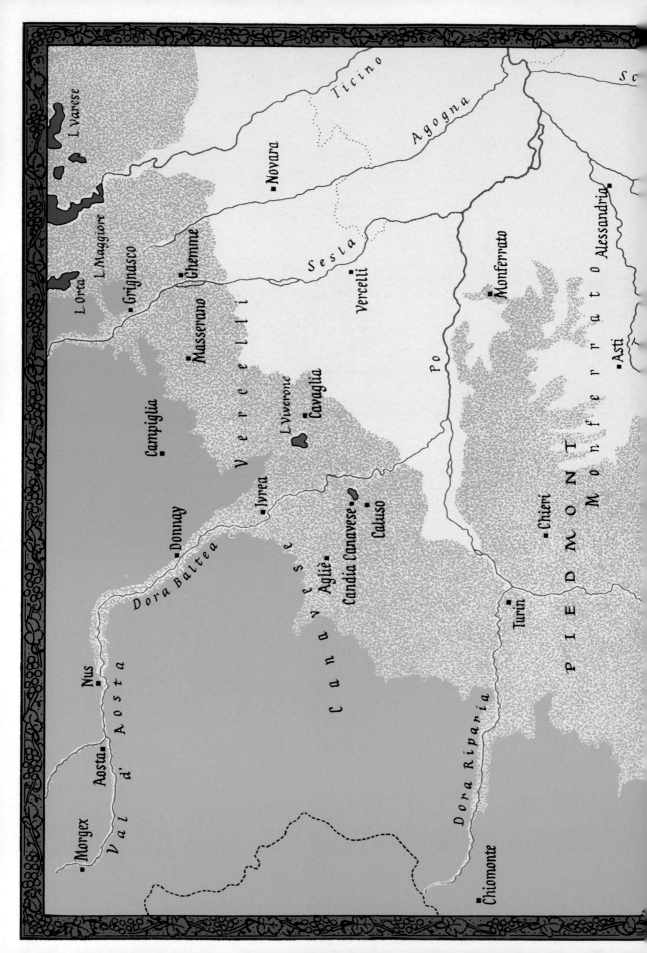

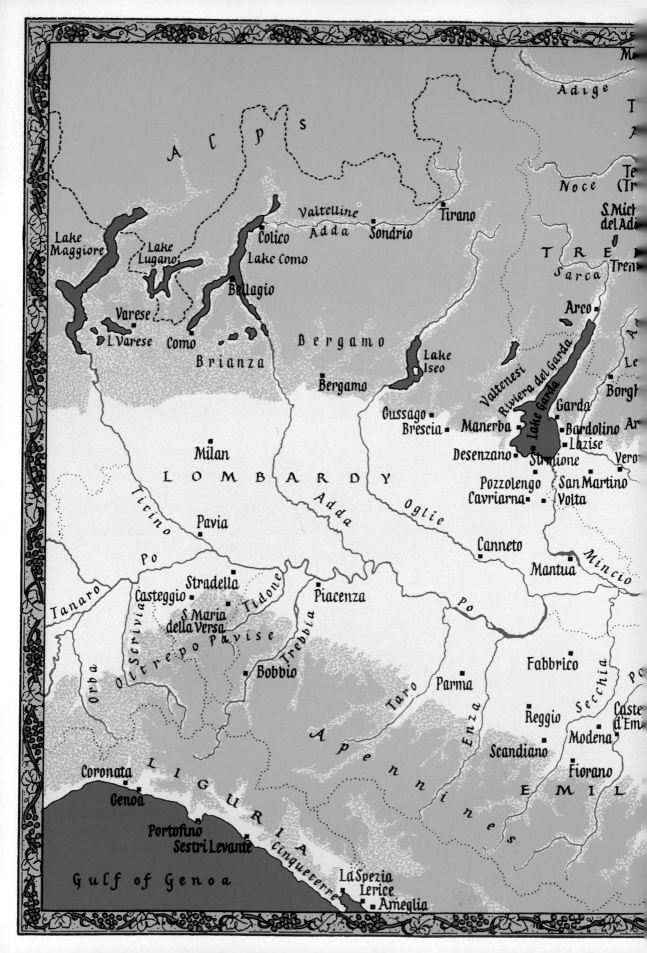

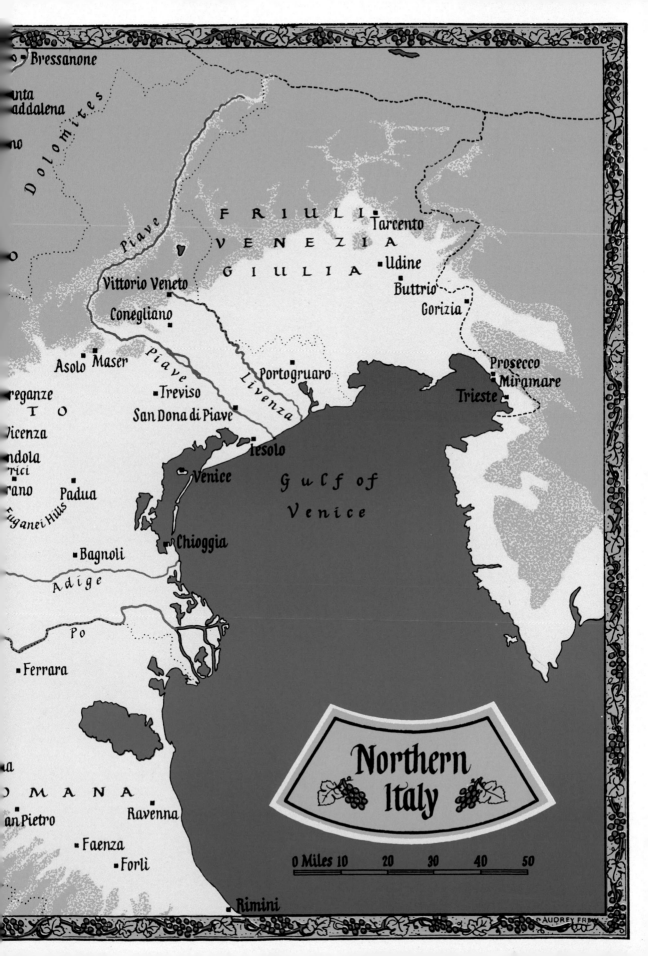

Bressanone

nta
addalena

no

Dolomites

FRIULI

Tarcento

Piave

VENEZIA

Udine

GIULIA

Buttrio

Vittorio Veneto

Gorizia

Conegliano

Asolo · Maser

Piave

Portogruaro

Prosecco
Miramare

reganze

Livenza

Trieste

Treviso

TO

San Dona di Piave

Vicenza

ndola

Iesolo

rici

rano

Venice

Padua

Gulf of

Euganei Hils

Venice

Chioggia

Bagnoli

Adige

Po

Ferrara

Northern
Italy

OMANA

an Pietro

Ravenna

Faenza

Forli

0 Miles 10   20   30   40   50

Rimini

AUDREY FREW